Africa's Freedom Railway

Africa's

Freedom

Railway

How a Chinese Development Project Changed Lives and Livelihoods in Tanzania

Jamie Monson

Indiana University Press
Bloomington & Indianapolis

Title page illustration: Woodcut by
Liang Yiqiang and Don Peigao depicting
friendship between African villagers and
TAZARA railway workers, from a collection
of poetry. *Rainbow of Friendship*, 107.

This book is a publication of

Indiana University Press
601 North Morton Street
Bloomington, IN 47404-3797 USA

www.iupress.indiana.edu

Telephone orders	800-842-6796
Fax orders	812-855-7931
Orders by e-mail	iuporder@indiana.edu

First paperback edition 2011
© 2009 by Jamie Monson
All rights reserved

∞ The paper used in this publication
meets the minimum requirements of the
American National Standard for Information
Sciences—Permanence of Paper for Printed
Library Materials, ANSI Z39.48-1992.

Manufactured in the United
States of America

The Library of Congress catalogued
the original edition as follows:

Monson, Jamie.
  Africa's freedom railway : how a Chinese
development project changed lives and
livelihoods in Tanzania / Jamie Monson.
    p.   cm.
  Includes bibliographical references and
index.
  ISBN 978-0-253-35271-2 (cloth : alk.
paper) 1. Railroads—Tanzania. 2.
Economic assistance, Chinese—Tanzania.
3. Economic development projects—
Tanzania. 4. Africa—Foreign economic
relations—China. 5. China—Foreign
economic relations—Africa. I. Title.
  HE3243.M66 2008
  385.0985—dc22

                        2008031559

ISBN 978-0-253-22322-7 (pbk. : alk. paper)

2 3 4 5 6   16 15 14 13 12 11

For Steve and Jenny

Contents

Acknowledgments

It may not "take a village" to produce and publish many kinds of books. This one, however, could not have come into being without the assistance, collaboration, and support of many colleagues and friends from three continents. The project began through my relationship with my friend and colleague, James Giblin, and his wife Blandina. The Giblins, and the community of friends they welcome into their home in Segelea, have been a source of intellectual engagement and friendship for many years. It was due to them that I first met and interviewed Philemon Kaduma in Mbeya in 1998. My conversations with Mr. Kaduma launched this book project, and I am indebted to him for the knowledge and wisdom he has shared with me, and for the friendship I have been blessed to have with him and his family. Mr. Kaduma introduced me to others who made substantial contributions to this book in its early stages, in particular Raphael Chawala. During a subsequent field trip to Tanzania in 2000, Du Jian of the Chinese Railway Expert Team generously shared with me important background information about the project, in addition to stories about his own personal experiences. These conversations persuaded me that this was a project worth undertaking.

In Tanzania I have been fortunate to work and collaborate with a community of scholars at the University of Dar es Salaam who have had a strong influence on my thinking about the history of TAZARA and Tanzanian history more generally. I am especially thankful to have had the opportunity to present my work at the university on more than one occasion, and appreciate the intellectual engagement I have had with faculty and students. I am especially grateful for the friendship and collegiality of Yusufu Lawi, Fred Kaijage, Isaria Kimambo, Eginald Mihanjo, and Rehema Nchimbi in the history department. Much of what I know about the practice of African history was learned during my dissertation research in 1990–91; both Seth Nyagava and Nestor Luanda taught me important lessons that have stayed with me. George Ambindwile has been an invaluable research assistant in the archives and around town during the pursuit of elusive research materials. Adrian Chamwela Mgulambwa made sure we got there safely. In the department of sociology Simeon Mesaki has been a longtime friend and shared his unpublished reports and documents with me. I owe a very special thanks to my friend Mrs. Grace Mshigeni, who has supported and encouraged me in so many ways all these years.

During the many years of fieldwork that we carried out in the TAZARA "passenger belt," our research team made our base in Ifakara at the Ifakara Health Research and Development Center (IHRDC). This center became our home in Tanzania, and we were privileged to benefit from the research-friendly amenities and also from the opportunity to engage with other field researchers based there. I am grateful to Hassan Mshinda, Rose Nathan, David and Joanna Schellenberg, and Hajo and Adriana Tami, who were among the many scholars we interacted with. The staff also made a great difference in our lives during fieldwork, and Veronica Mkopi was an especially important person to us not only at the center but also on our numerous field trips.

Our field research team included three invaluable assistants. George Mwambeta assisted with life history interviews; Onesmo Kwawira painstakingly collected parcel receipts data from the TAZARA stations; and Jesse Grossman piloted and completed the comparison of landscape cover change using satellite images. Each of these three individuals contributed a significant part of the primary evidence for this book.

I would also like to thank the TAZARA employees who gave me guidance and assistance during the project. The TAZARA public relations managers at headquarters in Dar es Salaam that worked with me, Conrad Simuchile and Mwase Lundu, and also James Mwitangeti, were very helpful to me. Mr. Nalitolela gave me guidance and assistance at TAZARA headquarters on many occasions. Many individual stationmasters and other TAZARA personnel in Tanzania and in Zambia have also made this project possible.

In China, I have been fortunate to have developed relationships of friendship and collegiality with scholars from the Institute for West Asian and African Studies (IWAAS) at the Chinese Academy of Social Sciences. This friendship began when Yao Guimei first invited me to give a talk on my TAZARA research at IWAAS in November 2003. Since that time I have appreciated the generosity and assistance of my colleagues there, especially He Wenping, Liu Haifang, Yang Lihua, and Wei Cuiping. In China I have also been fortunate to have met and worked with Africanist colleagues at Peking University. Li Anshan was very helpful during our visit to China in 2007. Li Baoping has made important contributions to this book by assisting me with contacts and interviews in China, helping me to locate Chinese sources, and reading chapters of this manuscript.

Several of my colleagues read all or part of this manuscript at different stages in its development. I thank Tom Spear, Philemon Kaduma, Steve Davis, Li Baoping, Xipeng Shen, Lorne Larson, Kennedy Haule, Ned Alpers, Naran Bilik, James Giblin, and James McCann for their helpful comments. Tom Spear has been an influential reader and editor of my work in other capacities and has also served as an important mentor to me over the span of my career. Lorne Larson has also been a careful and close reader of my work as well as a storehouse of knowledge on the history of the Kilombero valley and Mahenge highlands. There are many other colleagues who have contributed to my scholarly life and therefore to this project, including Kairn Klieman, Lessie Tate, Cherif Keita, Steve Lewis, Nancy Jacobs, Maia Green, Georg Deutsch, Heike Schmidt, Margot Lovett, Joseph Mbele, Cynthia Brantley, Michele Wagner, Sheryl McCurdy, Gregory Maddox, Jan Shetler, Andreas Eckert, Jan-Bart Gewald, Juhani Koponen, Thaddeus Sunseri, Cymone Fourshey, Kelly Askew, Pier Larson, Carl Weiner, George Yu, Zubeida Tumbo-Masabo, and Pamela Feldman-Savelsberg. The spirit of Susan Geiger has stayed with me over the years of the writing process.

During a remarkable year in Berlin in 2004–2005 as a fellow of the Wissenschaftskolleg (Institute for Advanced Study), my intellectual engagement with reading groups on globalization (the Global Girls) and experience were important in changing my thinking about this book; I am especially appreciative of the contributions of Maria Todorova on the topics of experience and backwardness, and of Lydia Liu, who read and commented on some of this work in its earlier stages. In Berlin I also benefited from my friendships with Michelle Moyd and Hansjoerg Dilger.

I have received support in many forms from Carleton College during the production of this book. Generous financial and leave support made field research and writing possible, in particular seed money for preliminary investigation. My history department colleagues form a lively and productive community of scholars who have stimulated my intellectual development in many ways. I have also benefitted from the contributions of Carleton College student research assistants, in particular Wayne Soon, who accompanied me on my first research trip to China and also to Tanzania in the summer of 2007, and Jennifer Cooper, who created the first full data analysis of the parcel receipts. Several student workers in the history department have also given their time and energy to the project, as has our assistant Nikki Lamberty, who has done much to make this project succeed.

The research for this book was made possible by fellowships from the Fulbright-Hays Faculty Research Abroad Program and from the Carnegie Scholars Foundation, in addition to generous financial support from Carleton College. A collaborative grant from the National Endowment for the Humanities also contributed to the progress of this research. The project was facilitated with the kind assistance of the staff of the Tanzania Commission on Science and Technology (COSTECH) and the Tanzania National Archives (TNA). I am also grateful for the assistance in Zambia of Marja Hinfelaar and the staff of the National Archives of Zambia, and to Giacomo Macola for helping me to access the UNIP archives in Lusaka. I thank Inka Praetsch and Meherun Ahmed for their work on the parcels receipts database.

This book would never have happened at all without the support of my life partner and husband, Steven Davis. He has been at my side as the driver of our Land Rover and as the photographer during fieldwork, in the archive helping me to translate German colonial documents, and in China as my companion. Most importantly, Steve has been a thoughtful critic and editor through the challenges of writing. This is really his book as much as it is mine.

Africa's Freedom Railway

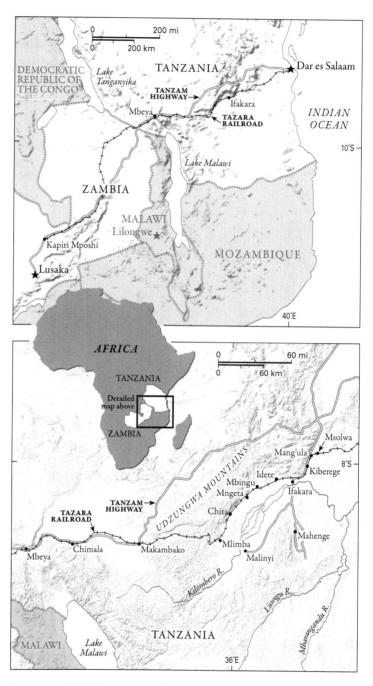

Map 1. The TAZARA Railway in Tanzania and Zambia (above); the research study area in Tanzania (below). Map by Jerome Cookson, 2007.

1

Introduction

Freedom Railway

On a hot afternoon in the early 1970s, a historic encounter took place near the town of Chimala in the southern highlands of Tanzania. A team of Chinese railway workers and their Tanzanian counterparts came face-to-face with a rival team of American-led road workers advancing across the same rural landscape. The Americans were building a paved highway from Dar es Salaam to Zambia, in direct competition with the Chinese railway project. The path of the railway and the path of the roadway came together at this point, and a tense standoff reportedly ensued as each side threatened to prevent the other from proceeding. According to one version of the events, reportedly from an eyewitness, the Chinese team had just completed construction of bridge number 117 over a tributary of the Great Ruaha River. They were busy planting grasses to secure the railway's embankment when they were approached by the American team. The trouble started, this eyewitness reported, when the Americans began to place survey markers on the newly planted embankment. The Chinese objected and quickly removed the markers, leading to a "heated quarrel."[1] A report in *Newsweek* magazine described the conflict somewhat differently, reporting that it was the Chinese team that encountered the Americans building a bridge across the river. The Chinese then "promptly laid claim to the site for their railroad and planted Chinese flags in the ground to reinforce the claim." And when the Americans then attempted to bulldoze the flags, "they found themselves suddenly surrounded by 200 screaming Chinese." The skirmish was only settled, both accounts agree, when the Tanzanian police intervened and made sure that both teams could proceed with their work.[2]

Stories of this conflict circulated widely during the time of the TAZARA railway's construction and afterward because of its powerful symbolism. For there was much more at stake in this confrontation than the simple logistics of one rural transportation project accommodating another; the disputed terrain was not just physical but also ideological. The confrontation came to represent a clash between a socialist vision of development, in which the state would play a prominent role in controlling development projects and subsequent economic activity, and a capitalist vision of free-flowing commerce. In these debates, railways were presumed to be ideal socialist projects: they were large-scale, state-funded, and centrally managed infrastructures. The scheduled stops that regulated passenger traffic and goods shipments were imposed by railway authorities, which in turn were state-governed enterprises. According to one Tanzanian economist, during the years of *ujamaa* socialism under the leadership of President Julius Nyerere, the state and the railway became so closely intertwined that "you couldn't tell which one was in charge any more."[3]

The paved highway, like other road projects favored by western donors, represented the freedom of the market. On road networks goods could be shipped according to one's own timetable, with stops anywhere along the way where market forces supported commercial activity. Feeder roads could link the highway to other areas, expanding the service area of the corridor and thereby increasing mobility and market choices. These two projects thus represented a rivalry between competing development visions: the socialist railway involving a state-managed infrastructure with centralized control; and the capitalist highway representing freedom of mobility and of economic enterprise.

That was not all. These two transportation projects were burdened with even more layers of ideological meaning and symbolism. The Chinese-sponsored TAZARA was known as the "Freedom Railway," the critical link to the sea that landlocked Zambia desperately needed in order to break free from her dependency on Rhodesian, Angolan, and South African rails and ports. TAZARA was therefore also an anti-apartheid railway, a symbol of revolutionary solidarity and resistance to the forces of colonialism, neo-colonialism, and imperialism. The Americans, on the other hand, viewed the construction of the TAZARA railway with growing alarm. As China's largest international development project and the third-largest infrastructure development project in Africa (after the Aswan and the Volta dam projects), TAZARA represented the "great steel arm of China thrusting its way into the African interior."[4]

The TAZARA railway (the acronym stands for the Tanzania Zambia Railway Authority, the binational administrative body that has overseen the railway since 1976) was constructed between 1970 and 1975 to link the landlocked Zambian copper belt with the Indian Ocean port city of Dar es Salaam in Tanzania. The 1,860-kilometer-long project was built with financing and technical support from China amounting to over $400 million in the form of a long-term interest-free loan.[5] China had agreed to finance and support the railway project in 1967 after several requests for assistance from western donors and from the Soviet Union had been rejected.

In the end, the distinctions that were drawn between the socialist railway and the capitalist highway, symbolized by the historic confrontation at Chimala, became obscured by the political and economic realities of post-colonial Tanzania. The highway was completed in 1973, two years before the railway, and was used by TAZARA vehicles to ferry materials and personnel to railway construction sites.[6] Thus the capitalist highway became an important if unintended partner in the building of the socialist railway. And after the completion of TAZARA, the highway was made less "free" and thereby less competitive by government attempts to control and regulate the transport industry.[7] Meanwhile, economic liberalization measures from the mid-1980s onward allowed TAZARA to play an important role in the expansion of independent small-scale trade and entrepreneurial activity. The highway, in other words, was susceptible to becoming controlled by the state, while the railway was capable in turn of serving a robust network of "free market" traders and other entrepreneurs.

In these and other ways, the story of the TAZARA railway brings to light dimensions of the Cold War era in Africa that go beyond the competition between socialist and capitalist ideologies. The railway was part of China's effort to combat what it termed the hegemonism and neo-imperialism of the two superpowers, the United States and the Soviet Union. At the same time, however, China's investment in African development assistance was part of a drive to be acknowledged as a world power. Meanwhile, in defining a legitimizing foundation for Afro-Asian solidarity, China claimed a shared history of imperial conquest and colonization with its "brothers" in the third world. The relationship between China and Tanzania at this historical moment was defined as one of "the poor helping the poor," as one underdeveloped country reaching out to another.[8] China thus claimed to be part of a common "third world struggle" against the forces of imperialism and neo-colonialism, while at the same time proposing to construct TAZARA as the third-largest development infrastructure project in Africa. In this way, through African development assistance China sought to retain two seemingly contradictory identities—that of a formerly colonized subject as well as that of a Cold War player. An article in Tanzania's *The Nationalist* in 1969 proclaimed that "New China has all the characteristics of a truly big POWER," including an independent industrial base, a self-reliant economy, and "the Bomb; today's status quo symbol in the world's real politic."[9]

TAZARA was not only a Chinese development assistance project in Africa but also, from its very beginning stages, a pan-African one. The Cold War era was a time of pan-African aspirations throughout the continent, and TAZARA represented the concrete realization of pan-African development cooperation. This contributed to the symbolic significance of the TAZARA project, for not only would Chinese and Africans cooperate together in an anti-hegemonic project, but Tanzanians and Zambians would dismantle the boundaries of colonial-era transport infrastructures. The project's pan-African foundations shaped the railway's construction process and ongoing operations in important ways: for example, in the use of English as the official language (rather than Kiswahili); in a careful division of labor and management between the two countries; and in the creation of a binational governing authority that included ministerial representatives from both Tanzania and Zambia.

And finally, the complexities of the Cold War era in Africa are revealed most clearly when the lens of analysis is shifted from the abstract level of state ideologies to local experience. The Chinese railway technicians who labored on the TAZARA project may have "allocated time for ideological instruction," as western observers had feared, but it was their everyday practice of teaching by example that is remembered more often by their African counterparts.[10] And once the railway was completed, it became as important to the rural communities located along the railway corridor as it was to the copper mines of Zambia or to the sawmills of Iringa. For over time, rural communities in the remote regions through which the TAZARA railway traveled came to depend upon the services provided by the Ordinary Train, the passenger train that stopped at the smallest village settlements and stations. And at the same time, the railway came to depend upon the agency and initiative of the rural users of the train for whom it was essential to life and livelihood.

The Ordinary Train

More than ten years after TAZARA's completion, Chimala—together with other small stations and settlements—was once again the site of conflict over the railway. This time, while similar issues were at stake—state control over transportation services versus market-oriented development—the protagonists were very differ-

ent. From the mid-1980s onward, farmers and traders along the railway corridor
had begun to generate a vibrant rural economy as markets were opened up in
response to liberalization measures. They did so by shipping their goods as parcels on the Ordinary Train. Meanwhile, railway management decided in 1994 to
impose "efficiency" measures that would save money by closing down stations that
had permanent staffing but infrequent train stops. The stations most likely to be
deemed "inefficient," according to this calculus, were those served by the Ordinary Train. Ironically, many of the nineteen stations slated to be closed were the
most active in small-scale trade in the form of parcels; indeed the bustle of local
economic activity on the railway platforms at some of these stations was slowing
down the train.

Angry residents responded to the threatened closures with a barrage of protests and complaints, lodged by individuals as well as by ad hoc committees. By
removing passenger services from their stations, they argued, this economic efficiency measure would be most devastating for local communities like Chimala
that depended upon the train for their small-scale entrepreneurial activities. In
their protests about the station closures, local people strategically deployed the
same language of freedom and socialism that had been used by the state during
TAZARA's construction. One local spokesman from Mbingu wrote to his member
of parliament asking that the station be reopened, "so that it can continue to provide important service for the citizens as it used to. Because the Freedom Railway
'TAZARA' was built for the benefit of Tanzanians and Zambians, not for the profit
of the IMF or to bring profits to private persons."[11] Using this language of state and
citizenship, local people made powerful claims to the railway and to the services
it provided them. As they did so, they reminded the railway authority and government officials alike of the obligations they were expected to fulfill as stewards of
the TAZARA project and its legacy.

Once again, a struggle over the railway embodied larger meanings. In this second conflict, local communities protested against railway authority actions that
threatened their livelihoods, livelihoods that they themselves had generated as
they farmed and traded in the TAZARA corridor. The struggle over station closures
illustrates the ways that this large-scale, state-driven project was both experienced
and shaped by the communities that lived in the railway corridor. Local people
were not passive recipients of transportation development in the railway corridor;
they engaged directly with it through their economic activities and their political
mobilization. Nor were they ignorant of the larger political and ideological context of the TAZARA project; far from it. Their protests show how they rhetorically
deployed the socialist legacy of TAZARA as they negotiated for services that were
vital to their current interests.

The Great Steel Arm of China

A succession of donors—including the World Bank and the United Nations—had declined to assist with the construction of a Tanzania-Zambia railway when they were first approached by presidents Julius Nyerere and Kenneth Kaunda at the time of independence. Nevertheless, when the news broke in 1967 that China had formally agreed to finance the project, some western observers reacted with alarm. The CIA had already warned of the leftward shift of Tanzanian politics in a 1965 report that devoted several pages to the friendly relationship between Julius Nyerere and China.[12] A *Wall Street Journal* article on the proposed railway project stated ominously in 1967 that "the prospect of hundreds and perhaps thousands of Red Guards descending upon an already troubled Africa is a chilling one for the West."[13]

Thousands of Chinese railway workers did make their way to Tanzania and Zambia during the years 1968–86, some 30,000–50,000 of them, depending on the source. Recruited from all over China, they arrived in Dar es Salaam on ships that had sailed for twelve to twenty days from the southern seaport of Guangzhou. From the harborside at Kurasini they were ferried in large grey trucks out to the twelve base camps that had been set up along the route to Zambia. The presence of these Chinese workers and their interactions with African communities—as the *Wall Street Journal* had predicted—generated one of the most significant and lasting legacies of the TAZARA project.

Chinese visitors to Dar es Salaam at the time of TAZARA's construction liked to remind their Tanzanian audiences of the voyages of Chinese admiral Zheng He, who had visited the East African coast in the fifteenth century. When Zhou Enlai visited Dar es Salaam in June 1965, he reminded the crowd that had gathered to greet him in the national stadium of these historical contacts between China and East Africa, as well as their shared histories of anti-colonial struggle, comparing the Maji Maji War with China's struggle against imperialism.[14] Zheng He did not come to Africa with the intention of colonization, Zhou explained, but rather sought to trade and interact with the African people as equals. Building on this tradition, Chinese development assistance in the post-independence period was put forward as having no strings attached. According to China's eight principles of African development assistance (these are listed in appendix 1), the role of Chinese aid was to help African nations to build self-reliance and to avoid dependency. And unlike the expatriate development professionals from other donor countries (the U.S. and the USSR in particular), who lived in well-appointed compounds, the Chinese experts would share the same living and working conditions as their African counterparts.[15]

During TAZARA's construction the Chinese railway technicians did indeed labor "side by side" with African workers, camping out with them in some of the most remote and rugged areas of the East African interior. They did not stand aside shouting out instructions, but taught the African recruits by example. They did not confine themselves to handling complex engineering technology, but were willing to pitch in on the most basic tasks. Chinese technicians remember assisting their young African friends with fatherly advice on matters ranging from saving their wages to repairing their shoes.[16] One African worker recalls the encouraging words his Chinese supervisor used to lift his spirits when he was demoralized by a minor injury. "Work!" the Chinese technician exhorted him, "because people will ride on this railway. Your parents will ride on this railway!"[17]

The relationships that developed between Chinese and African workers during TAZARA's construction were transformative in many ways. Yet they were not always transformative in the ways that western critics had feared, for despite the heavy ideological tone of China's official pronouncements (and the liberal distribution of Chairman Mao's books), African workers along the line do not remember having received a coherent "red" ideology. In practice, the work example modeled by the Chinese experts conveyed the values of modernity and progress through the practice of self-discipline and hard work. And while Chinese rhetoric put forward an image of egalitarian brotherhood, in reality most relationships between Chinese and African workers were hierarchical and highly regulated. Meanwhile, in the rural communities along the railway corridor, the Chinese experts remained something of a mystery. While the African workers moved more freely between the work camps and local villages after hours, the Chinese workers remained within the boundaries of their camp compounds. And when they did move about in local communities, they traveled together in groups and did not interact casually with the rural population.

Bamboo Railway

At the same time that reports in the United States were raising the alarm about the "great steel arm of China" extending into Africa, other critics were deridingly referring to the TAZARA project as a "bamboo railway." Delegates to the annual party conference of the Tanganyika African National Union (TANU) in 1971 were reassured by railway spokesman Waziri Juma that reports of a bamboo railway were "slanders spread by imperialists." TAZARA was not being built from bamboo at all, he explained, but was of the "highest quality and long durability."[18] In one sense, these two critiques were related. For it was the Chinese approach to technology—

constrained by foreign currency shortages and therefore labor-intensive—that resulted in the "thousands of Red Guards" penetrating into Africa's interior. This
labor-intensive technology was termed "deliberately backward" by one reporter at
the time, an inevitable if unfortunate consequence of the low availability of capital
and the high availability of labor. Yet one could also argue that the 30,000–50,000
Chinese railway experts dispatched to Dar es Salaam represented the project's most
significant technology transfer, when measured in terms of their contribution to
worker training in East Africa as well as by the cost to China of the withdrawal of
their labor and expertise.

Technology was transferred materially during the railway's construction, in the
form of rails and ballast (the permanent way) as well as wagons (the rolling stock)
and locomotives. Technology also took the form of knowledge, conveyed through
"teaching by example" on the part of the Chinese technicians, although this was
unevenly distributed. Both forms of technology came together at the base camp
at Mang'ula, where the Chinese established workshops and foundries for the production of TAZARA's concrete sleepers (molded concrete was used to support the
rails rather than the tropical hardwoods of colonial-era railways) and steel parts.
For many workers the most lasting impact of the project's technology lay in their
experience of a modernizing project—as one worker put it, the opportunity to work
on the railway had brought him and his coworkers into a "modern, civilized way
of life."[19] Modernization was experienced not just through handling machinery in
the foundry, but in the form of working for a wage, a new experience for many of
the young recruits, and following a work routine that was organized into hourly
shifts. The same experience that made working on the construction of TAZARA
modern for its workers—expressed by some as a coming-of-age—was very much
like what an earlier generation of African railway workers had experienced in the
colonial period: entry into a modern, masculine adulthood through wage labor and
a disciplined work regime.[20]

For the rural settlements that were located along the railway corridor, technology and modernization were experienced somewhat differently. The railway did
indeed reflect an expanding modernity, but it was one that sometimes threatened
the social and physical landscapes of local communities, particularly in those areas
where powerful ancestral spirits were associated with land features. There are many
stories of spirits that endeavored to stop the project by causing bridges to collapse
mid-construction, or by reversing the impact of excavation by restoring mountains to their original shapes. Upon its completion, the TAZARA railway formed
the backbone of a new spatial orientation for agrarian production and rural commerce. Entire communities were resettled along the railway in *Operation Kando
Kando ya Reli*, or "Alongside the Railway," the largest rural village resettlement

project in Tanzania. For the residents of the TAZARA corridor, the technological intervention of the railway was followed by a modernizing post-colonial agrarian reorganization.

How Development Worked

The story of TAZARA shows that state-led development projects in Africa could work in unintended ways, their outcomes diverging from the visions of their master planners. The communities living alongside the railway were not passive recipients of a technology transfer. From the time of construction onward they were actively engaged in the railway's development, in their multiple roles as suppliers of provisions to the workers, as the eyes and ears of a local security force, and as the producers and traders of agricultural products. Development also worked through contestation: there were conflicts in the workplace, on station platforms, and in rural villages as railway workers, users, and managers struggled over TAZARA's larger meaning and purpose.

Development worked initially in the TAZARA corridor through the work process itself; as the Chinese had argued, development took place through "deeds." The specific form of worker training during the TAZARA project, based on emulation or "teaching by example," resulted in the creation of a small but significant cohort of experienced African railway specialists who continued to work for TAZARA until their retirements.[21] And those who left the project after its construction took their new skills with them. Yet work for development was also contested and negotiated. During construction the labor conditions were so challenging that many abandoned the project or were fired for not measuring up. The insistent emphasis on "hard work" and work discipline, the same qualities that were associated with post-colonial modernity and progress, could also be experienced as oppressive and therefore resonate with memories of labor under colonialism. Conflict over labor conditions continued after the railway was completed, most notably during a protracted labor struggle between 1982 and 1992. Even the station closings of 1986 and 1994 were part of labor rationalization measures, intended to reduce the number of workers at isolated stations.

Development also worked through the visions and actions of the people who relied upon TAZARA for their lives and livelihoods. Farmers grew rice, maize, and bananas in the TAZARA "passenger belt" between Mbeya and Kidatu, products that were shipped on the train by small-scale commodities traders. These traders in turn brought consumer goods from the city to be sold in local markets. Fortune-seekers migrated to the railway corridor to try out gemstone mining, timber harvesting, fishing, and other forms of natural resource extraction. Others prepared cooked snacks and drinks for sale to passengers and traders waiting at the stations, as well as to those passing through on the trains. Over time, TAZARA's railway platforms became lively marketplaces filled with buyers and sellers on the days that the Ordinary Train passed through.

These economic activities could also involve tension and conflict, for the rural and urban users of TAZARA were located within larger social structures and political processes. Conflict was experienced most intimately at the local level, where differences between those with greater access to capital or political influence (resources that often went together) and those with less were keenly felt. At the larger level, interventions by the state and by market forces also played a part in structuring the ways development worked in the TAZARA corridor. The role of the state changed over the period of this study, with it intervening more directly and forcefully in rural life during the period of railway construction and *ujamaa* villagization through the 1970s, and less directly but no less significantly in the era of liberalization, structural adjustment, and political decentralization from the mid-1980s onward. In recent years people have felt the pressure of the state most often as the withdrawal of state support for agricultural production, while taxation and licensing fees have increased along with marketing structures that favor large-scale traders.

Whatever their social or economic position, the traders and farmers who used the TAZARA railway between 1975 and 2000 did so because it enhanced physical, social, and economic mobility. Over time rural actors were able to combine more than one form of livelihood, particularly small-scale trade with agriculture, resource extraction, and (less frequently) wage labor. Because the railway traversed several distinct agro-ecological zones, farmers and traders were able to shift not only from one sector to another but from one type of crop or product to another, depending upon the status of such uncertain variables as the local economy, national agricultural policies, and climate variation. In this way TAZARA's users crafted multi-spatial livelihoods, moving not only between rural and urban landscapes but also among diverse rural livelihood contexts.[22]

Mobility was central to lives and to livelihood practices in the TAZARA corridor. Yet equally important to corridor residents was a sense of physical belonging. In a rural economy filled with uncertainty and changing conditions, being connected with a place—particularly a plot of land where one could farm and build a home—was important to identity, community, and long-term security. As the TAZARA railway opened up access to fertile farmland, there was a dramatic expansion of small-scale landholding in areas that had been sparsely settled and difficult to reach in the past. Acquiring a plot of land was especially important for those who had moved away from areas of poverty and overcrowding, in particular for young people seeking a brighter future. One young trader described the acquisition of his first farm plot in the TAZARA corridor as a process of becoming a citizen, or *mwananchi*; another explained that by gaining a farm he had become a person, an *mtu* or human being. Migrants from other parts of Tanzania described their immigration into the TAZARA corridor as a shift in their sense of locality and belonging—they felt that they had become locals, or *wenyeji*, after acquiring land and settling there. The definition and meaning of locality was often debated in resource conflicts, as long-term residents who viewed themselves as truly local or indigenous attempted to distinguish themselves from immigrant newcomers making new claims to land and to nature.

The Book

This book begins with the story of the Freedom Railway. It frames TAZARA's planning and construction with reference to the colonial railway visions that preceded and shaped it. The second part of the book tells the story of the Ordinary Train. It chronicles the lives and livelihoods of those living in the TAZARA corridor as well as the landscape visions that guided rural settlement and resource use. This second half of the book focuses on a specific section of the railway in southern Tanzania, within TAZARA's "passenger belt," between the town of Makambako on the Njombe highlands and the village of Msolwa on the western boundary of the Selous Game Reserve.[23]

   This book takes on the challenge of writing about contemporary East Africa in historical perspective. To reconstruct the recent past, it employs sources that might commonly be found in social science analysis—quantitative data in the form of parcel receipts, for example, and comparison of satellite photographs that document landscape change. This book also relies heavily upon life history narratives as a primary source of evidence. The life history interviews allow people to speak about their own experience of the railway and its relationship to development. Life history narratives have been embraced by scholars of African history for a number of years as a form of evidence that allows historians to retrieve the experience of those left out of conventional histories.[24] Yet we know that accounts of experience, especially those recounted in the form of a life story, are in fact reconstructions of the self in the past that serve explicit purposes in the present.[25] In this book, I have tried not to extract personal experience *from* life history narratives as an authentic form of truth about the past, but rather to understand experience *within* narrative, including the contexts in which personal life histories have been solicited and recounted.

This book also relies upon archival materials, although these are predictably uneven for the post-colonial era. Official records from the railway's construction have not been released to the National Archives in Dar es Salaam. There are, fortunately, several important files on the railway in the National Archives of Zambia. In the Archives of the Ministry of Foreign Affairs in China, materials related to the TAZARA period are just beginning to be accessioned and may be made available to the public by 2008. There is also a small gallery of photographs with informative captions on view at TAZARA headquarters in Dar es Salaam. Despite the uneven availability of files in government archives, records from the construction period can be found in unlikely places. Some retired TAZARA workers have kept their own private collections of papers and reports. The M.A. thesis projects of graduate students at the University of Dar es Salaam reproduce important compilations of both documentary and fieldwork data in thesis chapters and appendices.[26] Newspaper accounts from Africa, China, and the United States also offer insight into the events as well as the propaganda of the time, as do reports from Chinese radio broadcasts.

Research on TAZARA is made more difficult by the secrecy and suspicion of outsiders that enveloped the project from its inception. The railway was designed and built at a time when China's activities in Tanzania were highly sensitive and it was difficult to gain access to data. As George Yu put it in 1968, "studying China in Africa is much like pursuing a dragon in the bush. The dragon is imposing but the bush is dense."[27] At the same time, the railway was a potential target of saboteurs from the white settler regimes in the southern African region because of its strategic and symbolic significance. Among the Tanzanian and Zambian contingents as well as the Chinese side, TAZARA was protected from potential enemy sabotage through secretive negotiations and planning. It was forbidden for anyone to take photographs of the railway itself or of the railway stations. Local communities were warned for years to be on the lookout for strangers asking questions, who may have been staking out targets for attack or subversion.[28] For these reasons, many of the reports that appeared in western-based newspapers and other media at the time were based on conjecture rather than hard evidence, resulting in conflicting accounts. Even today local villagers in the railway corridor can remain somewhat guarded in talking about the project, particularly with outsiders. I am therefore indebted to the individual TAZARA workers, retirees, and officials who have so generously shared their knowledge and experience with me in both informal conversations and formal interviews in Tanzania, Zambia, and China. The views expressed here are entirely my own.

Part 1 · Freedom Railway

2

Railway Visions

During the transition to independence in the early 1960s, Zambian president Kenneth Kaunda and Tanzanian president Julius Nyerere began to talk in earnest about constructing a railway that would link the Zambian copper belt with the Indian Ocean. The two leaders envisioned a post-colonial transportation infrastructure that would be based upon regional cooperation rather than colonial dependency. An alternative passage to the sea would free Zambia from its reliance upon existing routes through the white settler regimes and Portuguese colonies to the south. It would liberate both Tanzania and Zambia from the colonial division of transport infrastructures into southern and eastern railway networks, networks that operated on different-sized gauges.[1] And the proposed "Freedom Railway" would give lasting material form to the bonds of pan-African solidarity that had been established during the struggles against colonialism and imperialism. Political links could now be buttressed by structural links, according to Kenneth Kaunda, including not only the new railway but also new road systems, airlines, and telecommunications.[2]

These visions of post-colonial railway development were disparaged by the project's critics, who viewed them as ideological rather than economic propositions. The two initial railway surveys that were carried out in 1963–64—one by the World Bank and the other by the United Nations—concluded that the proposed rail link would be neither economically feasible nor sustainable. The World Bank survey isolated economic considerations from the overall political context, concluding that the existing Rhodesian Railways line to the south still had plenty of spare capacity to handle Zambia's copper exports. The World Bank report and its supporters implied that Nyerere and Kaunda had a political approach to railway development, while the approach of the World Bank and other western donors was based on rational economic decision-making. A CIA report at the time went even further, calling the African leaders "emotionally attached" to the railway project.[3] Yet the World Bank position on railway development was viewed by some as a political move in itself. Certainly many African observers saw it that way, and accused the Bank of supporting British mining interests in the region rather than the development needs of the newly independent states. One economic analyst accused the World Bank of being "out of touch with the realities of Africa."[4]

The participants in these early debates tried to distinguish the political from the economic in African railway development. In practice this was a false dichotomy, since railway development anywhere in the world is by its very nature a political as well as an economic endeavor. This is due in large part to the relative expense of initial investment in a railway compared with the rate of return. Railways quickly become permanent features of transportation infrastructures (indeed, the foundation of the railway together with the track is known as the "permanent way") and require ongoing subsidies. They concentrate administrative control over the movement of people and goods in ways that other forms of transportation investment do not. For these and other reasons, railways have always been highly political as well as economic projects. This was certainly true in the case of TAZARA.

These early debates also obscured the continuities between colonial and postcolonial transportation projects in East Africa. The construction of a southern railway in Tanzania—a link that would connect the port cities of the Indian Ocean with the shores of Lake Nyasa and beyond—had been envisioned from the very beginnings of European exploration in the region. From the German expedition leaders of the 1890s to the heads of independent East African states in the 1960s, a progression of public figures had put forward their visions for a southern East African railway link. In each successive historical context, contentious debate swirled around the railway proposals, debate that was dominated as much by political considerations as it was by the promise of economic gain. This background is important for understanding the place of TAZARA in the larger history of railway development in East Africa.

For the politicians, investors, and farmers who debated these issues, East African railway networks embodied both the symbolic and the material underpinnings of larger development paradigms. In the German colonial era (1885–1918) some viewed railways as a resource for white settler agriculture in the highlands, while others believed they should support African peasant production on the plains. German politicians had dreamed of an empire of *Mittelafrika* held together by transport connections, a span of territorial control that would stretch across the continent from the Indian Ocean to the Atlantic. In British-ruled Tanganyika, white settler farmers in the southern highlands lobbied with their Kenyan counterparts for a grand "Imperial Link" that would unite the settler colonies, consolidating economic and political interests from Nairobi to Capetown. Ironically, this same southern railway that was viewed as a backbone of support for white settler development in eastern Africa in the 1930s was envisioned only thirty years later as the "Freedom Railway" that would liberate East Africa's independent states from their dependency on white settler domination from the south.

In the colonial period in East Africa, there was intense competition among imperial rivals for control over trade, and therefore for control over trading infrastructures. Railway construction had been "the colonial war cry from the outset," a powerful symbol of colonization and progress. To construct a railway was to command a region—the most famous manifestation of this being Cecil Rhodes's dream of linking "Cape to Cairo" through a continent-wide rail connection. To control a region in turn was to keep rivals out, or at least to restrict their trade participation through tariffs and other regulatory interventions. The international rivalry in the promotion of East African railways that characterized the colonial era continued to play a role into the post-independence period, particularly during the Cold War. When China offered to fund the TAZARA line, part of the motivation behind the project was Sino-Soviet rivalry—China wanted to limit Soviet influence in East Africa. And while China did not seek to control southern Tanzania's economy or to profit directly from TAZARA's construction, it did expect through investing in TAZARA to establish itself as a regional strategic player in direct competition with U.S. and European interests.

The idea of building a southern railway—a "route to the sea" for the landlocked countries to the west of Lake Nyasa—therefore came to assume different meanings over time. The southern railway link was the infrastructural representation of a succession of visions for economic development and for strategic advantage, from the "Imperial Link" of colonial Tanganyika to the "Freedom Railway" of the post-colonial era.

The German Period: Constructing *Mittelafrika*

The possibility of developing a southern railway route in Tanzania was one that had fascinated planners from the beginning of German colonial rule. As Germans considered the potential forms of development that could be undertaken in their East African colony, three primary railway routes were considered. Each of these routes corresponded with a particular development vision, and each had its own proponents among German planters, industrialists, bankers, and politicians. The northern route would connect the growing German plantation economies in West Usambara, Kilimanjaro, and Meru with the coast. The central line, on the other hand, would be supported through the development of the interior by African farmers and traders from Dar es Salaam to Tabora. The southern line could favor either settlers or African producers, depending upon whether it traversed the southern highlands (settled by German farmers) or the areas further to the south (slated for peasant production). In the first round of railway investment, the northern route won out and was the first railway to be constructed in German East Africa, with work starting in the early 1890s. This line finally reached Moshi (with colonial government support) in 1912.[5] Meanwhile, the central route from Dar es Salaam to Lake Tanganyika was begun in 1905 under the auspices of the East African Railway Company (*Ostafrikanische Eisenbahn Gesellchaft*), after several years of discussion and surveying. The third colonial railway option—the southern railway—was never built, but extensive exploration and reporting on its potential reveal its relevance to German colonial development planning.[6]

German rail policy was heavily influenced by imperial rivalry with Great Britain. To the north and southeast, there was already competition with the British Uganda railway and the Shire-Zambezi railway respectively. A potential cooperative railway venture between Portugal and Britain through northern Mozambique was also making the Germans nervous in 1904, fueling fears that such a line would further divert trade outside the colony.[7] German colonial officials had talked since the late 1880s about the need to link their dispersed African colonies together, by obtaining parts of Portuguese-held territory in Angola and Mozambique or by carving out a section of the resource-rich Congo. As part of the *Mittelafrika* strategy, German politicians proposed railway projects that would stretch right across the continent from west to east. They later proposed a takeover of the Benguela railway that connected the Angolan coast to Katanga.[8]

Initial German plans for a southern rail route in German East Africa focused on the area traversed by the robust caravan traffic between Kilwa and Lake Nyasa in the 1890s. Several German expeditions had already explored this landscape by the time Paul Fuchs conducted the first survey of its potential for a railway in 1904.[9] Fuchs was employed by a group of German industrialists and bankers to carry out a survey of possible rail routes in the colony between 1904 and 1907. He published two reports, one on the economic development potential of the southern route (1905), and the other on the middle and northern routes (1907).[10] Fuchs was strongly in favor of developing a railway in the Kilwa-Nyasa corridor. At the time, the southern part of the German East Africa colony, with its rich agricultural and mineral resources, was believed to have the most potential for future economic development.[11] Fuchs's recommendations reflect German colonial development thinking—that transportation systems based on porterage should be replaced by railways, thus freeing up African labor for peasant and plantation agricultural production.[12]

Fuchs's vision of a dynamic peasant economy in the southern railway corridor never materialized, in part due to the outbreak of the Maji Maji War in the southern part of the colony between 1905 and 1907. An equally important reason for the abandonment of the southern corridor strategy was the intervening development of the central railway line. Once the central line had been constructed as far as Morogoro in 1907, attention turned to creating an alternative southern route, an extension from the central railway station of Kilosa southwestward to Lake Nyasa.[13] Thus rather than starting from a southern coastal port—for example, Kilwa or Lindi—this new southern line would begin from a station in the interior, passing through the Kilombero valley and terminating at Manda Bay. An alternative proposal was to develop a route from the central line south through the Iringa highlands and westward to Mbeya (both areas dominated by German settlement). These competing proposals for a southern extension of the central railway once again pitted settler and peasant agriculture against one another. In the end, neither railway was constructed, as resources were already committed to the extension of the central and northern lines. Plans for the further implementation of German colonial railways were subsequently terminated when the First World War ended German occupation of East Africa in 1918.

The British Period: An Imperial Link

With the advent of British administration in Tanganyika Territory in 1920, the era of imperial rivalry in the construction of East African railways came to an end. A new development vision had emerged: the possibility of creating a British-controlled regional network of railway systems, known as the "Imperial Link." Sentiment for building a southern railway was still strong, and the southern route was viewed as an important component of any British regional network. Colonel F. D. Hammond recommended in his 1921 report on East Africa's railways that a main trunk line connecting Dar es Salaam with the northern end of Lake Nyasa should have the top priority over all other projects, for it would provide an outlet to the sea for the British colonies of Northern Rhodesia and Nyasaland.[14]

Advocates for a southern railway line were divided into several camps. As in the German period, debate centered on settler versus African peasant production. Defending their own interests, the settlers argued that the colony would best be served by a railway link extending southward from the central line at Dodoma to Iringa (the center for European settler farming in the southern region) and then on to Fife in Northern Rhodesia. The alternative route ran from Kilosa through Ifakara to Fife, through territory viewed as unsuitable for European habitation because of its sultry climate and the risk of malarial disease. This Ifakara line would open up the fertile yet sparsely settled Kilombero valley for African resettlement and agricultural schemes, following the peasant model of colonial development. Advocates for the opposing sides in this debate had the opportunity to argue their cases before the Tanganyika Railway Commission in 1930.

These debates pitted prevailing development visions against one another—settler versus native production, peasant versus plantation farming, roads versus railways. Yet despite the extensive hearings and investigations, and the lengthy report that resulted from the work of the railway commission, interest in the southern line lagged during the interwar period. The economic crisis of the 1930s had resulted in reduced profits for Tanganyika Railways. Congolese copper exports that had once amounted to a third of revenues came to a complete stop during the depression. Crop exports also declined during those years after a series of poor harvests. To remedy the situation the Tanganyika Railway Administration was forced to cut back on staff (almost one-quarter of the total number of African workers), wages, and allowances. This was not a time for contemplating a costly new railway development project.[15]

After the Second World War interest in the southern railway was revived as the fortunes of Tanganyika Railways improved. During the war the territory had exported timber, sisal, and flour, products that were shipped on the central railway. In the postwar period a variety of development schemes were implemented that enhanced the prospects of both imports and exports—the Groundnut Scheme during the late 1940s required the shipment of large amounts of cement and petrol, bringing record profits for the railways. With the economic picture looking up, government engineers conducted a second extensive survey of the southern railway in 1950–51.[16] The field survey examined five different routes or sections of routes, a total of 1,867 miles, over a period of approximately one year, using aerial photographs. Yet even after this exhaustive engineering survey and report, the southern railway project still languished. A small portion of the surveyed railway was finally taken up—and constructed—to link the Kilombero Sugar Company to the central railway line at Kidatu in 1962–64, just prior to independence. The remainder of the line, however, was not built in the colonial period—it awaited support from China.

The Independence Period: A Freedom Railway

Following independence, the same southern railway plans that had represented a grand "Imperial Link" in the colonial period were revived, this time as a post-colonial railway of liberation. The link between Zambia and Dar es Salaam would be both materially and symbolically liberating, because it would end the division of Africa into competing spheres of influence. It would break the mold of colonial "divide and rule" policy, said Kenneth Kaunda upon TAZARA's completion: "Every time there is a communication network between African countries, that is a step nearer the end of our continent's balkanization on which imperialism has fattened itself."[17]

The end of "balkanization" was especially important for Zambia, a landlocked country whose dependency on Southern Rhodesia was due to a more complex set of factors than simple geography. Zambia's railways had been developed as an integral part of a larger southern and central African transportation network driven primarily by British and South African mining interests between 1890 and 1909. The British South Africa Company had a monopoly over both mineral and railway concessions at this time, and Zambia's railway development reflected the company's interest in mining revenues. Following the British takeover of government control in the Rhodesias after 1923, this railway system was consolidated under the management of Rhodesia Railways. This working company operated all of the railway lines in Southern Rhodesia and Zambia, and actively discouraged the development of alternative transport routes for Zambia's copper exports.[18]

Zambia's dependency on Southern Rhodesia's rail networks continued between 1953 and 1963, when the two countries were part of the Federation of Rhodesia and Nyasaland. During this period Rhodesia Railways relied on ports at Beira and Lourenço Marques (present-day Maputo) in Mozambique, and Durban in South Africa. Once the Federation broke up in 1963 and Zambia became independent in 1964, Zambia and Rhodesia shared ownership of Rhodesia Railways fifty-fifty. Both signed an agreement stating that if either of the two partners diverted their traffic from the Rhodesian network, they would be forced to pay compensation to the company.[19] Zambia therefore occupied a complex position of dependency on southern African railway routes as a result of the colonial development of railways and mining in the region. At the time of independence, Zambia had to contend not only with its geographical position as a landlocked country, but also with the legacy of a transportation system that was never intended to serve its broader economic and social development needs. As one transport economist observed, the pattern of transportation development around copper mining "has not been in the long-term interests of Zambia."[20]

The constitutional agreement on the future of Rhodesia Railways that was signed in 1963 placed limits on Zambia's ability to initiate new railway projects without paying a penalty to Rhodesia Railways. This presented a stumbling block for Zambia as negotiations began for the TAZARA project. According to a legal memorandum prepared at the time, Zambia's free participation as a partner in TAZARA would have required an amendment to the constitution of the Higher Authority of Rhodesia Railways.[21] This constitutional question complicated Kaunda's ability to express open public support for the railway link. In 1965 Zambia's diplomatic missions were instructed to respond that their government had "not yet reached the stage of 'viewing favorably' the construction of the link," when asked about the agreement with Rhodesia.[22] The British foreign aid office even discussed the possibility of intervening to resolve the constitutional question—but the problem resolved itself in 1966 when the Maxwell Stamp report concluded that a Tanzania-Zambia railway would not in fact divert revenue from the Rhodesian line.[23]

Meanwhile, Tanzania's leaders were also optimistic that the proposed TAZARA project could rectify negative legacies of colonial development planning. The southern region of Tanzania had been largely neglected following the Maji Maji War (1905–1907), and TAZARA's planners hoped that the railway would stimulate new development in the south. There were iron ore and coal deposits in the Ruhuhu-Songea area that could be tapped by the proposed railway, and the Usangu floodplain showed significant potential for agricultural and livestock development. Sugar production was especially important in the Kilombero valley, where mechanized rice production and ranching were also proposed. In the surrounding southern highlands maize farming and forest plantations were seen as productive options for Iringa, Njombe, and Mbeya. There were similar possibilities for rural development on the Zambian side, although the northeastern region had lower agricultural potential.

In addition to stimulating economic development in southern Tanzania and northeastern Zambia, the TAZARA railway was expected to be politically liberating for the entire southern African region. By breaking free from the hegemony of southern African mining interests, Zambia could provide inspiration for those fighting against white settler and Portuguese colonial rule in Rhodesia, Mozambique, Angola, and South Africa. The railway would also assist Zambia and Tanzania in their support for these liberation struggles: with an independent outlet to the sea, Zambia would no longer be as vulnerable to trade sanctions or border closings in retaliation for supporting the anti-colonial forces. Meanwhile, the railway could provide the means for shipping supplies, including military supplies, to the liberation forces in exile through a friendly neighboring country. For all of these reasons, therefore, Nyerere and Kaunda continued to move forward with their plans for constructing a railway link in 1964 despite the negative conclusions of the World Bank and United Nations railway survey reports.

Only one year later, the transportation picture in southern Africa was changed dramatically when the white settler regime in Rhodesia seized power and declared independence from Britain in November 1965 (The Unilateral Declaration of Independence or UDI). Zambia could no longer depend upon southern African transport routes for her exports and imports; indeed, the international economic boycott of Rhodesia in 1966 created a transportation emergency for landlocked Zambia. Rhodesia's oil pipeline from Beira to Umtali was blockaded by the British navy, requiring emergency airlifts of oil into Zambia by U.S., British, and Canadian military aircraft. Meanwhile, there was a scramble to improve Zambia's overland connections to Dar es Salaam. A joint road services company (ZTRS) was started in 1966 to improve the Great North Road to the coast, and the TAZAMA oil pipeline from Dar es Salaam to Ndola was completed between 1966 and 1968.[24] Yet despite these interventions Zambia continued to rely on Rhodesia Railways for much of her traffic. After 1965 only 50 percent of copper exports and 30 percent of general goods imports were diverted away from the southern routes. The picture looked brighter by 1967, when southbound exports had dropped to 34 percent and imports from the south to 37 percent. Yet the road services were simply not a viable alternative for all of Zambia's goods shipments, especially in the rainy season.[25] For Zambia in particular, then, the proposed Freedom Railway represented a lifeline for ending her dependency upon an increasingly hostile southern neighbor.

Faced with the urgency of this new situation, Nyerere and Kaunda accelerated their efforts to persuade the international community to assist them in constructing a railway link. It had become clear by this time that the southern routes through Rhodesia could no longer be relied upon. Meanwhile, the most promising alternative route, via Katanga to Lobito in Angola (the Benguela Railway), was disrupted by political instability and conflict in the southwest. Thus following UDI and international sanctions, analysts began to consider reports on the feasibility of a Zambia-Tanzania railway that were more favorable in their assessments than the World Bank study. The British Minister for Overseas Development, Barbara Castle, had already admitted that "there was now a growing realization that it was impossible to judge the project purely from an economic point of view."[26]

An inter-governmental committee to oversee plans for the railway link had been formed in April 1965, with two ministers each from Tanzania and Zambia. This committee also officially represented the interests of the other two members of the East African Railways and Harbors Corporation, Kenya and Uganda, until 1968 when the Tanzania Zambia Railway Authority was established. The first charge of the inter-governmental committee was to carry out a comprehensive engineering and economic survey. With funding support from Britain and Canada, the British firm Maxwell Stamp and Associates was engaged together with a Canadian aerial survey team, at an initial cost of £150,000. The Maxwell Stamp report would serve two primary functions: it would provide the information needed to make decisions about design and construction of the railway; and it could be circulated to interested governments and donors (in "cautiously worded terms") who desired to know specific information about the project's costs and feasibility.[27] Accordingly, in September 1965, a letter was sent out to the governments of Japan, Canada, France, West Germany, and China, inviting them to "consider participating in the provision of finance for the later stages for the project."[28] At the same time, the United Nations Special Fund and the United States were both approached about assisting the project, while an American firm, Kaiser Engineering Corporation, sent a team of engineers to gather data on the project.[29]

In the meantime, China had already begun to express interest in supporting the railway, initially during a state visit made by Julius Nyerere to Beijing in February 1965 and again in June of that year when Chinese Premier Zhou Enlai made a visit to Dar es Salaam. The initial twelve-person Chinese survey team arrived in Tanzania only two months after Zhou's departure, and although there was no formal commitment from China to finance and construct the railway at this time, Chinese interest in the project was becoming more evident.[30] What followed was a period of international speculation and confusion, what the Washington Post described as "part of the welter of political and diplomatic maneuvers that surround the railway and obscure the economic debate on it."[31]

Once the Stamp report was completed, it was apparently circulated to some interested parties abroad—Kaiser Engineering had reviewed it and responded positively to its findings in April 1967—while others did not receive the report at all until after China had already signed an agreement to support the railway in September 1967.[32] Internal memoranda from the Zambian foreign affairs ministry show that there were misunderstandings about when the Stamp report should be released and to whom, with the result that the report was temporarily "put away" and not circulated at all for a period of several weeks. This was apparently due to a bureaucratic oversight, rather than an intentional obfuscation, but that did not prevent rumors from circulating internationally about the way the agreement with China was handled. Representatives from western governments complained that they had "not been invited to say whether or not they were prepared to help."[33]

The first formal agreement between the governments of Zambia, Tanzania, and China for the construction of a railway link was signed in Beijing on September 5, 1967. According to a telegram posted to Lusaka on the day of the signing ceremony,

"The agreement was concluded in an atmosphere of mutual friendship and respect and to the complete satisfaction of the three governments. It marks the beginning of an important chapter in the economic history of this region of Africa." Under the terms of the agreement, the People's Republic of China agreed to extend an interest-free loan (of an unspecified amount) for the construction of the railway, which would take place following a detailed investigative survey and design phase. More specific technical and financial arrangements would be made following the analysis of the survey data.[34]

News of the signing of the agreement spread rapidly, and public reactions soon followed in diplomatic circles as well as in the news media. An article in the *Christian Science Monitor* accused China of being "coy" in its dealings with the African states, since the agreement did not commit China to anything beyond a survey: "The 'Cultural Revolution' may have produced a new ploy. China is not committed, at this stage, to more than the survey. Nevertheless, the Chinese have shrewdly exploited Black African nationalism with the survey alone. They can be expected to wring every last drop of propaganda juice from it."[35] Other reactions were more apprehensive, from western countries as well as from the Soviet Union, demonstrating according to Zambian observers "a feeling of desperation not only amongst the forces of the capitalist world, but unfortunately. . . . even the so called Socialist Camps such as the Soviet Union could on the issue of the Railway Project rally themselves with the Imperialists against the offer made by the Chinese."[36]

Even after the agreement with China had been signed in 1967, Zambia and Tanzania continued to correspond with interested donor countries and to circulate the Stamp report, stating publicly that offers for the railway were "still open." Copies of the report were sent out to all diplomatic and consular missions in Lusaka on October 26, 1967, with assurances of the "highest consideration" of the Ministry of Foreign Affairs. A Japanese firm requested copies of the agreement signed in China along with an official confirmation that the Tanzanian and Zambian governments would still accept offers from other governments and private enterprises. These inquiries, along with those from the United States and other countries, were viewed with skepticism in some quarters. "What were the Japanese doing before the Chinese decided to give us assistance?" queried Mr. Chimuka of the Zambian Foreign Affairs Ministry. A memorandum from the Permanent Secretary was more blunt: "It is now apparent that the Americans and the West in general are very disturbed about the whole railway project." The Americans were accused of having discouraged the project at first, but then, after the Stamp report indicated its feasibility, having "introduced a new phenomenon" in the form of a road transport survey. "The West has nobody else to blame but themselves," stated the memorandum, "since offers to build the Tan-Zam Railway were made to all potential candidates and only China has responded positively with a definite and unmistakable commitment."[37]

China's Development Vision: A Rainbow of Friendship

If Nyerere and Kaunda could be criticized at the time for their ideological approach to railway development after independence, the same charge could have been leveled at China, only more strongly. China's public statements about the TAZARA railway barely mentioned the railway's economic benefits, focusing instead on the need to combat imperialist influences. "The Tanzanian and Zambian people," one announcement proclaimed, "have built with the Chinese people's support and cooperation the over 1,800 kilometer long Tanzania-Zambia railway, smashing the imperialist slanders about the 'impossibility of a Tanzania-Zambia railway.'"[38] In another statement a Chinese correspondent made it clear that the Chinese viewed African development assistance in strategic terms:

> Under the cloak of "economic aid" and "military aid" the two superpowers, the Soviet Union and the United States, have been vigorously infiltrating into and expanding in Africa, interfering in the internal affairs of these countries and presenting a threat to their independence. The intentions cherished by the Soviet social-imperialists are particularly vicious, having the nature of greediness of arms peddlers, speculators and imperialists.[39]

In contrast to dealings with the Soviet Union, the relationship between China and Africa was consistently portrayed as one of cooperation and unity. Julius Nyerere distinguished Chinese assistance from all other forms of foreign aid when he stated that "China is a Third World country," and that although some other countries might use economic aid to exploit or to politically dominate Africans, "it is not China's policy at all."[40] The theme of "friendship" was used extensively to describe Chinese development assistance projects in Africa; according to Philip Snow, "friendship roads, friendship ports and friendship buildings sprang up all over the continent" wherever the Chinese invested in aid.[41] A book of poems about TAZARA's construction written by Chinese railway technicians was published in 1975 with the title *Rainbow of Friendship*. The woodcut prints that illustrated the poems depicted smiling African and Chinese workers toiling side by side.[42]

The TAZARA railway construction project came at a high monetary cost. It also diverted scarce technical expertise and industrial resources away from China when they were needed at home. What were the interests of China at this time that justified such a large-scale commitment of resources abroad? By the mid-1960s, having had friendly relations with many African nationalist movements during their

FIGURE 2.1.
Woodcut by Liang Yiqiang
and Don Peigao depicting
friendship between
African villagers and
TAZARA railway
workers, from a
collection of poetry.
Rainbow of Friendship, 107.

transitions to independence, China began to experience a low point in its diplomatic relations with Africa. Once African nations had become self-governing, the anti-imperialist and revolutionary tenor of Chinese foreign policy could be more discomfiting than inspirational for new African leaders. Zhou Enlai's comment during his historic 1963–64 tour of independent African nations that "revolutionary prospects are excellent throughout Africa," contributed to this anxiety.[43]

At the same time, there remained one region in Africa where the anti-colonial "racial line" was still relevant for Chinese diplomacy. In the still-colonized states of the south, support for the TAZARA railway link provided an opportunity for China to demonstrate continued support for liberation through a "just struggle" against white settler imperialism and Portuguese colonialism. China had already been providing support to the liberation movements, including both material assistance and military training, although this was complicated by the competition for influence with the Soviet Union.[44] Meanwhile, Chairman Mao's articulation of the "three worlds" theory of global politics allowed China to position itself as part of a marginalized "third world" united in solidarity against the hegemonism of the Americans and the Soviets. As "comrades in arms," stated one Chinese representative, China and Tanzania were working together to combat the "imperialism, colonialism and hegemonism" represented by the United States and the Soviet Union.[45]

China was also beginning to recognize that its lasting political influence in post-colonial Africa could come through development assistance, in particular from the positive example of China's own rural development experience. One after another, African heads of state had visited China to admire these accomplishments. Julius Nyerere was greatly influenced by the rural development he witnessed during his many visits to China, and commented often in public on the commitment to hard work and diligence that he had seen in rural Chinese villages. Kenyan politician Oginga Odinga stated in 1967 that "it was impossible not to be impressed with life in China. So many of the problems of poverty and illiteracy were those of our people, and those problems were being overcome at an impressive rate."[46] During TAZARA's construction in 1974, a delegation from Zambia to China reported positively on the model farms they viewed during visits to the Dazhai Production Brigade (a frequent destination for African delegations) and the Double Bridge Cuban Friendship Brigade on the outskirts of Beijing. They were impressed by the productivity of China's communes and hoped to apply lessons learned from China's development experience back home: "repatriation" of the urban jobless to rural areas, sending youth to the countryside between high school and university studies, and documenting the efficacy of traditional medicines.[47]

Some scholars have argued that the railway project also served an internal political function for China. Chinese railway workers in Africa were encouraged to study Mao's writings, in order to be inspired by him "to be determined, to be afraid of no sacrifices, to reject all difficulties and to achieve total victory."[48] Tanzanians were also expected to benefit from Mao's teachings, both by observing firsthand the model behavior displayed by Chinese technicians and also by reading for themselves from Mao's little red book (copies of the books, along with pins bearing Mao's likeness, were reportedly distributed widely in Tanzania in the 1960s).[49] Yet the bulk of the stories about the discipline, loyalty, and heroism of the Chinese railway workers were circulated not for an African audience, but for a Chinese one. News reports appeared almost weekly in Chinese publications, lauding the way the Chinese technicians were "imbued with Mao Tse-Tung's thought and working for the people of Africa. . . . not afraid of the hot burning sunshine."[50] The Chinese workers who reportedly toiled in the hot African sun while studying Mao's thought could be emulated by the Chinese who remained back home. In this way foreign assistance projects would project an image of "strength, unity and the revolutionary struggle."[51] Cultural performances, including the comedy routine known as "Crosstalk," introduced Chinese audiences to the geographical features of Tanzania, the challenges of railway building, and the Kiswahili language. In one routine Chinese actors undertook an imaginary visit to Tanzania to visit the railway, exclaiming about the beauty of the country, the hot sunshine, and the friendliness of the African people.[52]

For China's development vision, therefore, this large-scale "showcase" project was uniquely positioned to help meet strategic goals at home, in Africa, and in the world. A railway link that would liberate landlocked Zambia from dependency upon the southern routes enabled China to engage with her African comrades in a "just struggle against colonialism and imperialism" as represented by the settler-ruled states. By completing a project that had been rejected by other international donors, China had an opportunity to highlight its own approach to development assistance while exposing the "lies, slanders and maneuvers" of those who had claimed that post-colonial railways were not worthwhile. The construction of TAZARA would enable China to demonstrate to the world the beneficial application of the eight principles of development, including hard work, skills training, and brotherly solidarity. From the beginning China intended to complete the project ahead of schedule, in order to drive home these points and to instill pride and self-confidence in the newly independent African states.

The Three-Way Agreement

China had already made substantial commitments to development assistance in Tanzania by the time of the TAZARA negotiations. China and Tanzania signed a Treaty of Friendship in 1965, and by 1971 China had become Tanzania's largest single external donor, extending grants worth 5.6 million U.S. dollars between 1964 and 1966.[53] Most of this aid was in the form of agricultural and industrial development projects, the most famous of which was the *Urafiki* or Friendship Textile Mill in Dar es Salaam. China also provided Tanzania with military assistance and training at a time when this caused considerable anxiety among western countries. Some of this military support was sent onward to aid liberation movements in neighboring states.[54] China demonstrated a willingness to come to Tanzania's aid when western donors balked, particularly when political principles were at stake. When Britain failed to suppress Rhodesia's unilateral independence in 1965, Nyerere cut off diplomatic relations according to the principles adopted by the Organization for African Unity. In retaliation, the British froze their proposed loan support to Tanzania, worth about $21 million. The Chinese then offered, during the visit of the Tanzanian delegation to China, to fully finance the outstanding projects "which the British Government had promised to help build."[55]

One of the most important strategies employed by China in African development assistance was to offer generous terms of credit. The fifth of the eight principles of Chinese aid stated,

> The Chinese government provides economic aid in the form of interest-free or low-interest loans and extends the time limit for the repayment so as to lighten the burden of the recipient countries as far as possible.[56]

The cost of the railway was estimated at 988 million yuan, the equivalent at the time of £166 million or about $415 million. It would be financed by China through an interest-free loan, with the responsibility for repayment divided equally between Tanzania and Zambia over a thirty-year period and with a grace period of five years (this was later extended). Repayment was to be made in Tanzanian and Zambian currencies. The loan would cover equipment and technical services provided by China (amounting to 48 percent of the total) and local costs (52 percent).[57]

One of the major constraints faced by China in development assistance was its limited access to foreign exchange. For this reason China endeavored as much as possible to provide assistance in the form of equipment, materials, and technical expertise rather than monetary transfers. This resulted in some difficulties for recipient countries because Chinese equipment was not always standard, making it difficult to obtain spare parts and provide long-term maintenance. And sometimes the equipment provided was not well suited for local conditions, as was the case with the original Chinese diesel hydraulic locomotives supplied for TAZARA.[58] Meanwhile, China's own supply of industrial equipment was apparently limited, as evidenced by the Chinese transfer of ninety-eight Japanese-built bulldozers to Tanzania for the TAZARA project in 1970. These constraints were also one of the reasons for the labor-intensive approach to the railway's construction.

The Chinese developed a way of covering the local costs of the TAZARA project that relieved pressure on their foreign currency reserves. Local costs—including worker wages, housing, foodstuffs, medical care, and local building materials—would be financed through a commodity credit agreement. Through this arrangement, Chinese goods worth the full value of this portion of the loan would be imported into Tanzania and Zambia, and the proceeds from their sale would be used to pay for the local expenses. This required a complex set of arrangements involving Chinese commodity traders, national banks in China, Zambia, and Tanzania, and the Tanzania Zambia Railway Authority. Each of the two African partners would be committed to consuming around 8.5 million pounds of Chinese goods annually for a period of five years. By providing commodities that would be sold through

African government cooperatives, the commodity loan would ease the pressure on China's own limited foreign exchange supply.[59]

Arrangements for the purchase of merchandise from Chinese suppliers were made through the Canton Trade Fair, an import and export trade exhibition that took place twice yearly in the southern port city of Guangzhou. This system created communication difficulties for Tanzanian and Zambian state corporations in 1969, because they found it difficult to follow up with their Chinese trading partners.[60] Nevertheless, over a five-year period government cooperative shops in rural Tanzania and Zambia were stocked with Chinese textiles, housewares, bicycles, and pharmaceuticals. Ngila Mwase estimates that the proportion of Tanzania's total imports that came from China rose after the commodity loan agreement from less than 5 percent to over 22 percent. Chinese products did not replace Tanzanian manufactures but did reduce imports from neighboring African countries, particularly Kenya.[61]

Following the initial agreement between China, Tanzania, and Zambia that had been signed in September 1967, there were still significant issues remaining to be ironed out between the three partners. One issue had to do with the governance of the railway on the African side—and how to handle Tanzania's membership in the East African Railways and Harbors Corporation (EARH). A formal agreement was signed on March 12, 1968, to create the Tanzania Zambia Railway Authority, a corporate body that would coordinate the implementation of the railway project.[62] By passing this bill in Parliament, the Tanzanian government was freed from its earlier obligation to provide all of its railway services through the EARH.

A more significant issue that had been on the table since the start of talks about the railway link was its route. The original Chinese plan, like that of earlier colonial surveyors, had been to start building the railway at Kidatu, where it would intersect with the central railway line. This however would have created a costly transshipment problem, because it was also agreed that the TAZARA line would be built with the southern African wide gauge (3'6") rather than the narrower East African gauge (3'3"). A transshipment station would therefore have to be built and operated at Kidatu. The possibility of continuing the railway line all the way to Dar es Salaam, parallel to the central line, was raised as an alternative option. The Chinese were willing to consider having the railway begin on the coast at Dar es Salaam in Tanzania and run through the border crossing of Tunduma to Kapiri Mposhi in Zambia. This route was formally agreed to in a supplementary agreement signed in Lusaka on November 14, 1969. The new route would add approximately 340 kilometers to the total length of the railway.[63]

On the Zambian side, meanwhile, there had long been talk of routing the railway link to a terminus at Tanzania's most southern port at Mtwara in addition to or even in lieu of Dar es Salaam. This option was formally put on the table during discussions held in Lusaka on April 12, 1965, and continued to be discussed in subsequent meetings. If it had been adopted, it would have dramatically altered the geography of economic development in southern Tanzania. Some Zambians doubted whether the capacity of the port at Dar es Salaam would ever be adequately developed for the increased traffic created by the TAZARA railway as well as the U.S.-funded Tanzam highway. They proposed the development of Mtwara as a second East African port "which could meet any shortfall of capacity on the northern route or, conversely, the use of the Mtwara route to the fullest extent making use of the northerly route for traffic which could not be carried over the line to Mtwara."[64] The issue came up again in 1969, when a recommendation was made directly to President Kaunda that an alternative route from Kidatu to Mtwara be surveyed. Kaunda replied that the Mtwara option was a political "non-starter" in negotiations with Tanzania and China, and could only be considered after there was "practical proof" that the Dar port was inadequate—in other words, after the railway had already been built.[65]

The final agreement between the three countries was signed in Beijing on July 12, 1970, after the survey and design work had been completed and the specific financial and technical arrangements could be spelled out. The railway was now planned to extend the full 1,860 kilometers from Dar es Salaam to Kapiri Mposhi in Zambia. This meant that shipments could flow from Zambia straight to Dar es Salaam's harbor without expensive additional transshipment costs, thus also providing a realistic transport alternative for countries to the south that operated on the same gauge. China would provide the rolling stock and the locomotives, manufactured in China, as well as the steel rails, signaling equipment, and other materials. The cement sleepers and poles would be produced in a workshop in Tanzania, and timber and ballast would be obtained locally in the areas adjacent to the railway corridor.

China agreed to provide the engineering and construction expertise for the project by recruiting railway experts and technicians from throughout China. The exact number of Chinese railway workers who served during the construction period is not known, and has been the subject of some speculation. Published estimates range from 15,000 to 50,000 for the overall number of Chinese workers; this discrepancy reflects the difficulty in obtaining precise statistics as well as some confusion over the length of time of Chinese technical assistance being measured. There have also been political reasons for adjusting the numbers of Chinese workers: media reports hostile to the project may have exaggerated the numbers of Chinese present in East Africa at the time, while the Chinese and African governments tended to be secretive about them for security reasons. The CIA kept track of the population of "communist economic technicians" in less developed countries, and reported in 1974 that more than three-fifths of the 23,000 Chinese technicians working overseas, or 13,800, were involved in TAZARA's construction.[66] It is probably safe to state that in the years of intensive construction between 1970 and 1974 a total of some 30,000–40,000 Chinese worked on the project on teams that served two-year contracts; a Chinese source cites 50,000 as the total number of workers over the eleven-year period of surveying, construction, and management training.[67] These Chinese workers were accompanied by some 60,000 or more African workers from Tanzania and Zambia. Calculating the total number of African workers is also difficult, in part because there was high turnover.

Anti-Hegemonism

When they first proposed the construction of an alternative rail route from the Zambian copper belt to the Indian Ocean, Julius Nyerere and Kenneth Kaunda were accused of putting nationalist and pan-Africanist ideologies before economic efficiency. After 1965, economists were more willing to acknowledge the ways that a new East African railway might improve regional economies. Following Rhodesia's settler takeover it had become clear that strategic interests were intimately linked with economic interests in a region where colonial transportation infrastructure had been so profoundly affected by European mining investment and territorial rivalries.

When China became interested in funding the TAZARA project, public commentary once again focused on the political. Western analysts were concerned about the military and strategic consequences of the "Red Guard Line Chugging into Africa."[68] It was true that China was using development assistance in Africa to achieve larger international strategic goals—for example, to win a seat in the United Nations with the help of its African allies. And there was certainly a "thick ideological flavor" to China's public announcements of support for the railway link.[69] Yet even in this setting, economic factors remained important to the way China articulated its development vision, affecting the way the project was funded and the legacy that the railway project left behind in rural Tanzania.

Politics and economics came together differently in China's approach to development principles in Africa than they had during late colonialism. Chinese foreign policy did not divide the world into the binary Cold War categories of East versus West, but envisioned "three worlds." Mao had developed this "three worlds" theory in the mid-1960s because he viewed the United States and Soviet Union as having commonalities as well as differences. Chinese public statements described the Soviets and the Americans alike as expansionist, profit-seeking imperialists in Africa. The Chinese on the other hand were described as the sympathetic third world partners of African countries. As we will see in the next chapters, China was not just trying to create an alternative model that was anti-capitalist and therefore socialist. China's development principles were articulated as anti-hegemonic.

What, exactly, constituted an anti-hegemonic model of African development, according to China? The blueprint for anti-hegemonism lay in the eight principles of development. African and Chinese railway workers would live side by side in rural areas at the same standard of living. Work would be uplifting and would impart necessary skills; African laborers would no longer be treated as the toiling underclass of mining capitalism. The idealism behind these anti-hegemonic development principles was matched by economic practicality. Given China's monetary constraints, it made sense to construct the railway using African and Chinese labor rather than expensive foreign-built equipment. Local labor costs could be more easily supported through the sale of Chinese commodities. Thus development ideals and monetary realities came together in practice during TAZARA's construction. In rural villages along the railway line, China's unique approach to development—in particular the way the Chinese technicians worked and interacted with their African counterparts—shaped local experience and memory of the project. Local people did not have much direct contact with the Chinese technicians. Yet they remember the simplicity of their dress and comportment; the way they lived in local accommodations and grew their own food; and most especially their dedication to hard work.

3

Building the People's Railway

At the end of the dry month of August in 1965, a small team of Chinese surveyors and their African guides set off on foot from the town of Kidatu into the southern interior of Tanzania, heading southwestward toward the Zambian border. Carrying their supplies and equipment on their backs, this group would cover a distance of over four hundred miles before returning safely to Dar es Salaam nine months later. The team comprised twelve Chinese railway specialists accompanied by nine Tanzanian game scouts. Their job was to determine which of the many possible railway routes would be most feasible for construction. As they cleared their path across the landscape they reportedly left behind them a trail of bamboo marker poles with small red flags fluttering in the breeze.[1]

This Chinese survey team was ridiculed in the Kenyan press as an example of the ineptitude of "communist aid" in Africa. These were not genuine surveyors with proper surveying equipment, reported the *Kenya Weekly News* (a forum for the white settler community), but ordinary railway technicians imported from China who (the *News* implied) had no business carrying out such an enterprise.[2] A correspondent for the *Economist* complained that the 1965 survey report "turned out to be little help" to development analysts since it was written in Swahili and Chinese.[3] In fact, this first Chinese survey was never intended to be comprehensive; it was followed up three years later by a much larger and more thorough study of the proposed railway corridor.[4] Nevertheless, the image of this small team marching across the southern Tanzanian interior with their bamboo marker poles is an impor-

FIGURE 3.1. Surveying the railway line in Ulanga District. Photograph courtesy of Tanzania Department of Information Services (Maelezo).

tant one, for it symbolized China's approach to development assistance during the construction of TAZARA. The survey group modeled Zhou Enlai's eighth principle of development: the Chinese experts were to live and work according to the same standards as their African counterparts, without enjoying special amenities. The railway would be built using a labor-intensive rather than a capital-intensive model; themes of hard work and simplicity would guide the project from the survey and design phase through its completion.

The modest comportment of the Chinese surveyors provided a stark symbolic contrast with the prevailing tradition of European exploration of the African interior. From the nineteenth century onward, European survey parties had employed large convoys of porters, guides, and servants. Far from carrying their own supplies, European explorers had in many instances been carried themselves, in hammocks slung over the shoulders of their bearers, or on the backs of donkeys. Railway surveyors in the colonial period had always traveled with large retinues. During their reconnaissance expedition for the proposed southern railway in 1925, British surveyors were accompanied by "faithful Wanyamwezi porters."[5] The field survey party that studied the same route in 1950–51 under the direction of Sir Alexander Gibb and Partners included one assistant engineer and three surveyors (all Europeans) accompanied by fifty-six African porters and servants.[6] And the Anglo-Canadian survey team that produced the Maxwell Stamp report in the mid-1960s conducted much of their survey of the proposed railway line from the air.

The conduct of the small 1965 survey expedition hinted at the ways Chinese technical assistance in East Africa would endeavor to provide an alternative development model. During TAZARA's construction the Chinese experts would impart not only technical skills but also the values of simplicity, self-discipline, hard work, and brotherly solidarity. The comportment of the Chinese workers on the TAZARA project was of the utmost importance because the project was China's development showcase in Africa, closely watched by a world audience that, at least in some quarters, was highly skeptical. For Tanzania and Zambia, the construction of the railway was also an important opportunity to articulate and put into practice their own development principles as newly independent African states. The railway project symbolized the possibilities of new nationhood, and workers were recruited throughout Tanzania and Zambia to foster national commitment to the project. TAZARA was called the "people's railway," emphasizing not only the members of each nation but also the regional pan-African community of Zambians and Tanzanians.

The 1965 survey team introduced early on the theme of hard work that was to characterize the entire construction project. The Chinese emphasized this frequently as they pressed their work teams to complete the project ahead of schedule. Hard work was meant to be educational for African workers: by practicing disciplined work habits they were expected to accomplish their tasks early, and in the process to build self-esteem and to cultivate self-reliance. The challenge of building the railway under harsh conditions was intended to impart valuable lessons to Africans that would assist them in future development activities. As Tanzanian prime minister Rashidi Kawawa stated after construction was completed, the Zambian and Tanzanian workers had received "the best kind of training" during TAZARA's construction, and this could now be applied to other development work.[7] In practice, however, many African workers found work on the project to be grueling and living conditions to be intolerable; for this reason many workers ended up leaving the project altogether.

The theme of brotherly solidarity was also emphasized during the surveys and afterward, as Chinese and African workers labored side by side on the railroad. One group was not expected to serve or to be exploited by another, according to China's development guidelines. Although there were differences in age and experience between the two groups, and their tasks were not equivalent, they were expected to show one another mutual respect. Some African workers did work closely with their Chinese counterparts, frequently in relationships of instruction and tutelage. Many African workers described their relationships with the Chinese as those of juniors and elders, emphasizing the mentoring and teaching role played by the Chinese technicians. For these younger African men, building the railway was a coming-of-age experience, a time of moving into adulthood.

The experience of construction was also one of expanding modernity. For many of the young African school-leavers it was their first opportunity to earn a wage that could support them and their families. Rural modernization was also felt in the villages along the railway. TAZARA's construction brought strangers and new ways of working into places that formerly had been isolated. Local communities felt the beginnings of a long-term reorganization of rural life as new patterns of mobility, residence, and exchange were laid down alongside the rails. Even the landscape itself was transformed by the excavation of quarries, culverts, and tunnels. This experience of landscape change was a concern for the local elders who were the guardians of sacred sites disturbed by the railway's progress.

Survey and Design

With the signing of the first trilateral agreement in Beijing on September 5, 1967, the parties could begin making serious plans for the surveying and design phase. In 1968 a second and much larger survey team was sent out to chart the railway's path across the southwestern interior of Tanzania and through northeastern Zambia. The period of survey and design lasted from April 1968 through June 1970, as the surveyors scouted over eight hundred miles of potential track between Dar es Salaam and New Kapiri Mposhi.[8] The surveyors were divided into field teams that were spread out along the proposed line of rail, with each team responsible for a specific section, some operating from the Zambian side and others from the Tanzanian side of the border. The field teams were further divided into six subgroups: the flag team would go first, to clear the proposed route and to guide the others. They were followed by the traverse team, which carried out the line and distance survey using compass, rods, and steel tape. The topographical team and the drilling team took soil samples from land surfaces and from river bottoms for further analysis. There was also an electrical team and a base camp group, the latter made up of the engineers and technicians who did the design work and technical drawings.[9]

Carol Mpandamgongo remembers what it was like when the second survey expedition passed through his village of Ikule. "The Chinese came," he said, "and they told us, '*Jamani!* Hey everyone! We have come, we are ready now, we are bringing the news that we are building a railway!'" It was a time filled with excitement and expectation. Even the nation's leaders came through Ikule to announce that the railway was coming, Mpandamgongo recalled, including *Baba Taifa* (Julius Nyerere) himself. Martin Mtwanga of Mchombe remembers that he was so moved by these announcements that he decided to join the survey team. "I did that work because they told me that through cooperating with one another we would bring economic development and transportation" to the country, he remembers.[10]

Philemon Kigola also worked on the survey team. He was assigned in 1969 to survey the section between Mlimba and Makambako where eighteen of the railway's twenty-two tunnels would be built, as well as some of the most challenging bridges and earthworks. He remembers that the survey team had forty Chinese surveyors and about sixty Tanzanians. He was trained on site in surveying techniques and stayed with the team until they reached Igurusi and finished in 1970. The tunnels section was very difficult to survey. Here rugged hillsides were dissected by deep river valleys, and the entire area was sparsely settled. The surveyors used chain saws and machetes to clear a path through the dense brush as they clambered up and down steep slopes to mark the route. Kigola recalls that the Chinese team leaders were guided in some places by cement stakes that had been left behind by the British surveyors from the Gibb expedition. "In 1951," he said, "the British had surveyed this railway line. They had placed their own markers—cement stakes. The Chinese did not go far away from that line. They only diverged from that line along the Udzungwa mountains."[11]

The work of the second survey party was especially arduous for the Chinese workers, who were inexperienced with the East African terrain and its hazards. Retired Chinese surveyors retain clear memories of the dangerous and challenging conditions they experienced as they trekked through the Selous Game Reserve, crossed the Kilombero valley floodplain, and ascended into the rugged mountains above Mlimba toward Makambako.[12] In the Selous Reserve they had many encounters with wild animals; buffaloes in particular were aggressive and caused injuries to the workers. In forested areas visibility could be less than two meters, while in the waterlogged lowland forests it was almost impossible to make progress, especially during the rainy season. In the dry thickets of the foothills, Chinese surveyors were plagued by skin rashes caused by the pubescent pods of the buffalo bean, or *upupu*, plant.[13] Some were especially sensitive to this plant, and wore long-sleeved cotton jackets to protect their skin despite the tropical heat. One Chinese surveyor suffered a fatal allergic reaction.[14]

In the floodplains grasses grew taller than a man's height, requiring the survey party to slash their way through using machetes known as *pangas*. The grasses grew so thick and sturdy that it became too time-consuming to cut them all down, so the teams attempted to beat them back in order to make their way, or used local methods of grass burning in areas that were not forested. Vehicles were sent out ahead of the workers to clear a path through the dense growth, after which the surveyors would follow, riding in the beds of the Jie Fang or "liberation" trucks that carried them to their work sites. The Chinese engineers recalled lines from a classical poem while surveying this section: "wind lowers the grass to show the sheep and cattle." They joked that the grasses in Tanzania were so tall and thick that "wind lowers the grass to show the Jie Fang"; the trucks were so deeply submerged in the grasses that their tops were only made visible when the wind blew over them.[15]

High on the mountainous slopes of the Mufindi escarpment, the surveyors were challenged by the terrain and also by the cold temperatures that caused them to sleep under warm quilts at night. This was the famous tunnels section, and its challenges gained it a special place in news reports back in China. One news story recounted two dangerous incidents and rescues from this section in heroic terms: "First, a Chinese technician encountered unexpected danger; a Tanzanian worker stepped up in spite of risks to his own safety, and saved his Chinese comrade. Not long after, when a Tanzanian worker fell into trouble, a Chinese worker used his own body and saved his comrade's life. Now, these tales of love and support between workers from the two countries are being told on this road of friendship."[16] The behavior of workers during construction was held up in this way as an example of the larger principles of solidarity and friendship that guided the development project.

As the Chinese-led survey team traveled through the interior of southern Tanzania, the route they were clearing was already opening up new opportunities for trade and mobility in areas that had formerly been inaccessible. In those populated parts of the Kilombero valley where villages were already established, the survey line prefigured a new orientation for the transportation of goods and people. Where there had been no communication at all in the past, the surveyors created new thoroughfares. As they sited the locations of construction camps, railway stations, tunnels, and earthworks, therefore, the surveyors also charted the future patterns of settlement and exchange. These patterns began to take on a more tangible shape when the construction teams moved into the countryside in late 1969.

Worker Recruitment

Recruitment of workers for the construction of the railway reflected both the guiding principles of China's development policy and the political importance of nation-building in Tanzania and Zambia. Education and training would be provided on the job; recruitment criteria for the African workers therefore stressed good health, character, and discipline rather than extensive prior education or work experience. Physical fitness was one of the most important requirements for the African railway recruits, remembers Rogatus Nyumayo, who had to submit to a physical examination when he signed up to work on the railway in Iringa in 1971. "They measured us up like we were soldiers," he recalled. Those who didn't measure up were left behind.[17]

Chinese railway workers on the other hand were selected for their level of experience and technical specialization. There were two categories of Chinese railway workers, a smaller group of engineering "experts" assisted by a larger group of "technicians." All Chinese workers were expected to demonstrate personal character and ideological commitment, according to those who participated in the project: they should possess "strong bodies, strong minds, and strong skills." The TAZARA project took place during a time when life in China was unusually difficult, as the years of the railway's construction paralleled those of the Cultural Revolution (1966–76) and much of China was itself still underdeveloped at the time. Some retired workers described finding the living conditions in Tanzania and Zambia to be better than they were in parts of China. There were also material incentives for those who went to work on TAZARA: they continued to receive their normal salary from the Ministry of Railways, with an additional forty *yuan* per month as a spending allowance. Chinese workers remember saving these allowances until their departure, when they used them to make special purchases before returning home. Omega watches, Philips cassette tape recorders, cameras, and radios were popular luxury items that they remember buying from the shops of Dar es Salaam.[18]

In Tanzania and Zambia, recruitment for the railway was made a national and transnational priority. "The Authority considers it is important from the outset to give the service an international character in the recruitment drive," stated a 1970 report. "The recruitment will be done across the length and breadth of Tanzania and Zambia. This would avoid giving the impression that this railway is for the people in Dar es Salaam or Lusaka." Recruitment would focus primarily on young people, seeking to employ the "disciplined, loyal and dedicated youths of the ruling parties in both countries," especially those physically strong enough to endure the rough life of the work camps. To keep their political consciousness "constantly alive," these youths would be provided with political materials and training. They would be paid a wage of two hundred shillings per month plus a food and living allowance, a wage that acknowledged that the project's "emphasis [was] on nation building" rather than material gain.[19]

In Tanzania, recruitment was carried out through the offices of the national party, TANU. Announcements were sent throughout the country and posted at the local TANU offices. "Recruitment was a national effort," remembered Benedict Mkanyago, "so they advertised all over Tanzania and Zambia."[20] At the time there were few employment opportunities for young men, particularly those with minimal education and skills. Andrew Mangile learned of TAZARA through the TANU labor office in Dar es Salaam, where he had been checking every two or three weeks for news of a job. He was hired by the TAZARA project on October 31, 1969, and assigned to Kurasini base camp, where he was in charge of the storehouse of water pipes.[21]

Rogatus Nyumayo had also responded to an announcement posted at the TANU office when he signed up in Iringa. "They took eight hundred people from Iringa in one day," he remembers, "in about five buses from Iringa town. They took us straight to camp at Mkela Base Camp, to work on the tunnels. After about three days they divided us up into work teams."[22] Salum Mwasenga learned about TAZARA job opportunities in Mbeya, where the regional leaders announced the building of the railway. "So I came forward to cooperate with the Chinese experts," he remembered. He was posted to Mang'ula, where he worked in the foundry and learned engineering skills.[23]

Workers were also recruited through the Tanzanian National Service, or JKT (*Jeshi la Kujenga Taifa*). A group of seven thousand Tanzanian youths were recruited from the National Service in 1970, given a two-week training program including military drill, and then sent out to construction camps between Dar es Salaam and Mlimba.[24] Most of the recruits who responded to this national campaign were young men aged sixteen to twenty-five (this was in contrast with the Chinese workers, who tended to be in their thirties and forties), and few had much education beyond the primary level. The TAZARA project recruited these youths from the National Service, Daniel Mumello remembers, because they were supposed to have "discipline, dedication and energy." But when working conditions were difficult they became easily frustrated, probably because "they were young men and needed careful handling."[25] Some of them reportedly expected special treatment—for example, extra allowances for food, clothing, and accommodations. Those who made these demands were dismissed, while others were reported to be "hard working and well behaved."[26]

Daniel Mumello's view was confirmed by John Gilbert, who was brought from the JKT camp at Mgulani to work on TAZARA in 1971. While he stayed on and continued to work for TAZARA for many years, some others in his group did not. "We were brought here from Mgulani in the vehicles of the Chinese, and we arrived in a place that had a lot of forest. It was a place for soldiers; in fact when we arrived here we were a very large number [of soldiers]; I can't even remember the number of people. And among us, some of those who had come from the JKT ran away because the work was so difficult. Because often we were working night and day in shifts, rain or shine, as we were digging out the bridges and the culverts."[27] The workers recruited from the National Service were not segregated from other workers, but worked alongside them in the work teams. Christian Bulaya was recruited from the JKT camp in Masasi, where he had just been assigned after finishing secondary school in Mwanza. He remembers that during construction, soldiers like himself "came together with the common citizens. We all worked together; there were no differences between us."[28]

Christian Bulaya's memory of National Service youth working together side by side with the "common citizens" echoes the theme of worker solidarity that was repeated often during the project, whether in public statements from political leaders or in the announcements made at regular worker meetings. One of the stated goals of the project was to recruit a balance of workers from both Tanzania and Zambia, and for those workers to represent diverse regions, ethnic groups, and languages. In the end, however, the construction project ended up hiring more Tanzanians than Zambians. And within Tanzania, despite the intention of recruiting a national pool of laborers, the majority of workers came from the southern highlands region. In interviews with former workers, Ali Sendaro found that 54 percent had been recruited from the southern highlands, 43 percent from the remainder of the country, and 3 percent from the national service. Of this entire group only 14 percent had finished primary school. The project apparently avoided hiring workers from the areas immediately adjacent to the railway. According to John Gilbert, those who lived along the railway were a poor choice for recruitment "because the people here were fishermen, they weren't reliable workers."[29] Local workers would have been the least expensive to recruit and to employ because they lived so close to the project. Yet like wage workers in the colonial period, they were also most likely to leave their positions when they were needed at home. Their proximity to families and farms made it less attractive for them to stay on the line, especially during the planting and harvesting seasons.[30]

There were two competing factors at work during the recruitment efforts, explained Daniel Mumello in his report from Mkela Base Camp: politics and efficiency. "The Management had to choose between recruiting at almost no expense from areas near the railway route or recruiting at a high cost from all over Tanzania and Zambia," he wrote. While local labor was initially cheaper, these workers proved "to have a kind of laissez-faire attitude towards work, they tended to work for the sake of satisfying their temporary cash needs."[31] Some observers, like Gilbert, attributed local lack of interest in wage labor to cultural factors (residents of the

Kilombero valley had long been labeled as lazy and indolent). Yet local farmers also had much to gain by producing foodstuffs for the construction camps. Some of these camps housed thousands of workers who consumed quantities of rice, maize, and cooking bananas. As in the colonial period, the need for local food supplies could be a disincentive for local villagers in the TAZARA corridor to sign up for wage labor.[32]

Teaching by Example

Once TAZARA's construction recruits had signed on, they were transported in open trucks to the work camps, railway workshops, and warehouses where they would begin their new jobs. They were given intensive training in some cases, but more often they were simply sent out to the work site, where they would learn by doing. "The workers learn as they go about their job in the field," stated a report from the first base camp in 1969. "One person attached to Drilling Team No. 1 since December 1968 is learning how to handle the drilling machine with much success; and another man in the Pushers group is now able to drive a Pusher."[33] This form of practical training or "teaching by example" was the primary method used by the Chinese in development assistance; when theory was taught it was directly related to practice. "They preferred to teach without words," wrote Philip Snow. "A technician would assemble and dismantle a piece of machinery and encourage his African apprentices to follow suit until they got the procedure right."[34]

More formal job training for workers who had proven their ability was offered at the four railway training schools that opened at Mang'ula (1971), Mgulani (1972), and Mbeya (1974) in Tanzania, and at Mpika in Zambia (1974). The curriculum at Mang'ula included construction and maintenance of the permanent way and bridges, telecommunications, signaling, and locomotive driving. In all a total of twelve hundred African workers were trained in technology and railway management at these workshops during the construction and handing-over periods. A smaller number of workers were sent to China for further studies; some two hundred Tanzanians and Zambians were selected in 1972 to attend a three-year training program at Northern Jiaotong University in Beijing.[35]

Working on the Freedom Railway

In late August of 1969, the Chinese ocean liner *Yao Hua* pulled into Kurasini harbor in Dar es Salaam carrying over one thousand Chinese railway technicians.

Ankunft von chinesischen Eisenbahnbauern im
Hafen von Daressalam, der Hauptstadt Tansanies.
Jeder hat den gleichen Koffer, jeder trägt seine
Habseligkeiten selber. Die Chinesen bauen eine Bahn von
der tansanischen Küste bis ins 1500 Kilometer ent-
fernte Kupferrevier des Nachbarstaates Sambia

FIGURE 3.2. Chinese workers arrive in Dar es Salaam: "each has the same suitcase; each carries his own belongings." *Die Stern* magazine, 1974.

Experienced railway workers had been recruited from all over China, and their journey to East Africa from the southern seaport of Guangzhou took twelve to twenty days. Each Chinese recruit—they were almost all men—wore an identical grey cotton suit and cap, and each carried a small blue suitcase balanced on his shoulder. As they disembarked from their ship, martial music blared from the ship's loudspeakers. Large crowds of Tanzanian spectators gathered at the dockside to observe them. The uniform dress and strict discipline of the workers caused a buzz of rumor to spread that these strangers must be prisoners doing gang labor, or perhaps conscripted soldiers. The majority of the Chinese workers stayed only briefly at their coastal base camp before heading up-country in truck convoys. Cargo loads of construction equipment including rails, cement, and other goods were also unloaded onto the docks at Kurasini as Chinese ships arrived monthly from Guangzhou. Crowds of curious onlookers greeted each successive shipload of workers and supplies.[36]

The construction of the railway was inaugurated with two ceremonies, the first in Dar es Salaam on October 26, 1970, and the second two days later in Kapiri Mposhi, on October 28. To symbolize cooperation between the two countries, Zambia's president was slated to address the crowds in Tanzania, and Tanzania's president was to do the same in Zambia. Thus Kenneth Kaunda gave the first official address in Dar es Salaam, after which he and Julius Nyerere flew with their Chinese guests to Kapiri Mposhi. In his speech in Zambia, Nyerere pledged that the African people would show their appreciation to China "through our endeavors to speed the work which you are doing with us, and through our determination to use this railway for the exclusive benefit of the peasants and workers of Africa."[37] Nyerere's statement foreshadowed the contradictions that would later emerge between completing the project ahead of schedule and training a self-sufficient African railway management and labor force.

Meanwhile, heavy construction equipment continued to arrive at the port of Kurasini in Dar es Salaam. Supplies, equipment, and workers were carried up-country using three communication networks: by rail along the central railway line; by truck on the Tanzam highway; and into the interior along newly cleared roads that were built to support the construction. A British reporter who traveled on one of these roads described how he "swayed and sweated inside the vehicle, choking on the clouds of dust whenever we came up behind the convoys of Chinese trucks. The temporary dirt-tracks, hurriedly scraped on the mountainside by shovel and muscle, were beginning to show signs of the dry-season."[38] According to Daniel Mumello, the temporary road between Mlimba and Makambako was improved and kept passable only through the "unaccountable efforts" of road maintenance personnel during the entire period of construction, even in the rainy season. Once new sections of the TAZARA line were completed, these too were used to ferry materials to the next construction sites.[39]

Benedict Mkanyago explained the way construction proceeded from the coast: "Kurasini was the first base camp; that was where all of the equipment for the railway was unloaded. This heavy equipment was taken on the central railway line up to Mikumi and from there to Kidatu, where they built the second big base camp, at Mang'ula. It was a large base camp that also had a workshop with several factories." The territory that lay between the coast and Mang'ula base camp was almost all within the Selous Game Reserve, making construction work along this stretch of railway line both dangerous and isolated. Workers labored and camped here in the open bush, surrounded by wild animals and far from any population center where they might have found food, home-brewed beer, or the company of villagers. "I would have to say," noted Mkanyago, "that the environment there was extremely difficult for the workers, because there was not even a small village anywhere nearby."[40]

While the first tracks were being laid into the Selous Game Reserve, other work was commencing in the interior. The construction of access roads was followed by the establishment of twelve base camps. Each of these large camps had a resident work team and was responsible for a given section of the railway line.

Chinese railway experts supervised the workers, who were divided further into smaller sub-teams directed by Chinese field assistants. The sub-teams were each given a specific task to fulfill—some were assigned to build bridges, while others dug ditches, constructed the raised railway bed, or connected telephone lines. Each sub-team set up a temporary camp where they lived until they had completed their assigned tasks. They would then pack up their camp and move on to the next section. The sub-teams worked in even smaller gangs, sometimes as few as eight to ten people, supervised by Tanzanian foremen under the direction of a Chinese counterpart. The work gangs were spread out along the railway line during the day, some two to three miles apart. One field team could be made up of thousands of workers; at Mwale base camp in 1972, there were 64 labor gangs involving about 5,500 laborers.[41]

Despite the difficulties of working through the wilderness of the Selous Game Reserve, the 110-mile length of track from Dar es Salaam to Mlimba was completed within one year. The notorious tunnels section which followed, in contrast, took almost the whole of the following year to finish even though it comprised only half the distance. The engineering and construction challenges of this section had seemed almost insurmountable to each of the successive teams of earlier surveyors that had inspected the route. One-third of the civil engineering works for the whole line were built here: not only eighteen of the twenty-two tunnels but also several high bridges over steep ravines. The work required extensive road building and earthworks, and more construction camps per kilometer than any other section. There were also more casualties here than in other sections, including Chinese casualties. The Chinese press celebrated with relief once the tunnels section had been completed in 1973. "The victorious completion of the Mlimba-Makambako section ahead of schedule powerfully revealed the iron will of the Tanzanian, Zambian, and Chinese people to overcome all barriers and to be invincible in the construction of the railway," enthused the *People's Daily*.[42]

The tunnels had been measured and sited by the Chinese engineering surveyors who charted the route in 1968–70. During construction they guided the teams of workers as they labored to excavate from both ends of each tunnel at the same time, blasting through the rock until they met up in the middle. The Tanzanian workers described their amazement when they hollowed out a tunnel, each team working from the opposite side without being able to see the other, until they finally reached the point in the center where they came together. This was especially impressive for the teams working on the Iganga tunnel, which had a total length of 817 meters and curved three times.[43]

Rogatus Nyumayo was one of the workers in the tunnels section, where he was assigned to work on Tunnel Eleven at Mpanga. It took an entire year for his team of 150 workers to complete the single tunnel, which measured 513 meters in length. They blasted the tunnel open by drilling holes and stuffing them with dynamite, which they then exploded into the rock. Dynamite blasting was very dangerous, and the Chinese took the lead in detonating the charges. Nyumayo remembers that some workers were injured during the tunnel blasting. He also recalls a cave-in that trapped five workers without air for several hours. When the workers were freed, four of the five had died. The fifth, the only Chinese worker in the group, survived.[44]

The teams that worked in the tunnels section were under intense scrutiny, not only from their own supervisors but also from outside observers. "The whole world knew that the area through which Uhuru Railway construction [passed] is exceptionally tough, and the toughest section in the whole line is between Mlimba and Makambako," wrote Daniel Mumello in his final report from Mkela Base Camp. Given the challenges they faced, he wrote, the number of serious or fatal accidents was actually not high. From a total of 3,539 workers there were 17 accidental deaths listed in his report from Mkela, the headquarters for tunnel construction. Three of these were due to explosives, six to cave-ins, and four to motor vehicle incidents.[45]

The tunnels section and other major construction work between Mlimba and Makambako was completed in June 1973. The tracklaying reached Mbeya on the sixth of July that year, and crossed the Tanzania-Zambia border on the twenty-seventh of August. A ceremony marked the border crossing at Tunduma, with speeches by Nyerere and Kaunda. As construction progressed into Zambia, reaching Kasama in December, there was still much to do on the sections that had already been completed, including track alignment, spreading of ballast, and drainage works. Buildings had to be constructed for the repair workshops and depots, for training workshops, and for administrative offices and staff quarters.

The project reached Zambia in time to help alleviate the transport crisis caused by the closure of the border between Zambia and Rhodesia in January and February 1973. Once TAZARA had established a terminal within Zambia at Mwenzo, it was possible to provide emergency transit services for import goods waiting at the Dar es Salaam port, and for the export of over 4,000 metric tons of maize from Zambia between April and June 1974. After that date some trains continued to be made available for the transport of goods into and out of Zambia, but the primary purpose of the newly completed section was to help transport the materials needed to meet—and surpass—TAZARA's ambitious completion deadline.[46]

Hard Work

The Chinese stated frequently during TAZARA's construction that they were committed to following development principles in Africa that were based on solidarity

FIGURE 3.3. Presidents Nyerere and Kaunda (center), with Chinese construction leaders Jin Hui (far left) and Pu Ke (to the right of Kaunda), visit a tunnel at Kisarawe, 1970. Photograph courtesy of Tanzania Department of Information Services (Maelezo).

and friendship. In practice, Chinese railway technicians were expected to work shoulder to shoulder with their African counterparts, demonstrating in a brotherly manner new skills and new ideals of self-reliance through hard work. This construction work experience was meant to be an uplifting one, both for the individual worker and for the nation, thus representing an alternative to colonial and neo-colonial African work experience.

For many of the workers on TAZARA, these ideals were realized. The Chinese approach to work—especially the way they joined in on every task—did inspire the Tanzanian and Zambian workers. In response to a survey conducted in the mid-1980s, former TAZARA construction workers remembered that their Chinese supervisors had helped them the most by actually working alongside them, "not just standing aside, hand-in-pocket, directing workers by finger-pointing."[47]

Workers also appreciated the material gains they made on the job. They report being paid promptly with a good wage, and receiving substantial benefits. These included overtime, leave allowances, subsistence and night allowances, and workers' compensation. Wages were paid by Chinese accountants or Tanzanian foremen

FIGURE 3.4. Learning by example: a Chinese technician instructs a Tanzanian youth in the machine shop at Mang'ula Base Camp, 1970. Photograph courtesy of Tanzania Department of Information Services (Maelezo).

on site in cash. The Chinese were fair, recalled one worker, for they believed *ufanye kazi upate hela*, "if you do the work you will be paid." Those who were not doing their work were asked to leave.[48]

In practice, the Tanzanians recruited to build the TAZARA railway found the work to be challenging and exhausting. Each morning the work teams would be transported from camp out to their work sites. "When you arrived at the work site," recalled one worker, "you got hold of a shovel or a spade or any work tool and worked with it under the direction of the Chinese expert."[49] In uninhabited areas far from the reach of camps and settlements, workers were fearful of wild animals, especially lions. "A lot of the work was dangerous and difficult," remembers Raphael Chawala. "We had to use our heads and be watchful."[50] Some found the work to be so difficult, and the conditions so demanding, that they abandoned their jobs.[51] Hashim Mdemu worked at Namawala sub-camp digging culverts, a job he described as so physically strenuous that he did not continue after the first year.[52] Those who stayed with the project only managed to survive the suffering they endured in these sections, according to Gilbert, through their own fortitude: "We persevered here with the Chinese."[53] Rogatus Nyumayo used the same term when remembering the tunnels construction, where the work was extremely challenging, "but we ourselves just persevered."[54]

At the sites of large-scale tasks, such as tunnel blasting and bridge construction, the Chinese used electricity generators to allow work shifts to continue both day and night. John Gilbert remembers working at Kisaki building bridges as part of a twenty-four-hour crew. Here and in the tunnels section workers put in successive eight-hour shifts around the clock: "You worked for eight hours, you then rested eight hours, then you started again," recalled Beatus Lihawa.[55] During resting shifts the workers retreated to their temporary shelters in the worker camps. Electricity generated at the base camps also allowed for around-the-clock activity. At Mang'ula Base Camp, engineers who worked in the factories and workshops often put in similar eight-hour rotating shifts over twenty-four-hour periods.[56]

Even those who worked in clerical positions during the construction period remember their work as strenuous. As a stockkeeper in Dar es Salaam, Andrew Mangile was responsible for handling the supplies of fixtures, pipes, and tools that were imported from China. He carried heavy loads from the docks to the stores, kept the shelves stocked, and looked after the inventories and accounts as he tracked the supplies that came in from the Chinese ships and went out to the camps. "The work was very difficult," he remembers. "All the work was tough at the time."[57]

Work on the railway was difficult and rigorous in part because of the Chinese approach to the larger project of railway construction. The Chinese had committed themselves to building the railway using a labor-intensive rather than a capital-

FIGURE 3.5. Hard work: aligning the track at Wanging'ombe in Njombe District, 1973. Photograph courtesy of Tanzania Department of Information Services (Maelezo).

intensive model.[58] The labor-intensive approach meant that there were thousands of job opportunities for young Tanzanians and Zambians who had little previous education or work experience. Yet the vast majority of those jobs required back-breaking manual labor such as digging ditches, spreading gravel, and hauling heavy materials.

Strenuous working conditions were made more difficult by the determination of the Chinese authorities to finish the project well ahead of schedule. The Chinese management was willing to push the workforce night and day to show what could be achieved—and to build African confidence—at a time when the world was watching. The Chinese signed on to work at an accelerated pace, and they expected the Africans to join them. Tanzanians and Zambians, however, had a mixed response to this approach to labor. While many joined in the Chinese enthusiasm for hard work, they were not always willing to endure such a strenuous timetable. Conflicts took place, for example, when African workers completed their assigned duties before the end of the work shift. The workers felt that they had finished for the day and were entitled to rest; their supervisors insisted that they take on additional work until the end of their shift. During the colonial period, similar conflicts over the definition of work and the workday had taken place in eastern and southern Africa.[59] Compliance with colonial and post-colonial labor laws that sought to regulate the work day and other aspects of work also required some negotiation with the Chinese side.

In 1975, for example, this issue was brought to the fore when the Tanzanian legislature passed a directive requiring all employees in government institutions to work a seven-hour day. The Chinese supervisors, despite the fact that TAZARA was a government project, refused to implement this directive and instead tried to emphasize to the workers how valuable it was for them to continue to work longer shifts. They also dismissed some workers whom they identified as troublemakers. Eventually, however, they agreed to accept the shorter working day. By this time, the construction phase of the project was largely completed and it was almost a moot point.[60]

Labor relations were not the only locus of tension resulting from the Chinese desire for haste during TAZARA's construction. There was also a contradiction in the intention of railway authorities to accomplish their task ahead of schedule, on the one hand, and the Chinese development principle of conveying technical knowledge and skill to the African workforce. As Philip Snow put it, "Speed was a trademark of the construction teams, and training slowed them down."[61] Workers were reminded of the relationship between effort and good character at worker meetings, and similar ideals were conveyed through the sayings of Chairman Mao that circulated in a variety of settings. It remained difficult, however, for the Chinese to both mobilize and supervise a vast workforce with varying levels of experience, while simultaneously training that workforce to do the required tasks and to sustain the railway's operations into the future. These goals were often contradictory in practice: the Chinese were both supervisors and teachers; the Africans both laborers and students.

African workers remember Chinese railway technicians in ways that reveal these contradictions and the ideals that accompanied them. The Chinese are remembered as strict supervisors who doled out harsh discipline to workers who were lazy or errant. "They were very harsh," remembers Raphael Chawala. "If you were lazy or a liar or a thief, they would chase you away. They would send a report to other stations so that you couldn't work there."[62] Workers recall that the Chinese were tough but fair: if you did your job properly, you would be paid on time without questions. Those who failed to do their work, on the other hand, would be asked to leave. Stories circulated about particular supervisors who were unusually demanding: one was known as *kapitula*, or "short trousers," because he always wore safari-style shorts. When he confronted a worker who was falling down on the job, he reportedly reached into the pocket of his shorts, took out a bundle of shillings and handed it to the worker, saying, "take this pay, you are now dismissed."[63]

Thus a number of Tanzanian and Zambian workers who failed to measure up, or who were overwhelmed by the relentless pressure of the Chinese pace, left the project. There are also many stories of ingenious methods that African workers devised to avoid working at the Chinese level of effort. According to one widely circulated local story, if a worker wanted to rest all he needed to do was to open a copy of Mao's red book and seat himself in the shade of a tree. He could sit that way for hours, and his supervisor would let him be.

Conflicting practical and political pressures also shaped TAZARA's management structure: the Chinese had to balance their overall responsibility for completing the construction project with the political interests of the two African partners. In practice, these goals resulted in an elaborate managerial structure involving two parallel administrative bodies: the Tanzania Zambia Railway Authority, or TAZARA, and the Chinese Railway Workers Team, or CRWT. The TAZARA wing of management was run by Tanzanians and Zambians, and was responsible for local administration and security. The Chinese Railway Workers Team was responsible for the technical side of the railway's construction and operations, including worker deployment and supervision. At the field level each team had its own representatives: a team or sub-team leader from the CRWT, and an administrative assistant from TAZARA. The Chinese staff were the overall managers of the work teams in the field; the local Tanzanian trainee foremen reported to them. Because these teams were isolated from one another by the distances between camps and work sites, they had some degree of autonomy in their day-to-day activities. Each team was responsible for handling its own technical problems, along with everyday worker requests and complaints. The accompanying chart from a 1973 field report from Makambako shows how the field staff was allocated at one base camp.[64]

The Chinese approach to labor management on the TAZARA project was based on a set of principles that included political ideology, the development of personal character, skills training, and worker solidarity. In May 1971, a series of meetings were organized to assess the work process. At these meetings there were five main themes of discussion: 1. strengthening education about the importance of ensuring smooth transport in sections that had already been completed; 2. rigidly opposing arrogance and doing away with complacency, thereby constantly revolutionizing the leaders' team; 3. further implementing the guiding policy of hard struggle and self-reliance, and developing the spirit of perseverance and thriftiness; 4. efficiently organizing local workers and treating them well; 5. organization and adjustment of work tasks.[65]

Table 3.1. Allocation of Field Staff at Makambako Base Camp in 1973

TAZARA STAFF	Workers	CRWT STAFF	Workers
1. Administration		**1. Supervisory Staff**	
AdministrativeAssistant	1	Works Supervisor	1
Field Assistant	2	Trainee Works Foremen	4
Clerical Staff	2		
2. Police		**2. Technical Staff**	
Police in charge	1	Mechanical trainees	6
Deputy police in charge	1	Welder trainees	3
Police constables	11	Electrician trainees	3
Police driver	1	Carpenter trainees	15
3. Medical staff		**3. General Workers**	
Medical Assistant	1	Drivers	5
Rural Medical Aid	1	Guards, operators, examiners	20
Medical driver	1	Telecommunications	57
Cleaner	1	Permanent way, building, other	346
TOTAL WORKFORCE	**24**	**TOTAL WORKFORCE**	**437**

The transcript of a meeting held at Makambako base camp on May 23, 1973, reveals the way these meetings combined administrative briefings with appeals to political ideals and personal character. Administrative items on the Makambako meeting agenda included announcements about medical care restrictions, payment of salaries, and security. Workers were then urged "to cooperate among themselves as brothers, to work together as socialist brothers . . . to cooperate and work together as members of one family." They should also respect their leaders, and condemn "all bad practices."[66] These themes reflect the way that the transfer of skills and knowledge during the railway's construction included not only technical skills but also ideology, discipline, and virtue. The approach to work management on the Tanzanian side also emphasized solidarity, for example by using the term *ujamaa* or "familyhood" to refer to the communal dining groups formed by African workers. Political ideology was reinforced by creating a TANU party cell at the camp of each sub-team.[67]

While the emphasis in worker meetings was on solidarity and cooperation, in practice the structure of administration was hierarchical and directives always came from the top. African administrative assistants served as mediators between the Chinese and the African workers, and a large part of their job involved the transmission of policy directives from the top administrative levels down to the level of the workers. When the Chinese management style caused problems for the African workers, Tanzanian and Zambian administrators were called upon to mediate. Administrative assistants had to become skilled cultural translators in order to explain construction policies to the workforce in ways that could be understood and accepted.[68] During the survey and design phase, a Zambian administrative assistant found himself settling "squabbles" between farmers in Mkushi District and the Chinese personnel. In his quarterly report, Mr. E. C. Tembo listed the diverse range of duties he was expected to perform:

> He is responsible for general complaints between the local laborers and of course with the Chinese personnel or leader; attending to and assisting in settlement of complaints arising from local people in the field at different times; employing of general workers, marking of time books, cash payments, getting in touch with hospital for any sick reports; Administrative Assistant has also to join surveyors and share the same work being done by Engineers. We have to learn from our Chinese Engineers that when work is there no matter how simple or hard work might be, to keep it easy, we have to do it together rather than leaving everything for general workers.[69]

The contradictions that emerged in work relationships between Chinese supervisors and African workers resulted in some cases in conflict and insubordination. Occasionally a Chinese supervisor was reported to be contemptuous in his treatment of the workers; two Chinese supervisors were transferred for this reason.[70] In two other recorded incidents, Tanzanian workers assaulted their Chinese counterparts. One Tanzanian driver was sent to obtain diesel fuel with a Chinese supervisor, who complained after the driver repeatedly stopped the vehicle and disappeared to interact with villagers along the way (apparently these "villagers" were women). When the supervisor complained for the third time, the driver beat him severely. That driver was dismissed. In another case, a Tanzanian trainee foreman beat a Chinese technician so badly that he was hospitalized for two weeks. At Mpika Base Camp, workers threatened to kill the Tanzanian administrative assistant because of some new regulatory measures he had introduced. Police were called in to resolve the dispute.

Chinese supervisors were frustrated with workers whom they felt were lazy, disobedient, or incompetent, and normally requested their dismissal. In one report from 1969, an administrator explained why a worker had been dismissed: "I am informing you in writing about Mr. _____, one of our carpenters. He is a very complaining character, complaining on unnecessary and flimsy reasons, he is lazy and disobedient. Though he has been warned several times, he has not changed.

Finally the Chinese got tired of him."[71] Other workers were just plain rude. One worker jokingly knocked the straw hat from his Chinese supervisor's head several times, tossing it to the ground and stating that it was no good. He was given a warning. In more serious cases, the Tanzanian workers took liberties with moral conduct. Once a Tanzanian went with a Chinese driver to obtain drinking water for the camp. The Tanzanian worker had been drinking heavily, and along the way he made arrangements for himself and the driver to have intimate relations with young women in a village (an activity strictly off-limits for the Chinese). The Tanzanian was subsequently fired.[72]

Friends and Strangers

The construction of the TAZARA railway created the opportunity for an unprecedented cultural exchange. Over a five-year period, tens of thousands of Chinese and Africans lived together and worked side by side along the railway line. As they camped in rudimentary shelters, dug ditches, constructed bridges, and occasionally shared a meal together they had many occasions to interact. Friendship and solidarity were especially important themes in the isolated workplaces and temporary camps where the workers spent most of their time. African workers emphasized in interviews that the most positive aspect of their association with their Chinese counterparts was the educational instruction. "It was a true friendship," said John Gilbert of his relationship with Chinese technicians. "Even if you did not understand something, they explained it to you until you understood it." Another worker stated, "The Chinese [expert] taught us with honesty. He left you knowing that you had learned your job well."[73]

Many TAZARA workers remember this proximity in the workplace as a meaningful departure from the wage labor practices of the colonial era. Yet despite the ideology of brotherhood and the Chinese willingness to "muck in" to tackle difficult tasks, life in the construction camps remained largely segregated. While the living conditions of Chinese and African workers did not differ significantly in material ways, their housing was set up in separate sections of each camp and they ate their meals and enjoyed leisure activities separately. Here again, there were contradictions in the role played by the Chinese: at the same time that they were socialist brothers, they were also supervisors. They were older than their African counterparts and far more technically experienced. And despite the best efforts of Chinese and Tanzanian leaders to cultivate an ideal of friendship, antipathy occasionally slipped through. While the workers in camp were officially known as friends, their experiences on the ground were often like those of strangers.

This experience of closeness and distance is illustrated by memories of Chinese film showings that took place at the construction camps. As a film was being shown, the Chinese workers would seat themselves facing the front side of the projection screen, while the African workers sat in rows facing the back side. Because they could not recognize the Chinese characters, the African workers did not miss any of the text by viewing the film backward. Thus the Chinese experts and their African counterparts could spend an hour or two of their leisure time together watching the same film, sitting together yet spatially divided by the screen that stood between them. They could watch the same film over and over again as many as ten times, forward and backward, as there was little else to do during their off-duty hours. The African workers reportedly looked forward to the film showings so much that they began to seat themselves in rows on the back side of the screen long before the actual film showing began.[74]

When British journalist Dexter Tiranti visited railway construction sites in Tanzania in 1973, he witnessed a similar alignment of the African and Chinese members of the audience. During an evening of entertainment provided for the workers by a visiting Chinese acrobatic and juggling team, he observed, "Chinese and Africans sat at different sides of the hall as the artists spun plates, pedaled bicycles and juggled with fruit. But there was loud laughter from both sides when a group of Chinese actors, dressed as African workmen, appeared on stage with their faces blacked and struck militant postures with their shovels." Here again the African and Chinese workers sat watching the same show, but from opposite perspectives. As the groups faced one another across the performance space, the blackfaced Chinese pantomimes in the center intentionally crossed the boundaries of race identity.[75]

The relationships between Chinese and African workers depended to a large degree on the size and permanence of the camps where they were based, and on their positions within the labor hierarchy. African workers who were in leadership positions or who had developed more skills were most likely to have lived and worked closely with their Chinese counterparts. The majority of the rank and file, on the other hand, did not. This was due in part to the unequal ratio of Chinese to African workers: at the peak of construction in 1972, the Chinese working on the line numbered 13,500 workers, and the Africans 38,000.[76] The sub-teams that went out to dig ditches, reinforce embankments, and spread gravel typically included a large number of African workers with only one or two Chinese technicians. And when these teams returned to camp, the Chinese and African workers lived parallel lives.

In the dispersed mobile work camps accommodations could be quite spartan. Once a new campsite had been cleared and graded, tents and open-air shelters, or *bandas*, were erected across the compound in long lines. Accommodations were constructed on one side of the camp for the Chinese, and on the other for the Tanzanians. *Bandas* were built using locally available materials, most often mats woven from grasses or palm fronds and attached to simple wooden frames. The shelters offered little protection from wild animals or malaria-carrying mosquitoes. According to the memories of Chinese engineers,

> It took eight poles and a piece of cloth to build a temporary shed. Four poles served as the framing posts with one end buried in the ground; the remaining four poles were mounted to the shed frame with nails. With the cloth cover on top, a temporary shed was created. It might be too small to squeeze in four beds. But since it only served as a place for sleeping, people did not care about the size when they lay down. Sometimes it was hard to get the cloth, and you were stuck with no other choice but reed mats which were used to cover all sides of the shed. In any case, the rainy season had long gone and there was not too much wind, so it would be okay as long as it could protect against the dripping dew.[77]

The workers also constructed canteens, latrines, bathing facilities, and a medical dispensary at each camp. At the larger camps electric wires were hung overhead and diesel generators allowed work activity to continue through the night. In the early stages of construction there were housing shortages at some sites. At Signali, for example, the main camp accommodated only 86 of the 681 workers when construction began. Several Tanzanian workers roomed in the homes of nearby villagers. This was not an option for the Chinese workers, whose relations with villagers were carefully restricted.[78]

The work camps were located approximately forty miles apart along the length of the railway. Once a length of twenty miles of new track had been laid, it was time to pick up the camp and move it to the next campsite. The workers disassembled the *bandas* and other structures, carried the building materials to the next location, and then completely reconstructed their camp compound. Beatus Lihawa remembers packing up mats and poles and carrying them on foot from one section to the next while he was constructing tunnels between Mlimba and Makambako.[79] In the larger camps the housing structures were reinforced using durable but heavy wooden frames. When these camps were disassembled and moved, the portable wooden building frames were stacked on truck beds and ferried to the next camp location. On arrival the neat rows of shelters were laid out once again to create a new compound, with accommodations for African and Chinese workers separated spatially.

Life in camp mirrored the segregation of the compound housing. When they were not working, the Chinese enjoyed leisure activities such as reading, smoking cigarettes, and playing board games and table tennis. They also played active

FIGURE 3.6. Young TAZARA workers playing basketball at Mang'ula base camp while their Chinese counterparts look on, September 1972. Photograph courtesy of Tanzania Department of Information Services (Maelezo).

outdoor sports, especially volleyball. These games were occasionally shared with Tanzanian workers, but for the most part the Chinese kept to themselves. African workers, meanwhile, formed their own sports groups for playing volleyball and soccer. When they went walking outside the camp boundaries the Chinese workers always went together in a group, avoiding contact with local people. Chinese supervisors were very strict about the behavior of their workers, even off duty. A worker who did something out of line could be sent back to Dar es Salaam, and from there to China.[80]

At the largest base camps, where engineering workshops, training centers, and other permanent structures were located, housing was more permanent than in the temporary camps along the railway line. Some of these base camps could hardly be considered "camps" at all. Housing here was built to last using mud bricks, timber, and iron sheeting. Some of these structures are still standing today. When they were fully operational the large base camps could accommodate as many as 6,000 workers.[81] At Mang'ula, the railway's largest base camp in the interior, there were engineering workshops, a training institute, a quarry, and a sawmill. The three primary workshops produced concrete sleepers, bridgework, and machinery. The leadership-training institute offered courses in management, communications, and accounting. At these large camps, friendships did develop between Chinese and African workers who were employed as engineers and administrators, relationships that differed from those of the workers in the temporary camps along the line.

Salum Mwasenga, for example, was trained as an engineer in the foundry at Mang'ula. He developed a friendship with the Chinese technical expert who trained and worked with him, an engineer named Shao Xiong. Mwasenga was often invited to share meals with Shao Xiong at the end of the long shifts they worked together. A Tanzanian camp foreman also based at Mang'ula, Benedict Mkanyago, similarly remembers working closely with his Chinese counterpart. "This [railway construction] was a time of big changes," he stated. "We could ride together in the back of a lorry, we could eat together, even have celebrations together." This was a departure for him from the colonial era: "I did not expect that I would find myself sitting at the same table as a white person."[82] John Gilbert was a trainee foreman based at Ifakara who also has positive memories of working with the Chinese. They liked and promoted him, he said, because he was a good worker. "The Chinese truly had a heart of friendship," he believes. "Among those of us who were the workers and the citizens, nothing took place that was bad. It was true friendship; it was so good that you just can't understand it. . . . They taught us with goodness and left us doing our tasks well until today."[83]

These relationships were constrained by the language barrier. English was used as the common language at the higher levels of management and in print, and on the Zambian side of the border. Kiswahili was most commonly spoken among the construction teams and in the outlying camps in Tanzania. Chinese supervisors made an effort to learn Kiswahili, attending language classes where they learned to master Kiswahili greetings and other basic skills. "*Jambo, rafiki*" (hello, friend) was a popular phrase used by many Chinese workers to greet their African counterparts. According to Mkanyago, some Tanzanian workers also learned Kiwemba so that they could communicate with Zambian workers and their families. It was more difficult for the Tanzanians and Zambians to learn Chinese, but some did so. Once again, those at the more permanent camps in skilled or leadership positions were most likely to have this opportunity. The two hundred workers who went to China for further instruction brought back valuable language skills in addition to their technical training. More often, communication took the form of sign language combined with elements of both Chinese and Kiswahili. This three-way communication system met the fundamental communication needs of the construction work, according to both Chinese and African retired workers, despite the inevitable misunderstandings that took place.[84]

Because of the restrictions on their mobility and social interaction, the Chinese workers were observed mostly from a distance by local communities in the TAZARA corridor. Lao Wan, an independent Chinese engineer who worked at the Kidatu hydroelectric project at the time, observed that the Chinese who worked on TAZARA were never seen in towns socializing with Tanzanians. If an open truck carrying Chinese workers stopped at a local shop to buy soft drinks, the passengers did not disembark but drank their bottles of soda while standing in the vehicle. The Chinese were especially forbidden to have relationships with African women. They were respected for this by local communities, said Lao Wan (himself married to a Tanzanian wife and living in Ifakara in 2000), and were compared favorably with other development workers who reportedly "left many children" behind. The Chinese "were like soldiers," explained Lao Wan. "They were the cadres of Mao who came here only to work. They worked very hard, they only worked hard and stayed in camp. They did not talk or rest until all the work was done."[85]

Villagers also had restricted access to the Chinese workers in the camps. While there were no formal rules that prohibited them from entering the camps (and many did come to sell farm produce, as described below), security measures made this difficult. According to Benedict Mkanyago, security was important for protecting the Chinese technicians during construction. "I am grateful to them," he said of the Chinese workers. "They were people who observed the laws and the guidelines of our country. If they were just left on their own [i.e., without protection] surely harm would have come to them. . . . People could have hurt them or taken their things." Still, he remembers, they showed friendliness toward local people and learned how to greet villagers by calling out "*jambo*" (hello) or "*rafiki*" (friend). Small children greeted the Chinese workers with calls of "*mchina, mchina,*" and they replied, "*toto jambo*" (hello, child).[86]

The African workers, in contrast, mingled more freely with the local people. "The local people who were our neighbors," remembers John Gilbert, "showed kindness and helped us with many things." In the evenings at Mang'ula workers would go out to the neighboring settlements to relax and drink home-brewed beer (alcohol consumption was not allowed in the work camps).[87] In Mchombe village, women remember that workers from the railway often visited the beer clubs where they sold local beer. Samuel Undole remembers that women from Iringa carried pots of beer on their heads down the hillsides to Chita, where they sold it to the Tanzanian workers based there.[88] Several women remember young African workers who established relationships with girlfriends in the villages along the railway, and some of these partnerships are still intact.[89] Life for African workers thus differed from the lives of the Chinese workers in important ways. The two groups lived in similar conditions and worked side by side. In their off-duty lives, however, there was distance between them.

Food provision, meal preparation, and dining were a central part of life in camp for TAZARA's workers. At first, in the spirit of self-help and solidarity, workers ate their meals together. Communal dining was a common practice at work sites in China, and this approach was readily embraced on the Tanzanian side as reflecting the spirit of *ujamaa*, or "familyhood," that characterized Julius Nyerere's approach to African socialism. Common meals were "not alien to Africa," as one administrator put it, but were "inherent in the African way of life."[90] African and Chinese workers ate in segregated spaces for the most part, although some Tanzanians recall being invited to share meals with their supervisors. While working as a trainee engineer in the workshop at Mang'ula, Salum Mwasenga shared meals with the Chinese engineers: "We ate together [with the Chinese]; we ate with our hands and they ate with their sticks, but we all ate together."[91]

At this initial stage local workers ate their meals together in dining facilities or in canteens, where hired cooks prepared dishes such as *ugali* (boiled maize meal), rice, beans, and a stew made from small dried fish (*dagaa*). While the Chinese work teams imported tinned meat and fish, fresh meat was a rare luxury for the African workers and came mostly from wild game rather than by purchasing livestock. The project managers tried to encourage herders to open butcheries near the camps and to organize a steady meat supply, but they were apparently not successful.[92] The food supplies were purchased through a common fund to which every employee made a monthly contribution of twenty-five to thirty shillings. This system was designed to facilitate the distribution of food supplies to the various camps, to ensure the well-being of the laborers, and to cut down on absenteeism.[93]

Within a short period of time, however, the African workers became dissatisfied with these arrangements and argued that they should be allowed to prepare their own meals. Because workers from different regions preferred different staples and different cooking styles, they preferred to "depend on themselves" for their meals and to cook either individually or in small groups. Workers from Iringa, for example, preferred to eat *ugali*, while those from Njombe enjoyed Irish potatoes. Workers from Mbeya region felt that they had not really eaten unless they had been served cooking bananas. At Ruipa sub-camp workers complained, "the Ministry and the government force us to follow practices which go against our own culture," because they were not allowed to consume the foods they preferred. They threatened to "return to the village to till the land" if they could not prepare their own meals. Despite these different regional food preferences, however, Mkanyago believes that "the main foodstuffs that built this freedom railway were *ugali* and beans."[94]

The local workers were eventually able to follow their own cooking preferences, and each camp had the use of a truck on a monthly basis that they used to drive to towns and to village markets in order to purchase their supplies. Worker tastes stimulated the local production of such crops as cooking bananas, rice, and maize, even when these were not consumed by the local population. Maize and millet were especially lucrative because they were used to brew the beer that local women sold to construction workers in the camps and in the village canteens. For some local farmers, therefore, this was a time of increased production and sale of crops, and also a time of diversification into new crops. One local farmer near Ifakara told a government worker in 1972 that "These railway workers will buy all that we sell and all the time they will ask for more tomorrow."[95]

The different food preferences of the African workers led to a social separation of cooking and dining groups according to their places of origin. By eating familiar foods in smaller social groups, workers who had traveled long distances to work on the railway could create a connection to home. Stories of food provision, cooking, and dining were also reminders that the workers on the TAZARA project held multiple identities.

The Chinese workers also had diverse food preferences, and like those of the Tanzanian and Zambian workers their cuisines reflected their different places of origin and cultural practices. The cooks they brought with them from China prepared dishes from different regions to suit their tastes.[96] Some of the Chinese workers enjoyed cooking and gathered together to prepare favorites such as steamed dumplings with vegetable fillings. Local cooking assistants soon learned to steam rice, to make bean curd, and to prepare other Chinese dishes.[97] Vegetables were a particularly important part of the Chinese diet and were not always easy to obtain along the construction line. The Chinese therefore brought seeds for their favorite vegetables from home and planted them where they could, the varieties depending upon their personal and regional preferences. The Chinese workers carried individual sets of chopsticks and rice bowls with them during work shifts and out to camp. They also each carried an individual flask of boiled water infused with tea leaves, to refresh themselves with a clean beverage during breaks. "To be honest," remembered Jiang Chen, "the aid workers ate quite well, at least much better than what their fellow countrymen were having inside China," because they were able to eat canned fish or meat almost every day while those in China experienced food rationing. In China at this time fish and meat were regarded as expensive luxuries, and canned meats were highly valued as being both better-tasting and more technologically advanced than fresh varieties.[98]

Food was especially important for the Chinese workers during holidays such as the Chinese New Year, when they reported feeling far from home and loved ones. Holidays were also occasions when differences in cultural practice were more likely to be expressed. When Chinese project leader Pu Ke contacted his different field teams during Chinese New Year in January 1971, he discovered that while the bridge team was eating noodles, there were no fresh vegetables or meats for making dumplings. The workers on the third machine team, who came from Sichuan, explained to Pu Ke that they did not eat dumplings at all for New Year but preferred *tang yuan* (sesame paste balls), for which they had no sesame. Their paltry holiday meal consisted of "three whites and one red": white rice, white salt, plain (white) water, and red chilies. Pu Ke then contacted the Mang'ula Base Camp, which had its own farm, where workers were enjoying dumplings made with pork, shrimp, eggs, and vegetables. At his request the Mang'ula team sent two tons of food and other goods out to the camps so that the Chinese New Year could be celebrated properly by all the teams.[99]

The provision of foodstuffs for the Chinese and African workers alike was a logistical challenge for the railway administrators. The Chinese teams imported large quantities of foodstuffs from home, including soy sauce, shark fins, dried mushrooms, preserved meats, and 5,000 tons of sugar.[100] Other products were obtained locally. Truckloads of tropical fruits, especially mangos, were shipped to the Chinese kitchens from the coast. In camps that were near village settlements and farming communities, farm products were brought to the camps by local traders. The local rice-growing farmers and fishermen found a ready market at the TAZARA camps in the Kilombero valley, according to Samuel Undole. The Chinese were especially likely to purchase rice and were fond of fresh fish. "They didn't like dried fish," remembers Undole. "The Chinese also went around in their vehicles to get chickens. If someone killed a python, they could sell some to the Chinese."[101] Yohina Msaka remembers that local women at Mchombe sold rice and fried bread snacks (*maandazi*) to the workers there. She herself used to brew beer for sale, she said, initially brewing her beer from rice and later switching to maize beer to meet the tastes of the workers from the southern highlands.[102] The small-scale farmers around Mchombe brought eggs, milk, and other products to the camp on Sunday afternoons and set up an informal market next to the village where they sold rice, maize, and fish. "Therefore on days like Sundays that were our resting days, we would go and do our own shopping, sometimes at those villages that were nearby," remembered Moses Hassan.[103]

At Chita base camp, people brought maize flour and beans for sale to the workers. While rice was the local staple in the Kilombero river valley, many of the TAZARA workers preferred to prepare *ugali* with bean stew. A brisk trade apparently developed at Chita between the maize-producing highland farmers of Iringa and the workers at the camp. "They [the workers] preferred to buy maize flour, to cook *ugali,*" explained Samuel Undole. "They also bought beans. Here people do not grow beans; people brought beans here from Iringa. . . . Young schoolboys would come from Iringa carrying maize and beans; they used these pathways through the mountains." It was a long distance over rugged terrain, Undole explained, and a strenuous walk for an older person. A young man, on the other hand, could come early in the morning, sell his goods and then go back in the evening. "For a young man, it is about a seven-hour journey."[104]

At the camps that were located farther away from human settlements, procurement of food supplies was more complicated. In the tunnels section, workers would join together and send a representative to Iringa once a month to purchase maize flour, beans, and other bulk supplies. Even in places where there were local villages—for example, at Tunnel Three near Mkomaga village—the farmers did not produce enough surplus to meet the needs of the workers. Making sure that food supplies lasted in these remote areas took some effort on the part of the administrative assistants, according to Daniel Mumello. He had to monitor the cooperative shops in the tunnels section continually and make additional forays to Iringa when supplies were low. "Several incidents revealed," he reported, that without his intervention "the local workers sometimes failed to get food for considerable days."[105]

At the larger base camps and permanent settlements, workers could tend their own gardens and they had greater access to consumer goods. Workers at Mang'ula cultivated maize, bananas, and fruit trees on their days off. At camps with large numbers of workers, such as Mlimba, cooperative shops were opened where workers could purchase flour, sugar, and tea leaves. Cooperative shops were government-controlled, and during the construction period were stocked with the Chinese goods that were part of the commodity loan agreement. A report on items transported to shops by the Iringa Cooperative Society lists sugar, tea, beans, beer, cooking oil, and cigarettes as regular supplies. As the Christmas holiday approached, the shops also stocked Bee Flower soap, ladies' dresses, gentlemen's trousers, and *khanga* cloth wraps.[106]

The Chinese technicians established their own farms at the permanent base camps. On their farms the Chinese workers tended small livestock (mainly poultry and pigs) as well as vegetable gardens where they grew the Chinese vegetables whose seeds they had brought from home or purchased in Kenya. They even grew their own tobacco, from which they made hand-rolled cigarettes.[107] Poultry became a mainstay of the Chinese diet, and the 2,000 hens they kept at Mang'ula reportedly provided 1,000 eggs per day.[108] The Chinese farms are widely remembered throughout the railway region and have become part of local folklore about the way the Chinese conducted themselves. "I praise them," said Mkanyago, "because they were experts [i.e., they were trained specialists] who also liked to farm in their gar-

FIGURE 3.7. Chinese railway workers admiring the cabbages growing in their vegetable garden. *Die Stern* magazine, 1974.

dens very much. Truly we learned very much from their side. They were cultivating gardens that were flourishing during that whole time period . . . and they were also livestock-keepers. The Chinese are lovers of pork; therefore they kept many pigs, and on account of this they gave themselves a meat stew every week."[109]

Modernization

For the young men who were recruited for and stayed on through TAZARA's construction, the experience of participating in a transnational project of modernization was transforming. Most of them were from rural areas and had limited experience with technology beyond what they may have learned in primary school. For many of these young men it was their first time to be employed for a wage and to follow a structured and regimented work schedule. Workers themselves describe their experiences during construction as a process of maturation, as a coming-of-age. They remember joining the workforce as very young men, unmarried, many having served briefly in the National Service (most of the African workers were between the ages of sixteen and twenty-five). Their experiences were not unlike those of male railway workers in colonial Nigeria, described by Lisa Lindsay, who were attracted to railway work as a path to becoming "adult men."[110] Workers on TAZARA recall that the experience of construction was demanding and difficult for them. At the same time, they developed skills and in many cases developed a viable trade that gave them a new position in society. The experience of building the railroad, wrote D. E. Stambuli after TAZARA's completion, had lifted workers and their families out of their "deteriorated condition into a modern civilized type of life."[111]

Carol Mpandamgongo vividly described what it was like when he joined the hundreds of young men who descended on his village of Ikule in 1972 to take up residence at the Chita base camp. "We were there, we were there doing that work . . . working on the railway. Ah, ah, there was an *ngoma* here. We were still *vijana* [young men] when we worked here. We worked breaking up stones using *utambi* [explosives]. We also cleared the brush along the roadway so that the railway could pass." Mpandamgongo's use of the term *ngoma*, a community gathering based on dancing and drumming, conveys what the atmosphere must have felt like as large numbers of young men moved into the area and became engaged in noisy, pounding activity blasting rock, excavating ditches, and laying out the rail bed.[112]

Hosea Mngata described his construction experience this way: "I was still a very young man when I started working, I had just finished school. I had a very young age [he was 26], and then I had a great desire for work, and my Chinese brothers liked me very much." Mngata began working first at Mang'ula, breaking up stones at the quarry in the forest. After 1973, when the Tanzanian workforce was reduced, he was one of the fortunate workers to be kept on. "We kept working with the Chinese for a long time," he remembered, "almost three years, and then the Chinese left us on our own. Indeed, until today we are caring for the railway; we had grown experienced ourselves by that time." Mngata's memory conveys the coming-of-age not only of himself, as he learned skills and eventually assumed responsibility after the Chinese departure, but also the coming-of-age of the larger Tanzanian workforce.[113]

The rural communities in the TAZARA corridor also remember the time of TAZARA's construction as a time of dramatic change, one in which the earth itself was altered and reshaped in powerful ways. The Chinese engineers who carried out these disturbances were not members of local communities but strangers, with little knowledge of the physical, cultural, and spiritual landscapes they were affecting. A particular kind of story thus began to circulate, one that emphasized the strangeness, or *ugeni*, of the Chinese, and their unfamiliarity with local custom. Most often, these stories described the Chinese violation of local prohibitions, or their failure to consult with the community elders who mediated with local ancestral spirits. The stories reflect local perceptions and anxieties about landscape change, as well as the shifting economic and power relationships in the railway corridor. They comment on the realignment of patterns of settlement, trade, and mobility, as well as integration into a larger world through the presence of powerful strangers. In these stories, tensions between the acts of strangers and the local community were resolved when the Chinese agreed to respect the ritual authority of spirits and elders.[114]

In the tunnels section of the railway, for example, a story is told about how the Chinese were forced to consult local elders in order to transform a landscape in which spirits resided. As they were blasting dynamite to open tunnels through the mountainous region between Mlimba and Makambako, the Chinese apparently disturbed not only the earth but also a local spirit. At one of the tunnel sites on a mountainside, they blasted and hauled out stone during the day. When they returned the next morning they found that the mountain had been restored to its pristine state. Each day the Chinese worked hard blasting the tunnel only to return the following morning to see their work undone. Finally they decided to consult a higher power, according to a local story, and they gathered in a circle to divine what they could from their red books. When this approach did not resolve the problem, they turned for advice to the local elders. They were informed that in order to proceed with blasting the hillside, they must first ask the permission of the local spirit and make an offering (*tambiko*) in the form of a black ox. The Chinese consented to follow this advice and with the help of the local elders, they killed a black ox as an offering to the spirit. After killing the ox, they were able to go forward with their blasting without any hindrances, all the way to Mbeya. According to the story, the Chinese "medicine" (in this case the red books) was foreign and therefore did not have potency to deal with the local spirit. Once the Chinese showed their willingness to be guided by the local ritual experts, their problems were solved.[115]

There are many similar stories of trees that were uprooted during construction but grew back the following morning, for example, and bridges that would collapse overnight and require reconstruction again the next day. One of these stories is told about Mkela, the location of the base camp in the tunnels section. The settlement of Mkela was named for a resident who had lived in the area some time ago. After his death a tree grew at his gravesite, which later became a place where local people would come for propitiation of his spirit and the spirits of his lineage. Not knowing that this was a sacred site, the Chinese attempted to uproot the tree to make way for the tunnel. Yet each time they uprooted the tree, it replanted itself again overnight and stood upright the following day.[116] The Chinese were finally forced to abandon their effort. In another story, a powerful spirit associated with a pool of water misled a Chinese man when he inadvertently wandered into a sacred area of the Udzungwa forest near Mang'ula. The Chinese technician had decided to go for a walk by himself on his day off, but then completely disappeared after entering this part of the forest. According to some accounts he never returned.

These stories concern the spiritual forces that were present in particular landscapes during the construction of the railway. The landscape through which TAZARA passed was not neutral, but was a place imbued with meaning. Some selected sites in the landscape were places of ritual importance, which the Chinese as outsiders were unable to recognize. When the construction workers began to transform and realign this landscape, they disturbed these sacred sites. They also challenged the authority that local elders held over those sites. When the Chinese demonstrated that they were willing to honor local authority and to comply with the requests of elders, they were allowed to proceed with their project. (Some said that the Chinese were well disposed toward the concerns of the elders because they believed strongly themselves in the intervention of spirits, and carried charms for good luck.) It was not the construction project itself, but rather respect for custom and consultation with elders that these stories emphasized. The stories also reflect local anxieties about how changes in the landscape—and the advent of the railway itself—would realign relationships of power and authority in the TAZARA corridor. These concerns foreshadowed the events of the 1980s and 1990s that are the subject of the final chapter of this book.

CHAPTER

4

Living along the Railway

By the end of 1973, the TAZARA railway was nearing completion on the Tanzanian side, and construction was proceeding westwards into Zambia. For the thousands of Tanzanian workers who had been working on the project, it was a time of dispersal—around a third of them would stay on to continue working into Zambia, but for the majority it was the end of their employment.[1] Many of these former workers decided to stay and settle as farmers in the railway corridor, becoming a founding population for the settlements that would grow up around the railway stations over the next decades.

Meanwhile, Tanzania's political leaders had already begun to discuss the question of rural development along TAZARA. One party report expressed concern that TAZARA's construction was "proceeding faster than the country's ability to generate the wealth that the railway will carry."[2] Now that the Freedom Railway was almost finished, they asked, what form of economic development should be created to sustain it? Part of the answer lay in large-scale projects and in the extension of transportation linkages to existing enterprises. Among the projects already under way were a prison farm at Idete, the sawmill and machine workshop at Mang'ula, and an expansion of the Kilombero Sugar Company. But there was also a need for rural communities to play a role in the economic success and long-term security of TAZARA.

It so happened that the construction of the TAZARA railway in Tanzania coincided with one of the largest population relocation projects in East African history: *ujamaa*, or rural villagization. Thus when questions were raised about rural development in the TAZARA corridor, the solution seemed perfectly clear: *ujamaa* villages should be launched as quickly as possible all along the line, from Mbeya region to the coast. This policy was announced to delegates attending the fifteenth biennial TANU conference in September of 1971, when Waziri Juma (TANU's political coordinator for TAZARA) revealed that all TAZARA railway stations within Tanzania would be incorporated into *ujamaa* villages. This would ensure that the railway would become a foundation for socialist rather than capitalist development, he explained, warning the delegates that capitalists had already begun to take advantage of the young TAZARA workers who earned cash wages at the Mang'ula workshops.[3]

The news of planned villagization along the railway line had already reached TAZARA stations in Morogoro region three months earlier, when party secretary Major Hashim Mbita paid a visit in mid-June to encourage the creation of *ujamaa* villages there. Addressing a public gathering in Ifakara, Major Mbita urged the local citizens to stay alert, literally to "keep their eyes open," to be sure that outside enemies did not thwart the progress of TAZARA's construction. According to the party leadership, the *ujamaa* villagers living along TAZARA would serve as a first line of defense against potential enemy sabotage.[4]

At the time of Major Mbita's visit to Morogoro, there were already a few established *ujamaa* villages located near TAZARA. Among them was the village of Idete, which was selected that month as the best *ujamaa* village in the region, earning it a cash prize of 16,000 shillings.[5] For most rural residents along the railway line, however, relocation to planned villages took place between 1973 and 1976, and was carried out by force. Villagization along TAZARA eventually came to involve four provinces (Mbeya, Iringa, Morogoro, and Coast) and seven districts. In Ulanga District, seventeen *ujamaa* villages were planned along the railway. All families living up to ten miles from TAZARA were moved to newly designated plots located near railway stations. The project was called "*Operation Kando Kando ya Reli*," or "Operation Alongside the Railway."[6]

The *ujamaa* villages that were established throughout Tanzania at this time were, in anthropologist James Scott's view, part of a state effort to modernize and thereby "make legible" rural economies that were disorderly, inefficient, and poorly linked to state political and economic controls.[7] The national villagization project was based on the same principles of modernization that had prevailed in the colonial period: scientific agriculture, mechanization, and bureaucratic centralization. The image of the ideal rural landscape in the *ujamaa* era was one of orderliness and efficiency. Rural villages with individual and collective farms would be laid out in neat blocks and rows.

FIGURE 4.1. The housing structures of an *ujamaa* village, built alongside the TAZARA railway in Mbeya region, 1976. Photograph courtesy of Tanzania Department of Information Services (Maelezo).

Scott's view of villagization as an example of authoritarian "high modernism" holds true for *Operation Kando Kando ya Reli* in some respects. The citizens living in villages along TAZARA were to be educated "in a modern and economic fashion."[8] In the TAZARA corridor villagization had the additional modernizing benefit of the newly constructed railway to transport products and to provide development services. Not only that, but there were thousands of former railway workers who had experienced a new form of modernity as wage laborers in a transnational infrastructure project. Those former construction workers who chose to remain and settle along the TAZARA line had the potential to become both a population base for village-based productivity and a modernizing example for other village settlers. In an irony of history, this vision of rural settlement and modernity was remarkably similar to a proposal made by Paul Fuchs in his colonial-era study of the proposed southern railway in 1904–1905, when he argued that railway construction workers recruited from the north should be encouraged to settle and establish farms along the line.[9]

In practice, the implementation of villagization in the TAZARA corridor was anything but orderly and efficient. The Tanzanian government lacked the resources and deprived itself of the time needed to carry out resettlement in any organized way. An observer from the national party had cautioned that the railway "passes through some areas that do not have many people, therefore it will be a large effort to persuade people to move into these areas." This same observer acknowledged that villagization along the railway line would be by necessity a "rushed exercise."[10] This was an understatement. Families were swept up in large open trucks with few possessions, forced to abandon their dwellings and fields. In some instances homes and granaries were torched as they departed. On arrival at their new "villages" most found themselves in the midst of uncleared bush and forest. Rather than moving from disorder to a legible modernity, they experienced the opposite: they described living in a wilderness, far from civilization.[11]

For many, the experience of being forcibly resettled by the state into concentrated villages was much like what they had experienced during colonial-era resettlement schemes in Ulanga and Mahenge Districts. In this region of Tanzania there was a long history of concentrated resettlement dating back to the late nineteenth century, particularly during the British period. People remember being resettled in the 1920s and again in the 1940s during the sleeping sickness campaigns. "It was *kihamo* [forced removal]," exclaimed one man when describing *ujamaa* villagization, using a term that in his memory spanned the decades of colonial and post-colonial policies.

Local people were reluctant to remain in villages that, for a variety of reasons, did not meet their needs. Over time many moved back to their former homes and farms. Those who stayed in the new villages were frequently those who had recently migrated into the valley for wage labor, either on the railway or on the sugar plantations. A pattern thus developed of newly arrived families, initially wage workers and traders, living closer to the railway while the older, more established population lived farther away along the rivers and floodplain. This pattern would continue over the next two decades. When in later years the population of the villages around the railway stations began to grow in size and to produce more goods for shipment on TAZARA, this was not the result of centralized government planning but of spontaneous migration and resettlement in response to new economic and political challenges.

Settlement History

When the first surveyors set out to explore the route of the TAZARA railway in the late 1960s, they traversed a landscape they described as largely empty or sparsely settled. The construction teams that followed observed that in many of the areas where they camped, including the Kilombero valley, there was little evidence of close settlement. Foodstuffs were frequently difficult to come by, and wild animals still roamed freely through places like Ifakara and Mngeta. Yet while observers described much of the territory in southern Tanzania as isolated and barely inhabited, there were in fact several areas of population density, for the region had a long history of concentrated settlements.

Centralized settlement in the nineteenth century was associated most often with political leaders, who gathered their followers around them as they established control over trade, agricultural production, and the payment of tribute. The maps of German explorers from the 1890s illustrate the way that sparsely settled territory in southern Tanzania was punctuated by villages, described by mapmakers as "well populated" and labeled with the names of local headmen or family elders.[12] Traveling German officials admired and encouraged these chiefly settlements in the colonial period. In 1903 captain Gideon von Grawert wrote approvingly of the large area ruled by Bena leader and German ally Kiwanga:

I was convinced of the excellent order in the Sultanate. . . . The field cultivation has increased significantly recently. . . . Some years ago, this whole area [at the confluence of the Mnyera and the Mpanga Rivers] was completely uninhabited. On the suggestion of Kiwanga, people have now been settled here, on both sides of the river, and a large, very cleanly kept up village has developed.[13]

Chief Kiwanga had succeeded in establishing an orderly concentrated village. Yet the same regional dynamics that led to population resettlement in some areas had caused dispersal in others. Homes were relocated in response to the pressures of long-distance trade, chiefly imperatives, regional conflict, and colonization. During the battles of the Maji Maji War in 1905–1907, families and communities fled into the forests for protection. Not long afterwards the military campaigns of the First World War resulted once again in disruption of the population, as families fled to avoid the fighting, conscription for porterage, and food requisitions. By the time the British arrived and began to implement their administrative strategy of Indirect Rule in 1923, they found people living in small, scattered settlements.

For the British, these dispersed settlements were a hindrance to effective colonial administration and the collection of taxes. One Mahenge District administrator observed in 1923 that "The natives do not live in proper villages but in scattered family settlements of a few huts," and thus, "the sultans and headmen generally have not much influence over their people."[14] To remedy this situation the British officers of Mahenge District began to impose what would become the largest population resettlement scheme of the entire colony. They justified their policies by claiming that this was a return to the way people had lived before German rule, in concentrated villages under the close administration of tribal chiefs. They relocated rural populations near the headquarters of chiefs and headmen, in towns, and along roadways. Many families were relocated by force. A notorious colonial district officer known locally as *"Bwana Nyoka"* (Master Snake) reportedly set fire in 1922 to the homes of families that refused to resettle into designated villages.[15]

In the 1940s, the population in the Kilombero valley was once again the target of administrative resettlement policy, this time in the name of sleeping sickness control. During this decade the residents of Mahenge District experienced the second largest sleeping sickness resettlement effort in the entire colony of Tanganyika. The 1940s are remembered as a time of significant and widespread disruption in the district—a total of 37,188 people were relocated into nine sleeping sickness settlements.[16] The British district officer at the time, A. T. Culwick, admitted that the schemes were unpopular with local people. Despite their unpopularity, however, he persisted in carrying out the schemes.[17] Families were forced to abandon cultivated fields, cleared homesteads, and ancestral burial sites. Densities of settlement could be over one hundred times that of their previous pattern, making it difficult for families to retain their mobile and diversified farming systems. The forced resettlements, combined with wartime demands from the colonies for grain at low prices, led to severe famine in many parts of the district. As a result desperate families once again dispersed, in search of subsistence and to avoid grain requisitions.

Two decades later in 1962, a new settlement scheme was established in the Kilombero Valley that was also designed to establish social order, political control, and economic productivity. This time, however, the scheme included not only rural farmers but also the urban poor. Just one month after achieving self-rule, the TANU administration announced that they would resettle five hundred "surplus" urban dwellers in the Kilombero valley, where they would be sent to clear land and take up farming. An additional two hundred urban unemployed were settled in the valley on a 3,000-acre scheme in 1962.[18] These pilot schemes—there were about sixty of them throughout the country at the time—were designed to create order in both urban and rural areas, first by clearing undesirable elements from towns and second by putting them to productive use as agriculturalists in planned developments. The Kilombero Settlement Scheme was located on the main road between Mikumi and Ifakara, incorporating the villages of Ichonde, Sonjo, and Kichangani. In total the scheme comprised 1,000 acres of cleared land that was allocated to 250 families for development into "smallholdings," where they grew sugar cane as outgrowers for the Kilombero Sugar Company.[19]

By the time of TAZARA's construction, therefore, the residents of the Kilombero valley had experienced a series of efforts to resettle them into concentrated villages.

In the colonial period British administrators had attempted twice to relocate rural families into prescribed settlements. After the transition to independence, the TANU party had relocated urban dwellers and rural farmers into the Kilombero Settlement Scheme as sugar cane outgrowers. Thus when the Tanzanian government imposed *ujamaa* villagization in 1973, residents of the valley viewed it not as something new and modern, but as something old and familiar. For the rural residents of the valley, each of these *kihamo* resettlement projects resembled the ones that had gone before. The schemes are remembered as a series of forced relocations carried out by distant political authorities that used similar methods and achieved similar results.

Villagization: *Operation Kando Kando ya Reli*

Tanzania's national party, or TANU, had begun to actively pursue socialist objectives after the Arusha Declaration in 1967. As part of his vision for rural development Julius Nyerere proposed that rural areas be reorganized into collective villages based on his ideal of *ujamaa*, or familyhood. The engine of agricultural development would not be large-scale commercial enterprise, but rather family-based, village-level production. Young people would be trained through special programs in modern agricultural techniques, which they would impart to local villagers. The policy did not have positive results in the first six years. Rather than becoming more productive agriculturally, Tanzania experienced decreased food production and had to rely on food imports. Widespread drought and increases in the price of oil further eroded the productivity of the *ujamaa* sector. In response, the government decided to intensify villagization through a rapid increase in the number of *ujamaa* settlements. The government set a deadline of 1977 for moving the entire rural population of Tanzania into village settlements. If necessary, force would be used.[20]

In the TAZARA corridor, government surveyors began to map out homestead plots for resettlement near Chita railway station in 1973. The targeted population for the relocation campaign was a total of 344 families. Work went slowly for the villagization staff as well as for the relocated families. By October 3, 1973, officials had distributed only 35 plots to villagers and were in the process of completing surveys of an additional 12 plots. Once they had been allocated a plot of land, the families themselves were responsible for the arduous work of clearing the bush. Clearing was especially taxing for villagers resettled at Chita, because their plots were located in a dense forest. Of the 35 plots that had been claimed by villagers by October 7, officials reported that only about half (17) had been cleared, while the remaining plots were still under heavy forest cover. Only one plot had a house built on it; the others had no shelters or even the beginnings of construction. A few families here and there had started to gather wooden poles for house building.

There were clearly problems with resettlement at this early stage. The surveyors assigned to Chita village wrote a letter to their district-level leaders in late September, appealing for help with persuading people to relocate. Their job would be made much easier, they argued, if they had the use of a vehicle. The families that were slated to be moved to Chita resided an average distance of eight miles away, mainly in the settlements of Ng'ombo and Udagaji. Even those who had agreed in principle to take plots were not occupying them, according to a later report, because they were either fishing at the river, preparing their fields for planting, or working on the construction of TAZARA. Other problems that plagued the villagization team were the lack of a water supply system, a shortage of spare parts for the disabled tractor, and rumors of *uchawi* (witchcraft).[21]

The residents of Chita who lived through the villagization era have strong memories of what life was like before and after rural resettlement. Retired schoolteacher Samuel Mihanji Undole remembers,

> Before TAZARA, people lived *pembeni pembeni* [dispersed, lit. "in the corners"]. . . . The way people lived, one family would live together with their relatives, or with people that they knew very well. They would eat together—they would take the food to the father or *bwana mkubwa* first, then the others would eat together—the women and children. Not like nowadays, when you can live next to someone who is not a relative or close friend. [Back then] people farmed around their settlements.
>
> Where Chita is today, there were no people at all, it was a forest. It was called the forest of Ching'anda. It was a forest of big trees. There were wild animals like elephants, lions, buffalo, hippopotamus, and many snakes. Some people were living in the hills at that time, while others lived in the valleys.
>
> The operation began in 1974. The orders were to find a place here for people to move and to make villages. They chose this forest of Ching'anda. The leadership of the district came to oversee the operation, to educate and to inform people that they had to move here into villages and to live together. They first surveyed the plots, then later they moved the people using lorries. They brought you here and they dumped you out here. People had to live outside at first, without a shelter or a tent. You were given a plot in the forest, you had to clear it yourself and to build a house. Some people were bitten by snakes and they died. The people then began to build their shelters, and began to clear trees and to plant crops.
>
> Many of these residents moved back to their original homes. The people from Mkondoa, [a settlement on the floodplain], moved back and are now planning to initiate a new village there. The people of Undagaji, in the hills, also returned to their homes as did the people of the old Chita village that existed

before villagization. People who formerly lived at Mkaja, [along the escarp-
ment], were unable to move back to their homes because the land was used
by the Chinese for a quarry during the construction of the railway. Since that
time, it has been taken over by the National Service as a training camp.[22]

The *ujamaa* village at Chita gradually began to grow through the late seventies and
early eighties. A report from 1975 listed 478 households with 1,097 people, and the
following year 482 households with a total of 2,201 residents are listed. Yet the village
continued to have problems with production and population stability. A report in
1983 complained that there was no transportation to bring rice from the farms to the
village. Crops were producing poorly, the village shop was not making a profit, and
the cattle project was failing because of a disease outbreak. Because there was no
veterinary medicine available, three of the twenty cows in the project had already
died. The dreams of village prosperity were not yet realized.[23]

   To the east of Chita, people were also moved from outlying settlements to
newly surveyed villages alongside the railway in 1973. In Mngeta ward three villages were created for resettlement: Mchombe, Mngeta, and Mkangawalo. Prior to
the construction of the railway, people living in this area were living in settlements
that were governed loosely by extended family heads known as *wandzagira*. Some
heads of families, Chalachimu and Mtwanga, for example, had been government
jumbe representatives during the British colonial period, and their settlements were
named after them.[24] During villagization these settlements were abandoned when
their residents were moved to the new plots that had been surveyed alongside the
railway near the Mngeta station. Groups of people that had lived together in the
lineage-based settlements were divided in some cases rather than being moved
together as a group. Only those who had selected their plots early and voluntarily
were likely to secure adjacent plots for relatives. Most people found themselves
living next to people who were neither relatives nor friends: after moving, they
explained, they found themselves among strangers. The lineage elders and *jumbes*
who had governed over the earlier settlements were replaced by a new structure of
leadership created by the ruling TANU party: village chairmen, ward secretaries,
ten-cell leaders. In some cases, lineage elders themselves assumed new roles in the
TANU structure.

   At first, people around Mngeta were reluctant to move to the new plots that were
being surveyed along the railway. Only a few people volunteered to move, while
the rest had to be forcibly resettled. People and their belongings were packed into
lorries, then transported to their assigned plots where they were unloaded. "They
had to use force," remembers Mzee Majiji of Mchombe. "They went to people's
houses and took away everything they owned. They had no houses and they slept
outside."[25] The land designated for resettlement was undeveloped, making it dif-

ficult to get a start in farming. "It was so wild at that time," recalled Godfrey Mwa-kyoma: "there were buffaloes and hippopotamus walking around. This town was a big wilderness."[26] Because of the wild animals, farmers could only plant limited stands of rice and other crops. Many returned to their previous farmlands, where they stayed during the growing season in small raised shelters (lengo) to protect their fields from wild animals.

Even after Mchombe village became more permanently settled, according to Mtwanga, the area was never suitable for cultivation. "People go to other places to farm," he observed. "Here it is a town, there is no place for farming, so people have farm plots somewhere else." In Mngeta and Mchombe, a pattern emerged in which families held plots in ujamaa villages and eventually built houses there, but they continued to farm away from the town, toward the river. Men continued to travel to fishing camps during the dry season, leaving women with the work of harvesting and looking after the homestead. As the fish trade increased around the Mngeta area, men began to stay away for longer periods, causing strains on family life.[27]

For some residents of Mngeta and Mchombe, villagization was remembered as a positive change. Echoing arguments made by the national government, a few elders remember that people were brought closer together so that they could receive better services. Yokina Msaka stated that people came to Mchombe village to live voluntarily during Operation Kando Kando ya Reli because it was "a good place."[28] Others, however, complained that while they followed Mwalimu Julius Nyerere's directive to come together into villages, fulfilling their side of the contract, the promised services were never delivered. Godfrey Mwakyoma of Mchombe feels that TAZARA has disappointed the rural communities that helped to build and protect the railway in the early years. "We were asked by Nyerere to move alongside the railway," he says, and the villagers did so faithfully. "But now, the services have ended up being very poor."[29]

In the town of Ifakara, there was no need for large-scale villagization because the bulk of the population already lived in a concentrated community. Still, some neighborhoods were targeted for resettlement because of their geographical location. Families that lived in areas prone to flooding—for example, the neighbor-hoods near to the Lumemo river—were forced to resettle on drier ground along the railway line at Lungongole (a sub-village of Kikwawira about twelve kilome-ters from Ifakara). "I witnessed the kihamo, in Ifakara," remembers Joseph Haule. "People had their homes destroyed and they were moved to Lungongole. They were taken there to the wilderness [pori]. You were taken there with your family. They moved people who lived in places where there were floods, but they didn't move people who lived on dry land. The people who moved there weren't happy, they all moved back here eventually, now those areas are just farms."[30] One of the problems for families trying to settle at Lungongole was the abundance of wildlife, especially during the wet season. "The problem was that there were too many wild animals, like buffaloes and elephants," according to Mzee Moyo.[31]

Brother Edwin von Moos, a Capuchin missionary who has lived in Ifakara for over forty-six years, was a witness to villagization in Ifakara. "Villagization was a very bad time," he recalled. "Some people's houses were burned on the Mahenge side of the river, and people were moved forcefully at Kivukoni; the police came with guns to make them move. A lot of them did not move. They had to move to a place where there was nothing, no house, no water, nothing. They had to leave behind a house, trees, a very nice *shamba* [farm]."[32]

Villagization was carried out at several sites to the east of Ifakara along the all-weather road toward Kidatu. Here many of the *ujamaa* villages were created at existing population centers. Some villages were sited at TAZARA construction camps (at Signali, for example) or railway workshops (at Man'gula) that already had concentrations of population and adjacent cultivated land. At Signali most of the original *ujamaa* village inhabitants were migrant railway workers who decided to stay on after construction was completed. At Kiberege, an older settlement that had been the headquarters of Mahenge District under British rule, villagization involved the reorganization of the existing community into the *ujamaa* structure.[33] At Mang'ula, two villages (Mang'ula A and Mang'ula B) were created from the population of laborers that worked in the railway machine workshops and in railway construction. One of these villages, like Signali, was a former TAZARA labor camp.[34]

This stretch of road was also the location of the Kilombero Settlement Scheme (described above), where families were already farming sugar cane on one thousand acres of land in three villages. This scheme, once viewed as a model for the future of rural development in independent Tanzania, was completely dismantled during *ujamaa* villagization in 1969–70. Paul Bolstad, the Peace Corps volunteer assigned to work with the scheme at Sonjo from 1966 to 1968, remembers the transition this way: "By 1969, the government had abruptly abandoned the settlement scheme idea and was ready to roll out the Ujamaa Village idea. . . . When I returned in May of 1970, the whole scheme had suddenly been converted into a cooperative with no government funding at all . . ."[35] The land that had been cleared and developed for the settlement scheme was handed over to the *ujamaa* villagization effort, according to Juma Juma Kiswanya:

> During *vijijini* [villagization], they took the land of the settlement scheme to create the new villages. The village of Ichonde was called Mgudeni. They took the land from the settlement scheme because it was already cleared. They [the

settlers] received some compensation. The government saw that all people were *wananchi* [citizens], so it wasn't a problem for them to give the land to other people. Some of the settlement scheme members were angry that their farms had been taken, so they left.[36]

In the area around Mang'ula, therefore, villagization did not involve the relocation of people from their farms to a wilderness that needed to be cleared for settlement. Rather, *ujamaa* policies converted existing establishments (railway construction camps, the former administrative center of Kiberege, the settlement scheme) into new structures of economy and governance.

Living along the Railway

Operation Kando Kando ya Reli was similar in many ways to the *ujamaa* villagization programs being carried out elsewhere in independent Tanzania at this time. In other ways, however, it was unique. For the families that were relocated along TAZARA were expected not only to be rural producers, but also to provide security for the railway. The physical presence of village settlements was intended to provide protection from potential enemy saboteurs. Villagers were given responsibility for surveillance, and were taught to report strangers and any suspicious activity. Meanwhile, the residents of *ujamaa* villages had to adjust to the railway's presence in their everyday lives. Over time they began to use TAZARA in distinctive ways and to claim the railway as their own. The permanent way became a pathway for pedestrian travel in the lowlands, while in the highlands people used the tunnels as shortcuts to walk from one valley to the next. When in the 1980s officials endeavored to close some of TAZARA's stations, the villagers responded adamantly that TAZARA was "their" railway, the "railway of the people," and that therefore its policies should serve their needs. After all, they argued, hadn't they done their part in protecting the railway all these years?

The question of security had been a central one as TAZARA neared completion on the Tanzanian side of the border in 1973. Railways in southern Africa were strategic military and symbolic targets for the Rhodesian and South African military forces fighting against liberation armies based in Zambia and Mozambique. TAZARA was an especially important target for sabotage because its demise would leave Zambia's economy dependent once again upon the southern railway route through Rhodesia. Indeed, the bombings of TAZARA's Chambeshi bridge on October 12, 1979, and Lusemfwa bridge on November 9 that same year left Zambia without a transportation alternative for more than three months.[37] Julius Nyerere had declared in a 1970 speech that

It is quite likely that the agents of the Southern Africa regimes will intensify their efforts to sabotage our freedom and our work. It is therefore essential that, throughout the construction period, and when the railway is completed, all the peoples of Tanzania, and of Zambia, should accept a responsibility for guarding this railway. We must guard it against sabotage, and we must also guard it against the effects of hostile propaganda.[38]

In practice, it was the rural communities that lived alongside TAZARA that were given responsibility for everyday security. This approach made sense given the vast and often remote terrain that the railway passed through. Rural security policies were explicitly linked to the formation of *ujamaa* villages in the region. In a speech he made to villagers living along the railway in Kisarawe District in October 1971, Waziri Juma emphasized the connection between the security of the railway and *ujamaa* socialism: by practicing socialism, those already living productively in villages would encourage others to do the same, thereby expanding the presence of a watchful population of rural residents along TAZARA.[39]

When an unknown person was found in the area, villagers were expected to report them to local administrative leaders so that their identification papers could be checked. Any dubious person or activity was to be reported at once. D. S. M. Mumello, manager of the tunnels section based at Mkela, described his experience upon driving an unmarked Land Rover into a village to research local place names:

> The Mkomaga villagers stopped us from gathering any information concerning traditional names to be written on each tunnel until a detailed introduction of the idea was clearly explained to them. After introducing ourselves witnessed by other local workers around there then they became friendly and we managed to get the information required. This kind of security is excellent.[40]

The role of villagers in railway security also included the use of weapons for defense, according to one report. The head of Tanzania's police forces, Mr. Hamza Aziz, visited Mang'ula on January 11, 1973, to announce that the police would be facilitating coordinated security measures along TAZARA. As a result, local officers would be educating citizens living alongside the railway about "the importance and value of protecting this railway," a form of instruction that would include "lessons on how to use various types of weapons and devices of war."[41]

Moving people into villages along the railway line addressed one security problem by providing a population presence that could assist with surveillance of the stations and the track, but it created other security dilemmas for local leaders. People had to learn how to live alongside the railway—not only in order to protect the railway, but also to protect themselves. In the early years of train operations,

FIGURE 4.2. The youth of Ifakara demonstrate their readiness to protect TAZARA during a visit by TANU leaders to survey *ujamaa* villages alongside the railway, 1974. Photograph courtesy of Tanzania Department of Information Services (Maelezo).

there were collisions involving both people and livestock. Children, the elderly, and the intoxicated were at the highest risk for train accidents, especially at night when visibility was poor. There were three deadly incidents between August and December 1980 that illustrate the types of incidents that occurred. In the first case, a man walking along the track between Ruipa and Ifakara was struck by a moving train. The second incident involved two youths who were burned to death when they drew too close to a diesel engine fire near a station. In the third "accident," a murderer tried to disguise his crime by placing the victim's corpse in the path of a locomotive.[42]

Carol Mpandamgongo of Ikule remembers what it was like to live along the railway in the early years: "When the railway was started, many people and animals were killed by the train—buffalo, wild pigs, lions—especially at night. Even last year, there was a hippo killed at the crossing. Many people were killed because of alcohol [*pombe*]. They got drunk, went onto the rails, and got hit by the train. People could do bad things in places where there were no people to see."[43] TAZARA officials cooperated with government workers to teach the villagers living along the railway how to coexist with the passing trains. People were brought together in village-level meetings and taught both how to care for the train and also how to protect themselves. Education efforts focused on reminding villagers of the benefits of the railway, and their responsibility to help protect this national and international asset. Leaders exhorted villagers to protect the railway in their own interests, in the national interest, and in the interest of southern African liberation.

As they adapted to the presence of the railway in their midst, rural residents began to use it in ways of their own. The raised railway beds, built up high above the grass-covered floodplain, made excellent footpaths. The tracks and a wide reserve on either side were kept clear of brush and tall grasses, which improved mobility and visibility for pedestrians. Railway bridges and other raised structures provided foot crossings over the numerous streams and wetlands that filled the Kilombero valley. During the season of heavy rains and floods, the railway became a vital pathway above the marshes and was frequently crowded with travelers. On the rugged escarpment between Mlimba and Makambako, the tunnels that had been blasted through the mountains shortened the distances between villages considerably. Local residents used the railway tunnels as passageways through which they could walk from one place to another, traversing terrain that had previously been impassable.

There were other ways that residents used the infrastructure of TAZARA in their daily lives. For the temporarily homeless, stations were secure shelters where one could rest in shade during the day, or sleep safely at night. One woman trader slept with her children on *ukindu* mats on the floor of the Mlimba station for three months while she recovered from an economic crisis.[44] People also used TAZARA stations to obtain fresh water, and even to bathe. At Ifakara station, family members from nearby households came to collect the fresh water that was pumped by railway authorities from a well. In the 1990s this water use was becoming excessive and expensive, according to the stationmaster. While he had pumped one tank per week in the 1980s, due to a housing boom in the early 1990s one tank lasted barely a single day. The area residents were taking water for household use as well as for other purposes such as construction and beer brewing. In some instances they used stolen faucets at night to open the pipe valves. Some villagers carried the water away, while others bathed *in situ* from the pipes they had opened.

Thus local households used the TAZARA station both as a water source and as a nighttime bathing facility. When the stationmaster confronted some of those taking the water, they replied to him that it was the water of "the Chinese," and therefore anyone had the right to use it because its use was not governed by local law.[45] Their statement raised important questions about the ownership of TAZARA and its resources, questions that had also been raised during the time of construction.

Did the railway belong to China, to the nation (*taifa*), to the TAZARA authorities, or to the villagers who lived along the line of rail?[46]

Claiming the Railway

The residents who lived in *ujamaa* villages alongside the railway had been asked to provide security and surveillance in order to prevent international sabotage. Yet the majority of the acts recorded as "sabotage" against TAZARA in the Kilombero District books were carried out not by the agents of foreign settler regimes, but by local people. Many of these acts were random vandalism performed by young boys carrying out pranks. These youths enjoyed collecting stones (*kokoto*) from the railway bed and hurling them at the train with their hands or with slingshots. Others placed obstacles such as stones, metal bars, or branches on the rails, threatening derailment. A youth was caught placing a stone on the rails at Mang'ula station on August 14, 1989. He was seven years old.[47] In other incidents, vandals removed the nuts from bolts holding bridges and culverts together. Telegraph wire was cut and stolen, making communication between stations impossible. In August 1989, eighty-four nuts were removed from bridges near Mngeta. The same month, one hundred meters of telegraph wire were cut near Msolwa.

Some believed that the nuts were stolen by fishermen who used them to weight their nets in the fast-flowing rivers. Others said that telegraph wire was useful for tying snares for trapping wild animals, and in later years that it was used to make antennae for television sets.[48] TAZARA stationmaster Benedict Mkanyago felt that those who tried to disrupt the trains were simply ignorant people, who "didn't know the consequences of the things they were doing."[49] The solution to the problem in his view (and in the view of most TAZARA officials) was to educate the public about caring for the train through village-level meetings. Community education had already taken place in the 1970s after TAZARA was completed. It was carried out again in the 1980s when there was an increase in vandalism and consequent concern among TAZARA security police. Vandalism was an embarrassment to the nation and gave support to enemy regimes, wrote a TAZARA police officer in 1989:

> It is my view that we can stop these bad acts that are bringing shame to our nation in the full view of the world, especially in the view of our enemies who night and day are meeting secretly about the success that has been brought by this important transportation sector, i.e. the railway of TAZARA/freedom/liberation. We can achieve this if all the citizens who live alongside the railway, together with all the citizens of the district, will be educated about the importance of TAZARA.[50]

In the view of these TAZARA authorities, vandalism was caused by ignorance and therefore the solution was community education. Others, however, viewed vandalism as a symptom of a larger problem of discontent with the railway's functioning. Samuel Undole believed that some of those who threw objects at the train, unfastened the nuts, or placed stones on the rails had a quarrel with TAZARA: "This often took place when those people were fighting with the leadership" of the railway, he explained, and they were trying to harm the railway out of anger. He speculated that those carrying out vandalism may have been disgruntled workers who were let go after completing a temporary work contract, and who then decided to take revenge on the railway.[51]

The District Commissioner in the late 1980s, E. F. Tumbo, also believed that vandalism was a symptom of dissatisfaction with TAZARA's performance. She reminded TAZARA authorities that those who were resettled in *ujamaa* villages had been promised services in exchange for their security responsibilities. If the local people were expected to guard the railway and protect it from saboteurs, she wrote in a memorandum, then TAZARA itself needed to improve its performance. There had been many complaints, she noted: for example, the train often stopped outside the station rather than pulling in to the platform. This made it difficult, in fact dangerous, to load and unload passengers and goods. In other cases, the train was stopped between stations to load bundles of dried fish illegally. Following a meeting with TAZARA officials, Mrs. Tumbo reported that "we have agreed that we will provide education on both sides, for the villagers and also for the workers of TAZARA."[52] In her letters to TAZARA authorities Mrs. Tumbo articulated the widespread perception among local people that while they had fulfilled their obligation to serve the nation by relocating to *ujamaa* villages, the railway authorities had not provided an adequate level of service in return. Her memoranda emphasized the reciprocal relationship that local villagers understood to be the basis of TAZARA's authority: if they were asked to fulfill specific expectations on behalf of the railway, they had the right to expect a certain level of responsiveness in return.

In the late 1980s and early 1990s, local village leaders wrote a series of petitions to government representatives that accused TAZARA of neglecting the needs of local people. The letter writers were concerned by rumors of TAZARA's privatization and by closures of some smaller stations, moves that were rumored to be initiated by external donor pressures in the context of economic liberalization. The letters reminded government representatives of the reciprocity that had been established at the time of TAZARA's completion. The leader of a local ad hoc committee, J. M. Mukama, wrote the following complaint to his parliamentary representative in 1994, following the closure of Mbingu station:

We ask that this station at Mbingu be reopened, so that it can continue to provide important service for the citizens as it used to. Because the Freedom Railway "TAZARA" was built for the benefit of Tanzanians and Zambians, not for the profit of the IMF or to bring profits to private persons.

Mr. Mukama went on to remind the government that during villagization, rural people had been moved to live along the railway:

And that is why the government announced publicly that citizens who are near to the railway should build there and live alongside the railway, so that they can protect their railway.[53]

By referring to TAZARA as "their railway," as a resource belonging to the citizens who lived alongside it, Mr. Mukama expressed the claim of ownership made by local people as they attempted to influence railway policies that directly affected their daily lives. In these petitions and in oral interviews, local people remembered the period of villagization as a time of sacrifice by rural people who abandoned their established homesteads to serve the nation. They had been promised services in return, they argued, services that either had not been provided or were now being taken away.

Village protesters were correct in linking the station closures to the influence of external donors. The closures were one part of a larger process of commercialization and restructuring of TAZARA that was undertaken in the mid-1990s on the recommendation of an international team of consultants. The restructuring process aimed at making the railway more profit-oriented and more efficient, by reducing the number of departments, for example, and by establishing separate regional profit-and-loss centers for Tanzania and Zambia. The stations that were termed "economically unviable" under the new commercialization structure were small stations where railway employees were on full-time duty even though trains stopped only every twelve or twenty-four hours. Some of these stations were slated to be closed completely, while others would be partially closed, with staff available on part-time duty to receive and dispatch trains. A newspaper account described the actions of people living at Mbingu when their station was closed:

The [TAZARA] sources said the stations up for closure include Vigama, Kiberege, Mbingo [sic], Kibwe, Mahongolo, Wanging'ombe, Msesule, Chikola and Mpemba. These stations are said to be uneconomic while TAZARA spends a lot of money running them. Nevertheless, the people who live near the stations are opposed to the idea according to sources. Two engineers were sent to Mbingu Station on Tuesday this week to start dismantling the station, but the people set an obstacle and refused them to implement the plan.[54]

It should have come as no surprise to TAZARA officials that the residents of Mbingu protested the closure of their station by putting up physical obstacles and writing letters of protest. The railway restructuring process measured the economic viability of small rural railway stations based upon a comparison between the number of full-time railway personnel and the frequency of trains that stopped there. Yet it was precisely at those smaller stations that were served by the Ordinary Train (and thus those that had less frequent train stops) that local economic growth, migration, and settlement had been most noticeable.

Four years before the station closures were carried out, an in-depth study had been conducted by TAZARA's district traffic inspector, Mr. Ally Tajiri, to investigate requests made by local villagers for the improvement of railway services. There had been requests made to increase the number of "halt" stops—not formal stations but official stopping points for passengers and parcels—at four new locations. Mr. Tajiri analyzed the settlement patterns and economic activities in the recommended areas, and included this information in his report. He discovered that some of the recommended halt stations had higher population levels than existing stations, and concluded that the addition of new stations was in order.

Mr. Ally Tajiri made explicit the positive connection between transportation services and rural development: "The growth of population in these villages through migration is presently hampered by lack of transport service to the very areas. Once halts are opened up, those farmers living in Ifakara may decide to build their houses at Idete village and stay closer to their farms. The milling machines may also be set up with assurance of passenger services, and this is likely to tempt the inhabitants of smaller, nearby villages to join the one with the halt for easy travel via passenger train."[55]

Mr. Tajiri's final report echoed the language of reciprocal obligation used in the correspondence between local leaders and TAZARA authorities over improvements in service. "The time has come," Mr. Tajiri wrote, "for the Authority [TAZARA] to avail such services to the villagers who paid heed to the Government's directive to live together for easy provision of vital services, including transportation." He concluded that TAZARA should "include building of passenger platforms into the designated areas" in its next budget year.[56] The report was received positively by the TAZARA management at the district office and was forwarded to the regional manager in Dar es Salaam.[57] The halt stations were finally implemented in 1998, at Signali, Idete, Ikule, and Chisano, "as the people requested."[58]

As Mr. Tajiri concluded his report, he stated once again the claim that those who had "paid heed" to the needs of the nation during villagization should now benefit from services. Yet the economic justification he cited for the opening up of halt stations in 1990 was based not on the population that had moved into villages at the time of TAZARA's completion, but on more recent population growth through migration. As we will see in the next chapters, there was substantial immigration into the railway corridor in the 1980s and 1990s by newcomers bringing with them new forms of trade and agriculture. Thus while local leaders and government officials alike continued to conduct their negotiations over railway services using the language of reciprocity from the *ujamaa* period, it was the expansion of an immigrant population that created new demands on TAZARA.

Part 2 · Ordinary Train

CHAPTER

5

The Ordinary Train

The TAZARA passenger station in Dar es Salaam was designed to be an imposing landmark. A visitor to the station in 1976 described the station as "bigger and more splendid than any other building" in Dar es Salaam at the time.[1] The starkness of the station's concrete exterior was softened by the installation of graceful five-lantern Chinese street lamps throughout the forecourt. TAZARA's customers entered and exited the station beneath a broad balcony; the soaring windows above them allowed daylight to flood into the cavernous marble-floored entry hall below. Inside, a double staircase led to the waiting areas and loading platforms where passengers would board and disembark from the trains that traveled between Dar es Salaam and points westwards.

On the days when trains were leaving for the interior, passengers gathered in the departure areas with their luggage, waiting to board the train. Groups of families, friends, and other well-wishers escorted the travelers to see them off. Secondary school students waited with the suitcases and book bags that would accompany them to their boarding schools in rural settings. Families of parents and small children sorted their belongings, for if they were traveling in first or second class they would be separated into compartments by gender. Business travelers, traders, National Service recruits, TAZARA employees, and a multitude of other passengers awaited the train's departure, anticipating their upcoming journeys.

FIGURE 5.1. TAZARA railway station in Dar es Salaam, 1977. Photograph courtesy of Tanzania Department of Information Services (Maelezo).

Those traveling across the border into Zambia or headed for one of the large interior towns within Tanzania would be taking the Express Train—the passenger train that stopped at the largest stations between Dar es Salaam and Kapiri Mposhi. On alternate days, travelers would board the Ordinary Train—the slower train that frequented each of the small stations and halt stops along the route between Dar es Salaam and Mbeya. Even seasoned business travelers frequently preferred the Ordinary Train to the Express, for they could take advantage of the inexpensive and diverse farm products for sale on the different station platforms. Most of the passengers on the Ordinary Train were destined for one or more of the smaller settlements along the railway line, in particular those stations within the "passenger belt" that extended from the northern Selous Game Reserve boundary up to the regional town of Mbeya. Among them would be residents of these small settlements returning from the city to their rural homes, traders going there to purchase farm produce, and *wamachinga* peddlers carrying consumer goods for sale in more remote areas.

Some distance away from the TAZARA passenger station in Dar es Salaam was a second terminus for trains traveling to and from upcountry. The harbor at Kurasini was the final destination for TAZARA's goods trains coming in from the west. Goods trains arrived at the port loaded with ingots from Zambia's copper mines, or pulling wagonloads of bulk commodities from the regional trading centers in Tanzania's southern highlands. These goods wagons, or *behewa*, might be carrying stacks of cut timber from the pine forest plantations of Sao Hill in Iringa District, maize harvested in Iringa, Njombe, or Mbeya, or rice collected at Mlimba by one of the big merchant houses from Dar es Salaam. The wagons might even be carrying a shipment of live cattle transported by livestock merchants based in Ifakara or Usangu.

The goods trains carried products in large quantities that filled entire wagons, transported by agricultural projects and large-scale trading enterprises. Smaller traders on the other hand were unlikely to have enough volume to fill a goods wagon by themselves. In some cases they joined together in informal associations to share a wagonload shipment. Yet even if they did manage to have a large enough shipment, small-scale traders were frequently at a disadvantage when there were limited goods wagons available to customers. Most often, small entrepreneurs shipped their goods as "parcels" in the luggage wagon that was pulled by the Ordinary Train. These parcels were much smaller in weight and in bulk than the commodities carried in the goods wagons that rolled into the Kurasini terminus. And they were just as likely to be transported from one small station to another within the passenger belt as they were to be shipped all the way to Dar es Salaam or to Mbeya. The parcels were therefore a key component of the multi-spatial livelihoods that were fashioned by local communities along the TAZARA railway, as evidenced by the receipts that were left behind at each railway station after passengers boarded the Ordinary Train.

The Ordinary Train linked the rice farmers of the Kilombero valley floodplain with the maize and horticulture specialists of the Njombe and Mbeya highlands. In this way markets in the lowland settlements of Ifakara and Mlimba could play a significant role in the economic lives of Njombe farmers and traders, while traders based in Ifakara came to depend in turn upon regular supplies of beans, potatoes, or groundnuts from Makambako. The busy traffic in parcels that moved up and down the passenger belt therefore had broad significance for rural economic development within the southern region of Tanzania, and even further afield when traders extended their economic networks or traveled themselves to access more distant goods and markets.

The Ordinary Train provided a transportation infrastructure that enhanced physical mobility for goods and people across varied ecosystems, economic opportunities, and concentrations of settlement. Yet the train was much more than this. It was a resource around which people structured not only their material survival but also other important aspects of their lives—whether they were recovering from a sudden downturn or stroke of bad luck, were young traders just starting out in business, or were retirees settling down on a plot of farm land after a career in civil service. "I came here [to the railway corridor] looking for life," was one of the most common phrases used in interviews to explain the attraction of the Ordinary Train to its users.[2]

In life history interviews, respondents spoke about their experience of the railway and its relationship to development. Their narratives revealed the long-term strategies of diversification and of multi-spatiality pursued by individuals and families. Some were tales of personal progress, while others told of despair and frustration. Most followed cyclical patterns, contrasting times of plenty with periods of difficulty and want. Residents of the railway corridor remembered the histories of their life and livelihood experiences in rich detail. Their life stories affirmed the material significance of resources such as the railway and investment capital. At the same time, they described the larger meanings of these resources in the world of the railway corridor.

The TAZARA Corridor

After leaving the imposing setting of the passenger station in Dar es Salaam, the train begins its journey westwards by traveling through the expanding suburbs of the city. Soon the tracks gently ascend above the humid coastal plain to the progressively drier and cooler elevations of the *nyika*, or inland East African plateau. During the first hundred miles of its journey toward Zambia, the railway travels through the Selous Game Reserve. The Selous is the largest game reserve on the continent of Africa, and passengers on the train get a sense of its vastness as they traverse its wooded grasslands. During daylight hours giraffes and other wild animals can be seen from the windows of the passenger wagons, loping away from the noisy clatter of the passing train. As the train draws closer to the western boundary of the reserve, brush fires burning in the surrounding meadows can sweep perilously close to the tracks. TAZARA finally emerges from the Selous Reserve at the small town of Msolwa, located in the fertile floodplain of the Msolwa and Ruaha rivers. From here an expanse of bright green sugar cane extends northwards; these fields are the holdings of the Kilombero Sugar Company.

After leaving Msolwa, TAZARA passes along the eastern edge of the Udzungwa mountains—home to a uniquely biodiverse rainforest now preserved as Udzungwa National Park. In the corridor of land between the boundaries of this park and the Selous Reserve, the fertile alluvial landscape is filled in with a patchwork of rice and sugar cane fields, homesteads, and settlements. The sugar cane in these smaller plots is grown by outgrowers for the Kilombero Sugar Company.

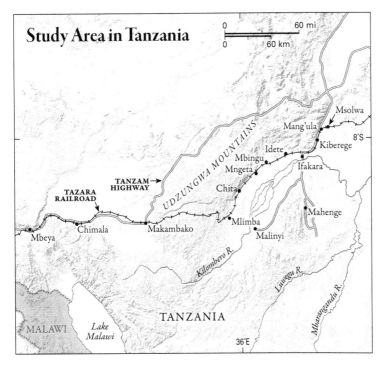

MAP 2. The path of the Ordinary Train through the passenger belt in Tanzania.
Map by Jerome Cookson, 2007.

TAZARA's tracks curve steadily southwestwards from here, following the pe-
rimeter of the Udzungwa escarpment into the wooded foothills on the outskirts of
the large town of Ifakara. The train does not pass through the low-lying center of
Ifakara itself, but stays to the north where the upland soils are drier and more stable.
The town of Ifakara, an historic settlement and trading center, serves as the main
bulking point for the loads of rice and dried fish that originate along both sides of
the Kilombero river. There is therefore considerable road and canoe traffic ferrying
goods from these areas to town, and from town to the TAZARA station. Overloaded
Land Rovers, bicycles, and pushcarts are employed to move passengers and goods.
The station platform becomes crowded when the train pulls through; a cluster of
restaurants and tea shops located just outside the station comes to life. Children and
other vendors parade with basket-trays of cooked snacks and drinks from window
to window alongside the waiting train for sale to travelers.

The train leaves Ifakara to continue its southwestward journey through the *miombo* woodlands of the Kilombero foothills. On the right side of the train the steep

FIGURE 5.2. Maize fields near Mang'ula with the Udzungwa Mountains in the distance, 2000. Photograph by Steven Davis.

Udzungwa scarp rises upwards, its rugged river valleys crowned by crystalline waterfalls. Here and there massive granite outcroppings loom into view from the forested slopes. On the left side of the train, woodlands give way to grasslands and eventually to floodplain as the Kilombero river stretches away to the southwest. The track is often elevated here above seasonally inundated valleys, formed by a multitude of braided streams flowing out of the mountains. The Chinese engineers and their African partners built miles of raised tracks, bridges, and culverts in this section.

A string of settlements lines the path of the railway here, buoyed by the presence of both road and railway links as well as proximity to the market in Ifakara. Idete, Mbingu, Mngeta, and Chita were all developed as *ujamaa* villages and have become substantial population centers since at least the mid-1980s. In the uplands adjacent to these villages residents tend fields of maize and bananas, while on the southern side toward the floodplain they cultivate rice. In informal settlements along the waterways there are fishing camps where men traditionally have gone for days at a time, leaving their wives and children behind to tend the rice fields. In the forests above the railway there are woodcutters and charcoal burners; in the grasslands pastoralists graze their cattle while wildlife poachers hunt for game where

FIGURE 5.3. *Ukindu* fibers used for weaving mats hang in a market kiosk alongside other consumer goods for sale outside the town of Mang'ula, 2000. Photograph by Steven Davis.

they can find it. Increasingly, however, the Game Controlled Area in the river valley is leased to tourist hunting concessions that work hard to keep unlicensed hunters out of their territory.

The last stop that TAZARA makes in the Kilombero valley proper is at the settlement of Mlimba. This booming town was once a small village off the beaten track, eclipsed historically by the more important chiefly centers of Merera and Utengule. Because of TAZARA's presence, Mlimba has now grown into a sizable settlement. The construction in 1995 of the nearby Kihansi hydroelectric project has also contributed to Mlimba's growth. The town is situated at the intersection of a number of diverse, overlapping landscapes on both sides of the river. To the south is one of the oldest and most productive rice-growing areas in the Kilombero region, the Malinyi alluvial fan. Between Malinyi and Mlimba, bicycle paths connect the TAZARA station to these rice fields and to important fisheries. Up in the hills of Masagati are legendary orange groves established by Italian Consolata missionaries in the 1920s, still producing sweet and thin-skinned fruits that are prized for their juice. Maize is grown in the higher elevations and in forest clearings to the north and west. Toward the Mpanga river, Sukuma agro-pastoralists use ox-plows to cultivate acres of millet, a grain they value both for subsistence consumption and for sale to beer brewers.

Westwards from Mlimba, TAZARA begins its famous climb up the escarpment to Makambako. Following switchbacks and traversing steep gorges, the railway passes through a region with only a few isolated settlements compared with the valley below. For most passengers this section of the railway line remains a mystery, for the passenger trains ascend and descend the escarpment after dark.

By the time it arrives in Mbeya, the TAZARA railway has passed through a succession of distinctive landscapes with unique ecological and socioeconomic attributes. The diversity of agro-ecological conditions has led to product specialization around each station. In the low-lying floodplain of the Kilombero river valley, rice is grown on a large scale and fish are harvested from numerous tributaries of the Kilombero river. In the foothills along the escarpment farmers grow maize and cooking bananas, while in the southern highlands the main staple products are maize, millet, dried beans, and Irish potatoes along with cool-climate vegetables such as tomatoes, onions, and cabbages. Stations that are located near more than one growing zone—Mlimba, for example—have become especially popular for rural settlement. As the TAZARA railway passes through the succession of distinctive landscapes that line the railway corridor, it provides a link between these diverse ecosystems and the product specializations that have been developed there.

TAZARA's Ups and Downs

Even before passenger services were officially inaugurated on TAZARA in 1976, rural travelers had already begun to use the train, riding in the open wagons that transported construction materials from the coast or copper ingots from Zambia. In interviews rural residents described the valuable services that TAZARA provided to them right from the beginning: they were able to reach the hospital in Ifakara without walking on foot; they could travel more easily between their homes and farms; and they could visit relatives some distance away. Samuel Mihanji Undole of Chita remembers riding atop goods wagons before passenger service began, although the trains made such infrequent stops that "you could pass your village unless you jumped out." Still, riding on a goods wagon was far superior to undertaking the four-to-five-day journey to Ifakara on foot.[3]

TAZARA has experienced uneven success with its operations since the railway was completed in 1975. During the first decade of TAZARA's operations, there were serious performance constraints that limited the services the railway could offer to rural passengers and long-haul transporters alike. TAZARA experienced a succession of performance breakdowns between 1975 and 1985, many of them related to technological malfunctions and management failures. During the same period rural economic growth was stagnating along the TAZARA line, as it was throughout many parts of Africa through the early 1980s. Political and economic difficulties in Zambia also affected overall railway operations, in particular the decline of the copper market and ongoing conflict with Zambia's southern neighbors. Things began to look up in the mid-1980s, as the ongoing Chinese technical cooperation was enhanced by generous assistance from other international donors. Yet while TAZARA's performance began to improve in the mid-1980s and record profits were recorded two years in a row, this success was not long-lasting. TAZARA's economic position was particularly vulnerable following the opening up of competitive transportation markets in eastern and southern Africa in the 1990s.

The physical infrastructure of TAZARA—the permanent way—was plagued early on by frequent landslides and washouts, especially during the heavy rains of 1979. While these problems were repaired relatively quickly with the help of Chinese technical assistance, there were other difficulties that were more intractable. The Chinese-built engines and wagons frequently broke down, and then languished in workshops rather than being repaired and sent back out on the track. The ninety-seven diesel hydraulic locomotives first sent by China lacked the motive power to haul heavy loads up the steep escarpment between Mlimba and Makambako. The original plan had been to have seventeen trains running per day, with an annual capacity of 2 million tons. At the end of 1978 only two trains were operating daily, with only 865,000 tons of cargo shipped in that year. As many as half of the available locomotives were stranded in workshops and out of service.[4] By the early 1980s, the railway's performance looked bleak indeed. Tonnage shipped on the railway had declined precipitously. The passenger trains—the services that rural communities depended upon for travel and for small-scale trade—plummeted to only one pair of trains per week rather than the expected six.[5]

Meanwhile, offloading and transshipment times were slow at Kapiri Mposhi in Zambia, causing delays in the return of wagons into Tanzania. There were inefficiencies at the port in Dar es Salaam, where congestion and mismanagement caused shipments destined for Zambia to pile up at the docks for months. These problems led to diplomatic tensions between the two countries in 1977–78, as Zambia's farmers waited in vain for some four to six thousand metric tons of fertilizers to be delivered in time for planting. In April 1978, five months after the start of the planting season, the fertilizer bags were still stacked at Kurasini, where they were finally covered with plastic tarpaulins to protect them from the heavy rains.[6] When Kenneth Kaunda announced the reopening of routes to the south on October 5, 1978, the Zambian people were reportedly "jubilant" that fertilizers, foodstuffs, and other commodities would be imported through Rhodesia.[7] Copper shipments also began to flow once again along the southern routes.

There were also financial conflicts between Tanzania and Zambia by the end of the decade, related in part to the way payments were made to the railway authority. Overall, the authority had been operating at a loss of as much as 200 million shillings between 1976 and 1980. Thus the agenda was a heavy one when Chinese, Tanzanian, and Zambian delegates sat down together in August 1980 in Lusaka to try to negotiate a new agreement for technical cooperation. The list of problems for discussion included ongoing need for spare parts, reliable locomotive power, expertise and technical support, and financial cooperation. The three delegations agreed to solve the locomotive issue by purchasing fourteen new diesel-electric engines from West Germany, to be put to work along the 546-kilometer stretch between Mlimba in Tanzania and Chozi on the Zambian side. China also agreed to continue to provide technical support, although at a reduced level, for the next two years. This would include personnel, materials, and loans for the purchase of spare parts needed to revive the railway's performance.[8]

The meeting in Lusaka was the start of a turnaround for TAZARA. The replacement of the fourteen diesel hydraulic engines did make a difference in the railway's performance. In the mid-1980s, a group of international donors joined China in extending aid packages for TAZARA's recovery that totaled $150 million (almost a third of the original cost of the railway itself). Following a ten-year plan adopted after a donors conference in Arusha in 1985, the railway authority undertook a series of ambitious projects for the rehabilitation of everything from the track to the wagon fleet.[9] In October 1987, USAID provided TAZARA with a grant of $45.9 million to purchase seventeen new diesel locomotives, bringing the number of high-powered locomotives to twenty-eight. The grant also supplied spare parts, a heavy-duty workshop in Mbeya, and equipment and technical assistance. The Chinese offered an additional $7 million for the purchase of spare parts, and promised fifty-seven Chinese technical experts to help repair and maintain equipment. Norway and Sweden joined in with support for training and for the rolling stock respectively.[10]

Following the adoption of this package, things began to improve for TAZARA, although progress was still uneven. Between 1985 and 1987 revenue increased as did cargo performance and the number of passengers. Passenger traffic along the length of the line had lapsed to below 500,000 in the early 1980s, but bounced back after 1986 to 860,000 persons in 1987–88 and had reached 988,000 by 1990. Local goods traffic within Tanzania also rose almost 50 percent between 1985 and 1988, according to TAZARA reports.[11] Yet by the end of the 1980s, TAZARA's performance was once again experiencing ups and downs. While passenger traffic was increasing yearly (and demand remained high), the railway's overall performance was "dismal" between 1987 and 1991, according to one report. The Swedish Aid Agency SIDA wrote a highly critical report in 1990 taking TAZARA management to task for not maintaining the rolling stock and the sleepers.[12] And despite improvements brought by donor initiatives and restructuring through the 1990s, there were still operational problems due to a combination of factors including low traffic levels, management problems, and escalating fuel and maintenance costs.[13] Tanzania's transportation minister acknowledged in 2001 that TAZARA was suffering once again from unsatisfactory traffic performance, a precarious financial situation, and declining customer confidence.[14]

Meanwhile, from the early 1990s onwards Tanzania's economic liberalization program had reached the agricultural sector, with crop marketing fully liberalized in 1991. This change affected trade and settlement along the railway in several ways. As markets for agricultural products were opened up, grain and other farm produce that had formerly been sold to government cooperatives and marketing boards could now be exchanged in local and regional markets. This provided new opportunities for small-scale traders to transport their products using TAZARA. Many of those who took up trading had suffered the negative effects of structural adjustment on employment, wages, and urban incomes in other parts of the Tanzanian economy. As opportunities in the formal sector declined, more people relied upon the informal sector to make a living, utilizing TAZARA to transport themselves and their goods.

In the highland maize-growing areas surrounding the TAZARA corridor, land pressures had already pushed many families onto farms that were only marginally productive by the 1990s. And after several years of successful participation in the National Maize Program, farmers in the southern highlands were no longer receiving government fertilizer subsidies and other supports after liberalization. In response, wealthier farmers in Njombe, Iringa, and Mbeya began to convert their maize fields to alternative crops such as Irish potatoes, while those with fewer means opted out of highland crop production altogether and used TAZARA to migrate into the railway corridor.[15] In the fertile soils of the Kilombero valley they could grow not only maize but also rice and other food crops without significant capital investment. Throughout southern Tanzania at this time, farmers were making shifts from "slow" crops and crops with heavy input requirements to "fast" crops that moved more quickly from field to market.[16] They were combining livelihood strategies in new ways, making shifts in agricultural and also in informal sector production. Families that had previously utilized the informal sector during breaks in the agricultural labor cycle were now combining agricultural and non-agricultural activities year-round.[17]

At the same time that these internal changes were taking place within Tanzania, the regional context of railway transport was also being transformed in ways that affected TAZARA's prospects. After 1990, as South Africa began the process of democratization, routes to the south promised to become competitive once again, causing TAZARA authorities to rethink the railway's regional strategy.[18] Participants in the 1992 TAZARA donors conference discussed plans to commercialize the railway and to enhance marketing strategies in the face of emerging competition with southern African rail and road transportation routes. In response to the "crumbling of apartheid and opening up of South Africa, and peace moves in Mozambique and Angola," according to one news report, "TAZARA has to launch an aggressive marketing campaign to remain competitive."[19]

Commercialization initiatives were announced by TAZARA authorities in 1994 and 1995. TAZARA would remain a unitary body, but would streamline operations in order to eliminate redundancy and to focus on commercially viable ventures. The head office would be reduced from nine departments to four, with two regional cost and profit centers, one for Tanzania and the other for Zambia. And because of the "cut-throat" competition that had developed in the southern African transportation industry, fully one-third of TAZARA's total 6,600 workers would be laid off in a period of fourteen months. At long last, wrote a newspaper commentator, TAZARA was waking up to the new economic reality:

> The announcement by the TAZARA management that it was trimming its workforce from 6,600 workers down to 4,000 comes as no surprise to those who have been following the railway line operations of late. The main problem with TAZARA has been that it has taken very long to transform itself from a political transport facility, primarily established to help Zambia loosen its dependence on the southern routes during the times of racial domination there, to a market-oriented facility when things changed.[20]

The railway was now officially re-inaugurated as a commercial enterprise.

Local pressures on TAZARA were as important during this period of transition as those from neighboring states. "This was a time of big change," remembers engineer Philemon Kaduma, because "under the open-market policies people could transport goods by any means possible," and TAZARA was forced for the first time into price wars with buses and trucks. In the 1990s passenger services became more important for railway services and revenues as Tanzania's rural economy was growing, while at the same time the price of Zambia's copper (and therefore shipment of goods from Zambia to Dar es Salaam) was going down: "Between 1995 and 1998, the local traffic was very important to the survival of TAZARA," according to Kaduma.[21] By the late 1990s, as the railway corridor became an important destina-

FIGURE 5.4. Traders and passengers on the railway platform. Photograph by the author.

tion for those from urban areas and from the surrounding highlands where rural economic conditions had faltered, TAZARA officials labeled the heavily resettled section between Mbeya and Kidatu the "passenger belt."

It was in this "passenger belt" that the Ordinary Train became an important resource for rural lives and livelihoods. It was also here that traders, farmers, fisher-

FIGURE 5.5. Sacks of rice waiting on the TAZARA station platform to be shipped as parcels from Mlimba in 1998. Photograph by the author.

men, timber cutters, and other users of the Ordinary Train shaped the railway in turn—as they crowded rural station platforms with parcel shipments, and as vendors of all stripes hawked their wares to passing trains. In response to this crush of passengers and parcels the TAZARA authorities inaugurated a shuttle train service in the mid-1990s, dubbed the *kipisi*, or "little piece." This was a shorter version of the Ordinary Train, plying the route between Makambako and Kidatu twice a week pulling two luggage wagons. The purpose of the *kipisi* was to expand services for the passengers and parcels that had been overloading the Ordinary Train, creating pressures that had affected the train's scheduling as well as security within the crowded passenger wagons. Unfortunately, after its initial success the *kipisi* did not always operate regularly—in fact, it was shut down for several months in 2000 and 2001—but the public outcry that followed disruption of the *kipisi* services (including intervention in parliament by the late Kilombero MP Abbas Gulamali) was moving testimony to its significance for local communities.

Trading with Parcels

When trader Rashid Rajabu was ready to take a shipment of cooking bananas from Mbingu to Dar es Salaam in the late 1990s, he first carried the heavy clusters of green fruits to the TAZARA station, where he stacked them onto the train platform. When he could afford it, Rashid hired a few of the freelance porters who were waiting for work around the station to help him carry his loads. He then had to register his bananas as "parcels," or small-scale goods shipments. He did this work during the day, often waiting long hours for his turn in line while the parcel clerk registered the accumulated bundles of goods on the platform awaiting transport. Rashid would then remain at the station until late at night, and frequently into the early hours of the morning, until the Ordinary Train finally passed through Mbingu on its way to the coast. Once his bananas were safely loaded into the luggage wagon, the parcel receipt was Rashid's only record of his transported property. Whether he traveled together with his bananas or sent them on a separate train, he could only claim them in Dar es Salaam by producing his parcel receipt.

Some years later, when he had shifted from the banana trade to trading vegetables from Makambako to Mbingu, Rashid followed the same procedure. "I pay for my luggage by the kilo," he explained. "When you leave Makambako, you pay 24 shillings per kilo for Mbingu . . . and you must also pay for your own [passenger] ticket." Once his goods shipments had been registered and paid for, Rashid alerted his customers at Mbingu so that they could go to the station and help unload the goods. "A person knows that they should go and collect their luggage on a Tuesday or a Friday [the days the train passed through Mbingu]," he said. "They remember on those days to go and collect their luggage." Occasionally a load was misdelivered, however, and this was practically impossible to remedy according to Rashid. When his luggage was lost or was dropped off at the wrong station, he would take his parcel receipt to try to locate it, but in most cases this was unsuccessful. "When they lose your luggage," he explained, "you have paid a lot of money and you don't get any reimbursement. This is the bad thing about this TAZARA railway."[22]

Official copies of the parcel receipts were retained at the stations of departure, which was part of the reason that customers had difficulties resolving problems at the delivery end. For the railway historian, on the other hand, these carbon copies of parcel shipment receipts are an invaluable form of primary evidence, illustrating the complexity and diversity of small-scale economic activity in the TAZARA corridor. The receipt books have not been kept in any formal or orderly fashion, but are stacked loosely on bookshelves or in cupboards in the offices of rural TAZARA stationmasters. They are stored for two or three years before being sent on to TAZARA headquarters in Dar es Salaam. While the books are not complete for each station, each individual receipt tells its own story about who traveled where, and on what day of the week, as well as the quantity of goods they carried with them. When these individual stories are aggregated, they illuminate larger patterns of small-scale and informal economic activity that would otherwise be difficult to quantify. The receipts are particularly helpful for understanding economic activity at the smaller stations and "halt" stops that are not represented in assessments of larger wagonload rail shipments. In fact, the receipts show that the majority of travelers carrying parcels were not going to Dar es Salaam but to a wide range of smaller stations in the TAZARA "passenger belt."

By documenting the ways that ordinary people moved their goods from one rural station to another, the parcel receipts make visible the details of exchange patterns and social networks. This project originally included receipts collected from five stations within the Kilombero valley section of TAZARA's "passenger belt" stations that were served by the Ordinary Train and by the "little piece" (*kipisi*) shuttle train: Mlimba, Chita, Mngeta, Ifakara, and Mang'ula. These five stations were selected because they represented diverse productive zones and settled communities. Each station also corresponded to a settlement that had been part of *ujamaa* villagization and had experienced economic and demographic change since TAZARA's construction. When it became clear that Makambako had played an important role in regional trade and in transshipment from road to rail networks, this station was added during the second phase of the study. The second phase also included samples of data from smaller stations and halt stops, as well as goods shipments from Makambako, for comparison.

These data have potential shortcomings, in particular biases in reporting. There are many anecdotal accounts of fraudulent activity on the part of TAZARA's parcel clerks as well as the passengers that engage in parcel shipments. Clerks have been accused of keeping incomplete records in order to disguise graft, while passengers are widely rumored to carry goods illicitly in passenger compartments. Women traders in particular have been observed carrying large parcels in first and second class passenger compartments, thereby avoiding legal payment of fees for parcels shipments. It was not possible to investigate these allegations during this project, but given their scope it is very likely that the receipt books underreport the actual volume of goods traded on the Ordinary Train. It is also likely that there is a gender component to this underreporting. Even with these shortcomings, however, the receipts depict overall patterns in consistent and useful ways.

Each parcel receipt includes the name of the traveler, the station from which their journey originated, the passenger's destination, and the quantity of goods shipped.[23] In the records for August 30, 2000, for example, the receipts show that quite a few traders were taking bananas from Mbingu to Kidatu and Mang'ula on the *kipisi* "little piece" shuttle train. Individual traders Salum Yusufu, Rashid Golo, Simon Magugu, Anzibeti, and Mohamed K. each boarded with bags of bananas weighing from 47 kilograms (for Simon) to 83 kilograms (for Rashid). On the same day traders Lucas and Athanas each took loads of paddy (unhulled rice) to Makambako, while a Mr. Moshi carried a basket of dried fish to Kiberege.

From Makambako, meanwhile, traders were carrying very different kinds of goods eastwards to the lowland stations. On the books for May 7, 2000, was a shipment of eleven bags of beans and one basket of tomatoes, carried to Ifakara by Joseph and weighing in at 1,414 kilograms. On the same day Mr. Mdemu transported eight sacks of peas, fruits, potatoes, and millet weighing a total of 840 kilos to Ifakara, while Miriam and Grace traveled to Mbingu with sacks of millet, potatoes, beans, and cabbages weighing 393 kilograms. Some of the receipts are enigmatic; for example, Mr. Muro was on the same train to Mbingu as Miriam and Grace, with ten sacks of "soft goods" and "so many indefinite things" weighing 300 kilograms. He was most likely a trader in consumer goods, taking wholesale products to smaller towns where he would sell them again at retail. Among the items shipped from Ifakara to highland stations during the week of June 17 that year were a large number of empty produce baskets, sacks of rice, a hen, two bags of fertilizer, one lemon, and a piece of iron sheeting.

Not all of the items shipped were intended for trade. Many travelers were carrying household goods and personal belongings, while others carried assets that would help to generate income at their destination—a sewing machine, a bicycle, or a water pump. The train was used to carry the sick from smaller villages to the hospital at Ifakara; it also transported bodies from the morgue back to rural villages for burial. The shipment of a corpse was recorded as a parcel and accompanied by a receipt.

When these parcels data are aggregated, they illustrate the patterns of trade and product specialization that have developed at individual stations and along the railway line as a whole. The receipts from Makambako document shipments of highland vegetables, maize, and consumer goods that are taken by traders to stations in the eastern lowlands. The importance of these shipments for Ifakara's consumers is made obvious when there are delays in the railway schedule: there are shortages of tomatoes, cabbages, Irish potatoes, onions, and beans in Ifakara when TAZARA stops running. The effects of shortages are felt from the stalls of the town's open market to the restaurants that sell cooked meals, for French-fried potatoes (chips) and tomato sauces disappear temporarily from menus. The trade from Ifakara back to Makambako consists mostly of rice and empty vegetable baskets (*matenga* in Kiswahili); these are taken back up to the highlands, where they are filled once again with new loads of onions, potatoes, cabbages, and tomatoes (see tables of selected parcel shipments in appendix 2).

Consumer goods or soft goods—a loose category that refers to a wide range of items including household utensils, beauty products, laundry soaps, packaged tea, and salt—are also shipped in large quantities from Makambako eastwards. These items are shipped not to the large towns like Ifakara, but to smaller stations where there is limited road access and there are thus fewer options for consumers to purchase goods from shopkeepers. Consumer goods are shipped from the larger stations located at the intersection of road and rail—Makambako, Ifakara, and Mang'ula—where wholesale goods are delivered by truckload. From there traders take them by train to smaller, more isolated stations like Mlimba and Mngeta, and to halt stops like Ikule. Trading in consumer goods at Mlimba is a lucrative enterprise, according to trader Selemani Mwelela, especially when the railway schedule is uneven. When there are shortages of goods due to train delays, those who have been able to stock up a surplus benefit from the higher prices that result.[24]

Rice is shipped eastwards from Ifakara and Mang'ula to the coast at Dar es Salaam, the largest market for inland grain. Paddy, on the other hand, is frequently shipped from the smaller stations where there are inadequate grain mills to Ifakara, where it can be milled and then sent onwards to grain markets in the city. Maize moves from the highlands (including the foothills around Mlimba and Mngeta) to the lowlands, where it is purchased for consumption and also for beer brewing. The smaller settlements between the highlands and the floodplain have their own product specializations. Mlimba sends out rice from the valleys and maize from the hills, together with the basketfuls of sweet oranges brought by bicycle from Masagati. Farther down the railway line to the east, Mngeta also ships a combination of upland and lowland staples: maize and bananas from the uplands; rice and dried fish from the valley.

At some of the stations traders specialize in particular products that are not found elsewhere. While these goods are not shipped on the same scale as staples such as rice and maize, they can play an important role in the livelihood strategies of specific producers and traders. A highly specialized product that is exported in some quantity from Mngeta is *ukindu*. *Ukindu* is the Swahili name for the leaves of the plant *Phoenix reclinata*, a small palm-like tree that grows wild in the floodplain (see Figure 5.3). According to local *ukindu* harvesters, this plant only grows in specialized habitats and cannot be domesticated. Therefore, its supply is limited and it has a high value. The leaves of the *ukindu* plant are dyed and woven by local women into traditional plaited mats or *mikeka* (Kiswahili, *mkeka*, singular). These mats are a specialty of women weavers in the Kilombero valley, and there is therefore a good market for *ukindu* in the marketplace at Ifakara and at other centers.[25] One of the most important source areas for wild *ukindu* is located some distance away from Mngeta station toward the river. Here at Mgudeni, a temporary camp for *ukindu* harvesting and other informal economic activities has grown in recent years into a semi-permanent settlement. Products like *ukindu* are an important part of informal economic strategies that link harvesters, traders, and artisans. The finished *mikeka* mats are sold in local markets and as far away as Dar es Salaam.

The parcel receipts that are kept at TAZARA stations are a useful resource for quantifying the transportation of small shipments of goods along the TAZARA railway, especially goods that were shipped on the Ordinary Train and on the *kipisi* shuttle train. Individual receipts tell important stories about what items were being transported, who was carrying them, and where they were going. Taken together, the receipts illustrate larger patterns of movement of goods and people, revealing the multi-spatiality of production and exchange in the "passenger belt" of the TAZARA corridor.

Life and Livelihood along the Railway

"I was one of the first to begin small-scale trading in this area," remembers Balista Kidehela, who finished primary school in Mbingu in 1985 (at the age of sixteen) and then began to trade in retail goods. He left the village to seek a better life in Dar es Salaam. "Because I was a young man, I decided to move to the city and lived far away from here for a time," Balista remembers. He tried to support himself as a trader in Dar es Salaam for three years, but found this to be a difficult challenge for a young man with few resources. So in 1988 he decided to return to Mbingu village once again to take up retail trading. He stayed with his uncle while he built up his own business, trading along TAZARA. "I was doing that trading until 1999," he recalls, "using the Freedom Railway to purchase goods at Makambako and Dar es Salaam. We went to Mzenga to get coconuts and bring them back here." He traded together with his wife, who took bananas from Mbingu to Dar es Salaam for sale. In the city she would purchase wholesale consumer goods and bring them back to Mbingu, where Balista sold them for marked up retail prices in a small shop.

Balista now has a small farm where he grows crops and keeps some livestock, and he has just launched a new enterprise: photography. "In this way," he explained, "when I combine all of these things together: farming, livestock raising, photography, and small-scale trading, I have the certainty of knowing that one way or another, tomorrow when I wake up I will be well (*mzima*)." Balista uses the Ordinary Train to transport the goods that he sells in his shop, to purchase feed for his cattle, and also to take his film to a photography studio for developing. "With the Freedom Railway you board here in Mbingu," he says, and "you travel directly (*moja kwa moja*) until you disembark at Makambako." When he wants to purchase molasses to feed his cows, he takes the shuttle train to Mkamba, where the sugar company is located. While he is there he also makes a visit to the photography studio. In Balista's view, Mbingu has changed a great deal since he first arrived there as a primary school student. "When I first came to Mbingu in 1978," he remembers, "there were very few people here. Now so many people are coming here to obtain foodstuffs. There are people coming here to get charcoal [and other items]. There are very many people coming here."[26] Some of these people are coming to Mbingu for short-term trade, while others are staying longer and becoming residents.

Rehema Mwabutwa is a small-scale trader who moved to Mlimba in the 1990s, following the death of her husband and the loss of her husband's inheritance to another wife. "I came to Mlimba to clear my mind of the suffering I had experienced," she says. She learned from other women in the market how to begin retail trading in dried beans, a product they obtained on consignment from larger wholesale traders. While she herself does not travel on the railway to obtain beans from Makambako, she is dependent upon the other traders who do so. "It is difficult to trade on consignment because I depend on them to bring the beans [from Makambako]. If they don't [bring the beans], I just stay home with my children with hunger," she explains. "TAZARA is very important, without it we would not have any business. We suffer when the train is not running, because we do not have any goods to sell."[27] While Rehema herself stayed in Mlimba and did not travel on the railway, her form of retail trade in the town marketplace required the mobility of others, and therefore reliable train services.

Among those who utilize TAZARA for their livelihoods are the *mama nitilie* (roughly translated as "mother serve me"), who are women (and sometimes men) who sell cooked food and snacks at the railway stations. One entrepreneur, Mwamini Salehe, tried a number of different enterprises in the TAZARA corridor before deciding to prepare hot meals for sale to passengers at Mlimba station in 2002. She had moved originally to Makambako as a young woman to sell used clothing, or *mitumba*, taking goods on consignment and walking around the town in search of customers. It was the promise of marriage that initially brought Mwamini to Mlimba in 1999, where she began farming and beer brewing while living with the family of her fiancé. She assisted her future husband with his trading enterprises: he would take the train to Makambako to purchase beans and other goods, which she would then sell in their small retail shop at Mlimba. After her marriage fell through, Mwamini decided to stay in Mlimba and take up food preparation, cooking meals for the passengers on the trains and for those waiting at the station. "I started out at first making soup, and then changed to cooking rice, bananas with fish, and millet porridge," she recalls.[28]

The income Mwamini makes from her profits is enough to help her to pay taxes, to have enough to eat, to purchase clothes, and to buy an occasional soda. "This work gets me what I need," she says, so long as she follows a budget. She hopes eventually to save up enough capital to move to Ifakara and expand her business. Unlike the traders in agricultural products who use TAZARA, Mwamini normally makes her biggest profits when TAZARA fails to keep to its schedule. When the train is stranded at the station for several hours, she explains, she benefits from the increased sales she is able to make to hungry waiting passengers.

The Ordinary Train has played a central role in the rural livelihood strategies of these traders, farmers, and entrepreneurs. The train connects rural communities with one another, and with more distant urban markets. TAZARA also connects them to services (such as Balista's photography studio), to social networks, and to other resources. Individuals and groups have used these connections as they develop strategies for rural survival and wealth accumulation. Most have used TAZARA to combine more than one economic strategy, whether at the same time or in succession. Many have collaborated in their economic activities with their spouses, extended family members, or other trading partners who linked them to more distant locations. As one man explained, describing the trading business he shared with a brother in another town, "business is going along well because we are two people in two different places."[29]

A key to success in the railway corridor, according to trader Eddy Nyaruke, was the ability to convert quickly from one enterprise to another in response to the rapid and unpredictable changes that regularly occurred in the rural economy. This reality placed consignment traders like Rehema at a disadvantage, because they had to sell all the stock they had taken before they could shift to another product, even if the prices were dropping. Products with slower turnovers were therefore less desirable in Eddy's view than those like the cooked foods prepared by Mwamini, which were sold out in a day. "Selling prepared food [along TAZARA] is the most lucrative activity because you make your investment and you sell your product on the same day . . . you can change according to changes in the market."[30] This view was confirmed by Mwajuma Malangu, a young woman who sold flat breads (chapati) at Mbingu railway station and reported that "cooking pays much more than farming."[31]

Eddy's observations emphasize the importance to rural actors of making timely conversions from one resource or occupation to another, in response to the "imperfections, discontinuities and fluctuations" that are characteristic of the rural economy.[32] For survival as well as accumulation, as Pekka Seppälä has observed in Lindi District, people in rural Tanzania need to be able to move laterally (from one product to another), sectorally (from one occupation to another), and geographically in order to make timely conversions. Diversification of this kind—what Seppälä terms "serial diversification"—can be a successful strategy for rural livelihoods. The railway facilitated such diversification by linking diverse physical locations as

well as economic sectors. TAZARA also provided a periodic communication network through which rural people could exchange information.

In life history interviews, respondents revealed that they possess detailed memories of these livelihood strategies, especially the shifts they have made over time
from one livelihood sector to another. They remembered and retold stories of the
circumstances that led them to start up and to diversify their enterprises, the social
networks and relationships they relied upon for assistance, and even the specific
amounts of money that they had invested. One trader in particular, Brown Mwasongwe, narrated very clear details of the history of his changing livelihoods. Although
my interview with Brown took place some seventeen years after his first business
transaction, he recalled this incident along with the many exchanges which followed in precise detail. His life history narrative was in large part a chronology of
these business events, recounting a succession of livelihood transitions. Brown and
other respondents used the term *maisha* in Kiswahili to refer simultaneously to life
and to livelihood; many stated that they had moved to the TAZARA corridor "in
search of life" (*kutafuta maisha*), a phrase that embodied both meanings.

Brown Mwasongwe began providing for himself at the age of eighteen, when he
went to work in a cement factory in Mbeya not far from his home town. He found
cement work to be grueling and unhealthy, and stopped working there after a short
time. He then worked as a security guard for three months before deciding to become a trader. Brown's sister, meanwhile, had moved to Ifakara with her husband,
who worked for the police force. When Brown's mother paid a visit to the sister,
they decided to begin a joint family trading business. Brown's mother brought 250
shillings in start-up capital back to Mbeya to give to Brown, so that he could begin
trading Irish potatoes. This was not a gift, he emphasized in an interview, but an
ushirika, a cooperative venture. After some time, his sister left Ifakara with her
husband and asked Brown to return her share of the business that they had started
together. With his own share he has been able to continue trading on his own.

After receiving the initial capital of 250 shillings from his sister, Brown bought
Irish potatoes in Mbeya and brought them to Ifakara by train. When he had sold
all of the potatoes, he returned to Mbeya to buy more. Soon he branched out from
potatoes to cabbages, trading both cabbages and potatoes until he saved enough to
buy *ulezi* (millet). When he sold the millet he had accumulated 600 shillings, and
decided to join together with some other traders from Mbeya to buy beans. Brown
now buys a number of goods from Mbeya, including millet, maize, beans, and
potatoes, depending upon their prices. He transports his goods by train to Ifakara,
where he sells them wholesale to traders who will sell them again at retail in the
local market. By 1993 Brown was able to purchase a rice farm and to add farming to
his economic activities. He rents a house in Ifakara, and plans to buy a house plot

in the future and build a home for his family. Brown says that he is doing very well with his business in Ifakara, much better than he could have done if he had stayed in Mbeya. Before coming to Ifakara, he says, "I didn't know what there was to do in life (*maisha*); after coming here I saw a lot of things, and learned a new way."[33]

Brown Mwasongwe's life story is similar to that of other young men and women who trade in the TAZARA corridor, in the way that he narrates an account of a difficult youth followed by a trajectory of betterment. These stories resonate with the theme of using cleverness and perseverance against challenging odds, thus conquering adversity through hard work. They also describe the gradual accumulation of wealth in the form of an *mtaji*, or purchasing capital; Brown's goal was to accumulate surplus through the marketing of one crop in order to eventually shift to a more lucrative one (and ultimately to take up farming). These life stories emphasize and acknowledge the support of relatives and other partners in economic pursuits. For many young people who pursued informal trading on the TAZARA railway, stories of *maisha*—of life and livelihood—are accounts of personal self-improvement. They describe feeling that trading allowed them to become positive and productive members of society.

Anua Mtengela is a mobile trader, or *machinga*, who uses TAZARA to trade between Mang'ula and Mngeta. He specializes in selling kitchen utensils, plates, and cups from his bicycle to residents of rural villages. Anua was born in 1982 in Ihimbo village, Iringa. He went to primary school for eight years, after which he worked as a wage laborer. He was first employed as a housekeeper in Dar es Salaam, then went south to Lindi, where he worked carrying water to timber cutters in the forest. There he rode his bicycle as many as fifty kilometers per day, carrying drinking water from a well to the timber-cutting site. He left that work after a short time and moved into trading. Anua began his bicycle trading business in the TAZARA corridor in the small village of Ikule, near Mngeta. There is a TAZARA halt station at Ikule, and he normally traveled from Ikule to Mang'ula or Makambako to obtain his stock of consumer goods. After trading in Ikule for some time, Anua found that it was a good place to stay and try his hand at farming, so he asked the village leaders for a plot of land there. By 2001 he had planted two acres of maize, and had built himself a small house (*kibanda*) at Ikule village. He now combines maize farming with his business as a small-scale trader.

Anua normally sells his wares either by bicycle or on foot. He travels from his base at Ikule up the road to the National Army Camp (JKT) and onwards as far as Chita, looking for customers. On other days he goes in the opposite direction to Mngeta, where there is an active market on Sundays. "The good place to sell [on Sundays] right now is at Mngeta," he said in July 2000. "At Mngeta there is a place near the market where many people bring their goods and spread them out along the ground, selling to people coming out from church, coming to town." On Mondays he and his fellow traders go back to walking around the neighborhoods (*mitaani*), trying to sell their goods. Anua says that the *wamachinga* can offer their products at cheaper prices than those found in shops, and this helps them to get many customers.

Anua would like to diversify his livelihood strategy in the near future, to move from consumer goods into trading maize. He says there is a good market for maize at Mang'ula, Mngeta, and Ikule, where many people purchase maize for brewing into beer. He intends to purchase maize at Makambako and to take it by train to those stations where the prices are good. He plans to use the *kipisi* shuttle train, because it has two luggage wagons and is most reliable for shipping parcels. The Ordinary Train has only one luggage van and this makes it more difficult to receive shipments on time. Once he has traded maize for a few weeks, Anua will go back to trading consumer goods. He normally follows such market trends in small-scale trade, he says. He obtains information about markets and prices from his fellow traders, especially those with whom he occasionally cooperates, and whom he trusts. They help one another by exchanging information and ideas about their businesses.

Anua's long-term goal is to earn enough money from trading to build a better house, and then to hire an assistant who can stay at his house and protect his home and farm while he is traveling and trading. It is expensive to hire such a worker, he says, and he is already using many resources to pay for the train fares to travel back and forth between the stations where he conducts business. He says there is also competition from other traders, as more and more young men and women come into the valley to take up trading and farming. "We are used to it [doing this work]," he says, "and there isn't any other work. You can find people who have finished Form Four, Form Six, and they can't find any work.[34] These are the youths who can end up becoming thieves, gangsters, and *bhangi* (marijuana) smokers." Some young people like himself are trying to survive through trade, and others are coming into the Kilombero valley to grow maize and rice.[35]

Anua's life story shows that small-scale trade has been an important livelihood strategy for him, and that TAZARA has assisted traders like the *machinga* to reach formerly inaccessible markets that continue to be cut off from road traffic. In these isolated villages they are able to sell goods more cheaply than in shops, and thus they generate some income while also improving local access to consumer goods.

Life stories like those of Brown Mwasongwe and Anua Mtengela resonate with hopefulness and possibility. Mwamini Salehe also spoke about her dream of moving to Ifakara and expanding her business. Yet the progressive themes of these narratives belie the harsh reality of economic life in the TAZARA corridor: for

many economic actors, the path of development was not one of continuous progress and uplift, but one of cycles of prosperity followed by cycles of despair. It was
during the downturns in their economic circumstances that livelihood conversions
were most significant for those living closest to the margins of survival. For even
without much in the way of material resources, a person like Rehema could move
to Mlimba, begin taking beans on consignment, and start to accumulate a small
amount of profit.

The Importance of *Mtaji*

Life history interviews emphasize that one of the most important resources in the
TAZARA corridor was accumulated capital for investment. It was also clear from
the interviews that there were sharp differences between those who had secure
capital resources (for example, retirees with access to government pensions) and
those who did not. Those with resources were much more likely to be able to use
livelihood conversion to build and expand their wealth—moving into an additional
activity or expanding the scale of an existing one. According to a retired civil ser-
vant at Mbingu, Michael Mweji, those like himself who have resources "have goals,
and farm with a purpose, knowing what they wish to achieve." Mweji compared
himself, a retired worker with savings and a pension, with those he called "everyday
farmers" who had no capital. "The everyday farmer only farms to get *posho* (daily
rations); to get enough to eat for himself and his family. But for the [retired] worker,
even if he doesn't succeed he thinks it through that he is farming so that he can
build a house, or so he can educate his children, or he wants to construct something
or to do something. He is undertaking one thing so that he can achieve a second
thing that he has envisioned."[36] In Mweji's view, capital was important not only for
material investment but also because it enabled one to think differently about the
future: it allowed a person to plan ahead, to have a vision and to carry it through.

Those with the fewest resources were most likely to use livelihood conversion
to maintain their subsistence, often uprooting self and family to take advantage of
a rumored shift in market prices or a newly discovered source of income. Many
life history accounts from the railway corridor describe a cyclical pattern of crisis
and recovery. In these stories TAZARA and the possibility it offered for livelihood
conversion are most significant in the way they allowed an individual facing a crisis
or downturn to recover and start over once again. At the same time, they remind
us that mobility for many was not a strategy for accumulation but a necessity for
survival. Lazaro Mbilinyi, a farmer originally from a village in Iringa, told a story
that followed this pattern.

Lazaro's first source of income after finishing his education was as an hourly worker. He took a job as a tobacco harvester for a Greek farmer in Iringa, but soon realized that he desired "more from life" and decided to learn a skilled trade.[37] Lazaro chose to train as a carpenter, and took up that occupation for a short time. When his employer failed to pay him for his work, he left carpentry and became a self-employed tailor. Tailoring was a good enterprise for him, he remembers, and he was able to build himself a shop and to take care of his wife and small child. His prosperity did not last long, however. While he was out of town one day, thieves broke into his shop and took everything he owned, including his sewing machine and his entire stock of fabric and clothing. He was left with only the empty shop.

Without any capital, Lazaro had few options. Like many others in the same position, he decided to move to Ifakara to become an informal trader. He had a friend who was a teacher near Ifakara, and this friend helped him to get a start in trading fish. After trading fish for two years, Lazaro began to trade in maize. Three years later he had earned enough from maize to begin trading in charcoal. He traded charcoal for two years, and was then able to open a small shop in Ifakara. He now owns and operates the shop, but has not been able to develop his business further because of pressures from extended family members.

Once Lazaro became moderately successful in his trading business, his family members began to look to him for assistance when their own life circumstances became difficult. Lazaro has been caring for the five children of a sister who recently disappeared, along with children of other relatives who have been sent to stay with him. To support this growing family of dependents, Lazaro began growing rice on a nearby farm. He has been redirecting the profits from his trading business into farming, and hopes to save enough to hire a tractor to farm a new plot of land he has just acquired outside of town. Farming makes sense for him economically now that he has so many dependents, he says. He can use their labor in the fields, and his harvest provides enough food for the large family.

Lazaro's story describes how he was able to use his own social network (the teacher friend who had knowledge of the fish trade) together with the established trading networks along the TAZARA railway to get a new start in life after a devastating downturn. Once he was established in his trading business, he became an important resource in turn for other friends and family members who needed assistance. This story thus has two important themes: the opportunity to start over in informal trade along the railway; and the cycles of alternating success and adversity that can occur in individual lives as well as extended families. Life stories like this one from the TAZARA corridor make it clear that prosperity and poverty were not permanent conditions in rural Tanzania, but rather fortune could reverse itself dramatically and without warning. In such situations the railway facilitated connections between families and friends while serving as a resource for rural economic networks, both critical for rural livelihoods.[38]

A recurring thread throughout the life history narratives from the TAZARA railway corridor was the importance of having an economic foundation for investment—an *msingi* or an *mtaji* in Kiswahili. Acquiring an *mtaji* was the goal of those who sought to get started in an enterprise, to expand an existing project, or to move from one form of livelihood to another. Socioeconomic mobility—and with it to a large extent geographical mobility—was dependent upon an *mtaji*. The larger one's *mtaji*, the more resilience one would have in times of economic turbulence. And a strong *mtaji* was the key to being able to invest quickly in response to changing opportunities. As retired officer Michael Mweji told us, "If the people here had a good *mtaji*, this [Mbingu] would be the number one village here in Kilombero District."[39] He emphasized that while Mbingu had abundant natural resources (fertile well-watered soils, transportation connections, fisheries, and forests), these could not be mobilized without capital.

Many people described their personal economic success in terms of their acquisition of an *mtaji*. Often, however, stories about the importance of *mtaji* were stories of hardship and constraint—about the struggle to get ahead and the devastation of loss, about inequities in the distribution of wealth, and about the failure of the state to provide resources to rural areas. References to *mtaji* were part of the stories people told about the enormous hurdles faced by the rural poor. An *mtaji* was most often material—a reference to wealth in the form of money, land, livestock, or other assets. The term was also used to refer to hard work and perseverance, and was thus a reference to a form of moral capital that was revealed through one's personal character.

As they had been during TAZARA's construction period, notions of hard work and self-sufficiency were invoked by rural people in ways that resonated with the exhortations of Tanzania's first president, Julius Nyerere: hard work was "the poor man's capital."[40] One older man stated that "*mtaji wa maskini ni nguvu zake*," or "the capital of the poor man is his own strength." "Even if you have nothing," explained Yohana Paul Nyakunga, "just take up a hoe and you will farm and you will gain wealth that will help you."[41] The importance of hard work was the moral of the story Mzee Nyakunga told about his own life. He had misspent his youth pursuing wealth through mining, he said—initially at the gold fields of Chunya, and later in search of elusive profits through gemstone mining throughout the southern highlands. It was only when he settled down and began a life of farming that Mzee Nyakunga found prosperity: "After I finished all the work of the gemstones," he said, "I didn't have anything. I then used my strength to farm and by continuing with farming I don't have any problems."[42]

For most rural Tanzanians struggling to maintain a livelihood in the railway corridor, discussions about *mtaji* were a way of speaking about hardship and constraint, about the way that access to opportunity was differentially structured and therefore elusive for many. As Rehema Mwabutwa put it, "The conditions in Mlimba are good if you have *mtaji*, but they are not good if you don't." When she first came to Mlimba she was almost destitute, having sold all of her belongings (including most of her clothes) to survive following her husband's death. She and her children had no place to stay for the first three months, and slept at night on mats on the floor of the TAZARA station. "If I did have some money," said Rehema, "I would buy rice from the people in the villages. Right now there are many bags of rice. You can go into the villages with used clothing [i.e., for barter]; this is what pays now." But without savings for such a prospect, Rehema continues to sell beans on consignment in the retail market, the form of trade that Eddy Nyaruke described as the most vulnerable to economic fluctuation.[43]

There were definite disparities in wealth in the railway corridor, and these were discussed in life history interviews. Those living along the railway with the most security were the retired workers, such as Michael Mweji, who were supported by various combinations of pensions, savings, and other assets. Many railway workers, military officers from the JKT facility near Chita, teachers, and other civil servants acquired land and settled along TAZARA, often having accumulated their land and other assets during their working years. These wealthier farmers employed casual laborers to work on their farms. "If I didn't have these casual laborers [*vibarua*]," to work my fields, says Michael Mweji, "I would have nothing, nobody here would be able to farm four or five acres" without additional help.[44]

The poorest residents of the TAZARA corridor regularly supplemented their other economic activities by working for their wealthier neighbors. In Mikoleko village, 80 percent of farmers worked as casual laborers on the plots of neighboring landholders in order to sustain their households.[45] In villages of the most severe landlessness along the Selous Reserve boundary, residents migrated seasonally using the railway to other parts of the valley to find available land or to work as casual farm labor. They traveled the length of the valley from Mang'ula to Mlimba, returning to their homes after the harvest.

These examples show the ways that TAZARA contributed to survival and accumulation, not only for those who traveled on the railway but also for those whose livelihood pursuits depended upon the mobility of others. Thus retail traders in the marketplace required the reliable transportation of wholesale goods in order to flourish. Farmers and laborers alike depended upon the mobility of casual workers from homes to farms. Even the outgrower system of the Kilombero Sugar Company depended upon the reliability of transport for the outgrower farmers and their dependents to travel from sugar farms to the outlying fields where they planted their food crops.

The term *mtaji* was deployed in life history interviews to convey many diverse meanings. *Mtaji* was described as a vehicle for material advancement as well as a precondition for being able to envision a future of progress. It was used in accounts of livelihood transitions both to describe events and also to discuss morality. It was widely used discursively in critiques of the difficulties faced by the rural poor as they struggled to "get more out of life."

People also used references to *mtaji* to critique the absence of state support for rural economic development along the railway. They expressed frustration that the government does not assist small-scale traders and farmers with investment resources. They made both implicit and explicit comparisons between the role of the state during the time of *ujamaa* villages and its function in the post-liberalization era. The absence of government support for small farmers and entrepreneurs, they said, causes the poorest farmers to be made more vulnerable and the wealthy to have even greater advantages. The support farmers need most, in their view, is that of agricultural inputs or *pembejeo*, especially tractors and other technologies. The state was also criticized for not making credit available to small farmers and to small-scale traders. Rather than helping to support rural enterprise in the TAZARA corridor, said interviewees, the government seemed to be aiming to suppress entrepreneurship through charging high taxes and raising train fares. "You can say that you will do trading on TAZARA," explained Michael Mweji, "but you will reach a point where you are stuck, and you cannot succeed with your goal. The fares are too high and . . . you pay *ushuru* tax to the council; you pay to the village; you pay to TAZARA; you pay to the porters; you pay to the person doing the [wholesale] trading; you pay to the person who takes the money and to the person who owns the goods. That is five people, this makes you just stop doing trading."[46]

Government exactions are a special burden for young entrepreneurs, according to Selemani Mwelela, causing them to abandon their paths of self-betterment and to turn to illicit and immoral activities. "First of all," he explained, "many young people exert themselves to obtain an *mtaji*; they struggle with farming and are able to gain a profit of perhaps fifty thousand shillings. Now, that [young person] might wish to set up some form of small business, to keep himself [productively] occupied. But when he starts out with this *mtaji*, of fifty thousand, he finds that the place where he wants to set up his business will charge him rent. And at the same time, the government wants him to pay for a license and the license may cost him forty thousand shillings. Therefore, young people become fed up and stop doing business sometimes, because they fear the costs of licenses and of taxes." What Selemani Mwelela would like the government to do, instead of charging for licenses and council taxes, is to provide young people in rural areas with small business loans—resources that are made available to those in towns and those who are wealthy, but which in his view need to be provided to young people living in villages.[47]

Thus *mtaji* is a term that takes on an array of meanings in local communities in the TAZARA corridor. It refers to the material wealth needed to expand an enterprise or to move from one form of livelihood to another. It also has a moral meaning, referring to the perseverance needed by the rural poor in order to survive in an uncertain rural economy. It is used to discuss and critique differential access to wealth and the uneven opportunities for rural development that exist in the railway corridor. The government is an object of this critique, because it has failed to provide support for youth and others who seek to get a start in economic activity.

The concept of *mtaji* is one of many that rural people employed in life history interviews as they discussed their lived experience of rural development in the TAZARA railway corridor. Their personal narratives explained the ways that they fashioned social networks, retail and wholesale trading opportunities, and farming and other livelihood options as they used the Ordinary Train. The stories that people told about their own lives and livelihoods—*maisha*—situated them within larger economic, social, and political contexts. The stories they told were at times heroic narratives of progress in overcoming hardship, and at other times filled with despair and devastation. As they recounted their life histories people frequently critiqued the structures around them, whether the social differentiation that constrained opportunity at the local level, or the indifference of a government that exacted multiple forms of taxation without reciprocating through support programs.

Conclusion

The traveling traders, farmers, and laborers who used the Ordinary Train were part of a larger context of economic development in the TAZARA corridor that radiated outwards into the surrounding regions. The stories of their livelihood strategies, together with the carbon-copy records of their transactions that they left behind in the TAZARA stations, are compelling evidence of their participation in shaping the outcome of the railway project. These were not passive recipients of transportation infrastructure and technology, but shaped the railway itself as they shaped their own lives. As they depended upon TAZARA to provide them with reliable transportation services, the railway in turn required the initiative and agency of the railway's users. This was as true at the end of construction in the 1970s when rural villagers were relocated into *ujamaa* villages as it was in the 1990s when TAZARA authorities responded to the commercial potential of the "passenger belt."

Yet the passenger services of TAZARA could hardly be called dependable over the three decades since the railway's completion. Living along TAZARA has meant living with the railway's ups and downs, including repeated schedule interruptions due to internal management problems and failures to keep up with the maintenance demands of the permanent way and the rolling stock. The railway's services have also fluctuated with the shifting ways the railway authorities have defined their customers and markets over time. The rural communities that depend upon the railway have been buffeted by shifts in railway policies, shifts that were themselves frequently a response to the larger transformations taking place in the political economy of the southern African region from the mid-1970s through the 1990s. Railway users have also been affected by changes in the mechanisms the state has used to intervene in rural economic life, as policies shifted from villagization and nationalized agricultural programs to liberalization and structural adjustment. The strategies pursued by the railway's users—together with their local knowledge and experience, including their deployment of social networks and local understandings of capital formation—have all been part of the story of how development worked in this context of uncertainty. The railway has been a key resource for rural populations as they have endeavored to survive and accumulate wealth in uncertain times and places. Yet the railway, like the other resources they have depended upon, has itself often been unreliable.

CHAPTER

6

Landscape Visions

A visitor to the outskirts of Mngeta village in the year 1999 would have found there an unlikely cluster of grey industrial buildings, most of them in disrepair and inhabited by fruit bats. This was the former headquarters of KOTACO, a large-scale mechanized rice project established by North Koreans in 1988 and then abruptly abandoned in 1994. The huge rice fields that had been cleared and drained by the North Koreans were barely visible in the distance, most of them having already reverted back to wooded grassland. Beyond the gates of the main administrative compound stood rows of disabled Chinese tractors, and several of the windows of the management offices were broken or missing.

Inside the lobby of the main building was an image that provided a surprising contrast with the surrounding environment. Painted on the wall in tranquil greens and blues was a large mural—a depiction of the rural development vision that the North Koreans had hoped to implement here at Mngeta. The mural portrayed a tamed and ordered landscape: in this image the swift-moving Mngeta river had been dammed and put to use for hydroelectric power; the woodlands and grasslands of the valley were cleared; and rectangular rice fields were laid out in parallel rows alongside drainage canals. The Chinese tractors were busy in the fields, while the grey administration buildings overlooked the scene from high on a hillside. Running through the center of the mural—providing the backbone for the entire enterprise—were the tracks of the TAZARA railway. A passenger train was shown gliding over a bridge on its way to the west.

FIGURE 6.1. Section of a mural depicting landscape vision of North Korean irrigated rice development project (KOTACO) at Mngeta, 1999. Photograph by Steven Davis.

This image of rural order and industry represented yet another kind of railway vision for TAZARA—this time a vision of landscape change that would be shaped by the intervention of large-scale, state-sponsored agricultural projects. For while the *ujamaa* village development schemes alongside the railway were intended to mobilize rural resources and to distribute development benefits, large-scale irrigation projects were also deemed necessary by the state in the period after TAZARA's construction "for the achievement of longer term objectives."[1] Like the planned villages that preceded it, however, this large-scale irrigation project ended up having a very different effect on the landscape than the one that its planners had envisioned. The North Koreans originally contemplated a much larger project of 15,000 hectares, but settled for 5,000 and ended up clearing only half that area along with developing a road and culvert system. During the first growing season 400 hectares were cultivated; that amount reached 860 hectares the following year. The Korean rice fields were plagued by the same birds and wild animals that raided the *shambas* of local farmers—flocks of small quelea birds could devastate as many as 50 hectares at a time, with the help of hippos, wild pigs, antelope, and buffalo. In the end, according to farm manager Moses Kisugite, the project was a disappointing failure, not only because of the problems the Koreans encountered in the rice farms but also because of their sudden departure. "When the Koreans learned that the country was turning to multi-partyism," he explained, "they ran away. They abandoned us, so the project never reached its goals."[2]

In satellite images taken in 1996, the large rectangles of the KOTACO rice fields are still clearly visible in the midst of irregularly shaped smaller rice farms and the tangled pathways of pastoralist grazing lands. Yet despite their size and their imposing geometry, these fields were ultimately far less significant in the transformation of the landscape of the TAZARA corridor than the activities of small-scale cultivators. For by the late 1990s the rural landscape alongside the railway had been altered most not by the large-scale mechanized interventions of state-sponsored enterprises, but through the cultivation by small farmers of thousands of rice, maize, and banana fields. Farmers had transformed the landscape surrounding each station along the railway line—not only at big towns like Ifakara, but alongside each smaller station and halt stop served by the Ordinary Train.

A comparison of satellite images from 1975 through the 1990s shows that the most visible and extensive landscape conversion in the corridor study area was from grasslands or woodlands to small farms. In the narrow corridor between the Udzungwa National Park and Selous Game Reserve boundaries, the land area under cultivation grew from 109 to 385 square kilometers during this period, while open grassland declined from 57 to 19 square kilometers and bushed grassland virtually disappeared. There was also significant change in places like Mlimba, where there had not been much settlement before TAZARA's construction. In the countryside around Mlimba station, cultivation increased from 49 to 212 square kilometers during the same period. Along with oral interviews and demographic data, this landscape evidence illustrates how people living along the TAZARA railway— both newly arrived migrants and longer-term residents—transformed the physical landscapes that surrounded them as they fashioned the multi-spatial livelihoods described in the previous chapter.

The migrants who moved into the TAZARA corridor in search of a better life dreamed of one day acquiring a plot of land where they might establish a farm, build a home, and raise a family. For the mobile population of the railway corridor, a farm was a firm foothold in an uncertain world. Wage workers used farming as a form of security during their working years and into their retirement. Traders invested their accumulated savings or *mtaji* in farms that they hoped would generate future resources for their trading enterprises. Young school-leavers, weary of chasing one livelihood trend after another, found respite in the stability that a small farm offered. Newcomers to the TAZARA corridor described the acquisition of land as a process of belonging, of feeling at home in their new surroundings. This process could be both individual and collective, for people frequently resettled close to relatives and neighbors from their places of origin, and in this arrangement they felt more like "locals" than like "strangers."

Meanwhile, those long-term residents of the TAZARA corridor who considered themselves to be truly "local," as members of founding lineages and ethnic groups, struggled to retain their own control over resources in a rapidly changing demographic context. As the landscape alongside the railway became settled with increasing numbers of newcomers, members of long-established lineages critiqued the changing exploitation of nature, charging that outsiders disregarded local customs and violated sacred sites. In their critique they reconstructed narratives of locality and resource rights that had been deployed in the colonial and even in the pre-colonial periods. In this way concepts of belonging became important both to long-term residents and to the new arrivals who sought to utilize farmlands, forests, and fisheries in the changing environment of the TAZARA corridor.

Satellite photographs taken between 1975 and 2001 illustrate how changes in demography and in resource use altered the landscape alongside the TAZARA railway. In contrast to the railway vision depicted in the mural at KOTACO, the landscape images revealed from space were filled with farms that were irregular in shape, spreading outward from floodplain settlements in unplanned and undisciplined patterns. On hillsides and in forest clearings maize and upland rice farms appeared as dispersed clusters, linked by foot and bicycle paths. On the ground, local residents and newcomers alike shared their own visions of landscape change along the railway in oral interviews. Their accounts emphasized the importance of a plot of farm land in their everyday lives—as a source of livelihood, as security against adversity, and as a place to call home. This was the landscape vision of the Ordinary Train.

Hoe and Wage

The North Korean rice project at Mngeta was one of several state-supported agricultural enterprises that were established in the TAZARA railway corridor. The oldest of these projects, the Kilombero Sugar Company, predated the railway (it was established in 1962) and then underwent an expansion in 1976 that coincided with TAZARA's completion. To the west in Mbeya region, an irrigated rice farm was created at Mbarali in the late 1970s with Chinese assistance. In 1993 the Kilombero Valley Teak Company began planting on the first 24 hectares of cleared *miombo* woodland in Kilombero and Ulanga Districts; teak plantations would cover over 4,000 hectares by 2004.[3] Long-term rural development projects were also established on the sites of former TAZARA construction camps and workshops: a national service camp and farm at Chita, for example, a prison farm at Idete, and a sawmill and engineering workshop at Mang'ula. Each of these enterprises affected the rural landscape through its own productive activities. Meanwhile, outside the boundaries of the projects themselves there was another land use transformation taking place—on the small farms established by active and laid-off workers, retirees, and frustrated job seekers. Like their counterparts in other parts of Africa, laborers in the TAZARA corridor strategically combined the resources of "hoe and wage."[4]

During the construction period and into the mid-1980s, most of those who migrated into the TAZARA corridor were workers employed by the railway or by one of the other state-sponsored development schemes and projects. The largest employer among these was the Kilombero Sugar Company. Like the railway workers, those hired by the sugar company came primarily from the surrounding highland regions of Mbeya, Iringa, and Ruvuma. They were most likely to be male heads of households who were seeking not only wage labor opportunities, but also farms that could serve as a form of livelihood security. In a study of migration along the railway carried out by Rudolf Mayombo in 1988, a decade after TAZARA's construction, the majority of those interviewed cited wage employment as their primary reason for coming into the Kilombero valley. At the same time, a majority also said that they hoped to settle more permanently in the valley and to engage in agricultural production.

Most of the respondents who participated in Mayombo's study had come to the TAZARA corridor as secondary migrants, having moved already at least once after leaving their place of birth. Many came from Dar es Salaam and Tanga, and were moving back to the countryside to seek work with the secondary goal of finding a plot of land on which to settle. Mayombo speculates that those from Tanga and other sisal growing areas may have intended to find work as cane cutters at the Kilombero Sugar Company following the collapse of the sisal industry in the 1970s.[5]

Mayombo's data show that the majority of migrants to the TAZARA corridor in the 1970s were mature adults between the ages of 25 and 49. Most were male (76%) and were married (73%). Thus male household heads were moving into the Kilombero valley to seek work while also establishing a household and an agricultural base that would utilize family labor. There were far fewer women household heads in the Mayombo survey. The women household heads were younger than the men and tended to be single (65%); many had experienced divorce, separation, or widowhood. Women migrants, like men, were seeking economic stability, but were less likely to have a partner or to be able to rely on household labor. The majority of migrants into the railway corridor in the later 1970s and early 1980s were therefore mature adult male heads of households with their families and dependents, in search of employment and a place to settle and farm. A smaller group of migrants were female heads of households, many recently divorced or widowed, coming into the valley to establish themselves economically and to find a place to make a new home. Once they became settled, these newcomers provided a demographic base that facilitated the resettlement of extended family members and others from their home areas.

In interviews workers and retirees described the ways they had combined agriculture with wage labor, both during their working years and after retirement. Augustino Magwaja was employed by the sugar company and also by TAZARA during his working life. He retired from TAZARA and settled at Mlimba, where he obtained a farm and grows rice and maize. Many other TAZARA workers also acquired farms near TAZARA stations on their retirement. Shabani Mseja chose to stay in Mlimba after retiring because he had lived and worked there for many years. He grew a combination of rice, maize, and vegetables on his farm. Bernard Katabi worked for TAZARA as a civil engineer for twenty-one years, from 1970 until 1991, before retiring to live on the farm he had acquired near the TAZARA station at Msolwa. He had been given a land grant and support for resettlement when he retired along with thirty other TAZARA workers, he said, which made it very attractive to stay at Msolwa. He was happy there, he explained, and felt that it would be difficult to go back to the southern highlands after living at Msolwa for so long.[6]

The pattern of "hoe and wage" documented by Mayombo began to change following the imposition of structural adjustment in Tanzania after the mid-1980s. The large-scale, state-owned enterprises that had offered employment to wage earners in the 1970s and 1980s no longer served as the same source of security in the 1990s. There had already been a reduction in employment opportunities in the railway corridor after TAZARA's construction was completed in 1975. Meanwhile, the railway had opened up new possibilities for settlement and farming in areas that were still undeveloped. By the 1990s more residents in the Kilombero valley had come seeking land for farming (45%) than jobs (25%), according to a study by Kennedy Haule. Migrants were also interested in finding access to grazing lands (11%), fisheries (6%), and timber (6%).[7] While retirees—civil servants and others with pensions—continued to settle in the corridor, the migrants of the 1990s were more likely to be young single men and women unaccompanied by family. Many were temporary residents, seeking a living through the seasonal exploitation of natural resources such as fisheries, forest reserves, and wildlife areas. Thus the pattern of migration and settlement shifted from a more stable, household-based pattern in the 1970s and early 1980s to a more dynamic and less stable pattern by the end of the millennium. At the same time, the primary resource for livelihood security—fertile farmland—was beginning in some areas to be in short supply, causing families to spread their farm holdings out over larger distances.

The example of the Kilombero Sugar Company illustrates the way economic policy in the liberalization period caused some rural workers along TAZARA to move into agriculture. It also shows the role played by the railway as a link between farm and workplace. For almost four decades the Kilombero Sugar Company was run as a government enterprise with some guarantee, however symbolic, of worker protections. When the South African company Illovo purchased the company in 2000 they immediately reduced the size of the labor force as well as the short- and long-term security of those who remained employed. Some three thousand of the company's workers were laid off as part of a bitter and violent labor dispute that took place in June 2000 following the plant's acquisition.[8] Most of these labor contracts were replaced with casual day labor arrangements; thus workers who had depended upon the security of salaries were either unemployed or hired back on much less secure terms.

In response to these changes in worker security, both former and current workers from the sugar company moved into the farming sector. Many used severance pay they received from Illovo to acquire land in the area, where they established new farms and homes. For others, however, it was difficult to find a place to farm in a valley bounded by two wildlife reserves, where the available space was already claimed by sugar cane plantations and outgrower schemes. Newcomers therefore began to acquire and clear land for farming at some distance away. TAZARA played an important role in facilitating these farming arrangements: casual workers were able to maintain a residence near the Kilombero Sugar Company while using the railway to travel to their more distant farm plots. Frequently families were seasonally divided as some members remained close to the factory while others lived some distance away on the farms.[9]

In life history interviews, workers explained how they managed after being laid off by the sugar company. Elisha Kidumbe took up farming in Mwaya after being laid off in 2000. He had moved to the Kilombero valley from his home in Njombe in 1985 to seek work. After working for three years as a seasonal worker for the sugar company, he was able to obtain a permanent salaried position in 1989 as a survey attendant for the entire sugar estate. When Ilovo purchased the company, and he was laid off, Elisha decided to stay in the area rather than return to his home at Wanging'ombe: "I saw that it was difficult to return to Wanging'ombe," he remembers, "because the area was having a drought, the soils were worn out." The price for fertilizer in Njombe was very high compared with the price he could obtain for his maize. In addition, there was a shortage of available land in Njombe—his own family's land was already divided among his siblings.[10]

Elisha Kidumbe felt that he could get a better start in farming if he stayed on in the Kilombero valley, and he purchased a plot of land near Mwaya village using his severance pay from the sugar company. He said that the land there in the river valley was still fertile, and he could grow his crops without purchasing fertilizers. He used TAZARA to travel to the Njombe highlands to visit his family, and his relatives came to visit him in turn, especially during times of family celebrations or difficulties. At the time of his interview he hoped to begin to use TAZARA to conduct small-scale trade along the railway (drawing on income he generated from farming), but had not yet started this new enterprise.[11]

Like Elisha Kidumbe, Richard Mwailunda was also a worker at the Kilombero Sugar Company and had worked there for fifteen years before he was laid off in 2001. He also decided to remain in Mwaya and purchase a farm there, rather than return to his home area of Kyela, having lived away for so many years. He purchased a three-acre farm in a forest about one hour from Mwaya village, using his severance pay, and began to clear the forest and to build a house. Richard Mwailunda used casual laborers to help him to clear and farm his land. He was not interested in returning to Kyela, also a rice growing area, because it was already overcrowded. One could only obtain a farm there through inheritance, he explained. "I like it here" at Mwaya, he added, "because it feels like home."[12]

The acquisition of land could be a livelihood alternative for workers who had been laid off from the Kilombero Sugar Company in 2000–2001, as well as for casual laborers who continued working but sought a more secure economic foundation. Workers who acquired farm plots discussed the limited agricultural options available to them in their homes of origin, particularly in densely settled areas of the southern highlands like Njombe and Kyela. While many of these workers were able to buy land near the sugar estates, over time they were moving farther and farther away in search of farms as the valley filled with cultivators. Martin Kabida, who was raised in Sonjo, moved back there after his retirement so that he could live near his birthplace, where he "began life." He noticed many changes that had occurred in the landscape and settlement since the time of his childhood. The railway attracted many people to settle in that area, he says, and farms were decreasing in size and availability. The next generation, which includes his own children, is moving out westward to Mngeta, Chita, and Mbingu, where open land is still available for settlement. These young farmers visit their parents and send them letters using TAZARA; thus the railway is an important means for family communication in a changing rural landscape.[13]

These life stories show how salaried and casual sugar company workers relied upon TAZARA as they combined "hoe and wage" in their rural livelihood strategies over time. Meanwhile, the sugar company employed a third category of worker in the railway corridor: the outgrower farmer. Like their wage worker counterparts, outgrowers also sought farmland for subsistence security and used the TAZARA railway to support their agricultural activities.[14] Outgrower schemes had been part of the sugar company's production strategy from the beginning: the Kilombero Settlement Scheme described in chapter 3 was an outgrower project. After its acquisition of the company in 2000, Illovo expanded its use of outgrowers in an effort to lower labor costs and to shift the risks of production to local farmers. According to oral interviews, producers who converted their farms to sugar cane sought additional farmland elsewhere for subsistence agriculture. Many outgrowers cultivated grain on second and third farm plots at different locations. To reach these farms, some of which were some distance away, they used the railway to travel from one rural area to another. The produce they harvested provided them with food for subsistence and also for sale, forming an important supplement to the income they earned producing cane under contract to the sugar company.[15]

The example of the Kilombero Sugar Company shows how people living in the TAZARA railway corridor implemented their own rural landscape visions by combining agriculture with changing forms of wage labor. As national economic policies, regional demographics, and local livelihood strategies shifted over the three decades following TAZARA's construction, the responses of workers and farmers transformed the countryside in new ways. The enduring landscape legacy of development projects such as the Kilombero Sugar Company was therefore embodied not only by the mechanized sugar plantation fields but also by the multiplicity of small farm plots spreading out along the railway.

A Place to Call Home

For those without access to a wage, farming could be even more important to rural livelihood. Many of those who migrated to the TAZARA corridor after 1985 had few resources and were in search of a "good place" to acquire land, settle, and take up agriculture. Shaha Salum Mnauye explained that he was told by friends that he should move to Mbingu to get a start in farming, because it was a good place for a person who didn't have much wealth to invest. He moved there in 2000 and has stayed ever since, although he has little capital and has not yet built a house—he sleeps in a small shelter in his rice field. Gerodi Pius Mikupi explained that "in other parts of Tanzania, people are unable to find a place to farm. They have left those places, they are coming here." This is the reason, he said, for the steady population growth in the communities along TAZARA where land was still available.[16]

Interviewees frequently used the concept of home to express their experience of farming in the TAZARA corridor, whether they were describing a feeling of being "at home" in their new surroundings or feeling like "strangers" when they returned to their place of origin. Because farmlands were fixed in location, discussions about them were part of a larger discourse of belonging and locality. This was true whether or not the farm was the place of actual residence; belonging was associated with a larger sense of place that included soils, climate, crop selection, and neighbors. As Michael Mwaniko explained, "Many of the citizens who live here in Mbingu come from Mbeya region, and they come here in order to farm. They tell their friends and relatives that this is a good place to farm. . . . They are attracted here by the quality of the soil, because it is the same as the soil from home, especially for growing rice and bananas."[17] This combination of qualities was what made Mbingu and Mngeta feel like home for people from Mbeya, according to Josefina Mwasulama.[18] TAZARA workers who had stayed for a number of years in the railway corridor also used the idea of "home" to explain why they had chosen to remain there, especially when they retired near TAZARA stations. As Shabani Mseja said, describing his retirement on a farm in Mlimba after working for TAZARA for thirty-one years, "if I go back to the place where I came from, I will be a stranger."[19]

The idea of "coming home" to work and farm in the rural areas is echoed in life history interviews with traders and others who spent their early earning years struggling for a living in the city or at the coast. The life story of Hamisi Mkoka is a good example, for he was born in the TAZARA corridor at Sonjo in 1963 and then left for several years to trade at the coast before "coming home" to grow crops in Mbingu. Hamisi decided to move back to the TAZARA corridor in the late 1980s when "TAZARA was built and trade was good." He jokingly referred to himself in an interview as a *muhamiaji mwenyeji*, or "immigrant local," playfully combining two identities that are often contested in the context of immigration and demographic change in this region.[20]

Yohana Nyakunga returned to farming in the TAZARA corridor after trying several other livelihood strategies, including prospecting for gemstones. He now has a farm near Mlimba, where he grows rice in the rainy season and irrigated market vegetables during the dry season. Yohana still continues to mine for gem-stones, and he uses the proceeds from one economic activity to support investment in the other.[21] Another farmer at Mlimba, Mohamed Manjenga, decided to settle there after a lifetime of extensive travel. As a young man he worked for shipping companies and cruise lines that took him to Namibia, Mozambique, Rwanda, Kenya, Uganda, and Madagascar. He hopes that his farm at Mlimba can help him to earn enough capital to start up another small business of his own. Mohamed was inspired by the farms that he saw during his travels, especially those he visited in Windhoek, Namibia. "I enjoy farming, I feel it in my blood," he said. He would like to have an extensive mixed farm with chickens, dairy cows, rice, and sesame. He hopes to invest some day in a flower farm like one he saw in Windhoek. "I want to be a good example for young people," he said, who can also be successful in farming.[22]

Familiar physical landscapes and communities of neighbors sharing cultural and linguistic qualities contributed to a sense of belonging for the farmers who settled in the TAZARA corridor. Land acquisition could make one feel at home in another way as well. When a newcomer wished to acquire land from a village administration, he or she was expected to go through a process of application and in some instances a probationary period. For Hussein Ally Mgeni, this process resulted in a feeling of citizenship that had eluded him during a life of itinerant trading and fishing. Now that he has been accepted into the village and is cultivating his five acres of land at Mbingu, he said with some pride, he is recognized as an "official villager" and lives there very well with his fellow citizens.

Hussein was born in Ikwiriri in Rufiji District in 1969, and spent his early adulthood working as a casual laborer and fisherman at Dar es Salaam and in Rufiji District before leaving the coast in 1996. "I was saying farewell to my parents," he explained, telling them that "I had to go away to look for another life." Hussein sought that new life in the TAZARA railway corridor, where he tried out farming in two other locations before coming to Mbingu in 1998. When he asked the village leadership of Mbingu for land to cultivate, he was told to settle in the village for a time so that they could judge his character. He then enrolled in training for the village defense squad (*mafunzo ya mgambo*) and proved to the villagers that he was a good farmer and neighbor. "The village has now seen that I am a good citizen," he explained. "After seeing that I was good, they gave me their approval and included me in the *mgambo*." He described his sense of pride at being accepted into Mbingu village and said that he planned to marry there and to stay for many more years. He earned enough profit from his rice farm to buy a house plot and to start building a home, and then purchased a bicycle. Hussein said that he feels a strong sense of belonging in Mbingu. The process he went through to acquire land for farming required him to become a member of the community in an official way. It was a process that made him feel like a fellow citizen and no longer like an itinerant or stranger.[23]

Demography and Landscape Change

In oral interviews, residents of the TAZARA railway corridor described the material and symbolic importance of farming in their daily lives. The significance of farming is also reflected visually in the comparison of satellite images from 1975 to 2001, illustrating broad patterns of land use and landscape change during the first twenty-five years of railway operations. This study used photographs from the year of TAZARA's completion (1975), 1990, 1996, and 2001. Because photographs were not available for all years for each area, the comparisons drawn here are suggestive rather than conclusive. Nevertheless, patterns can be discerned in these images of landscape cover that can enhance our understanding of the relationship between the railway, human settlement, and natural resource use.[24]

For the purposes of comparison, landscape cover was classified into eleven broad categories. This classification was done by comparing the digitized satellite images with field observations carried out in July and August 2002, and through interviews with valley residents. The study area was then divided into four sub-areas or "complexes" that correlated with the primary service areas for the TAZARA stations that were included in the parcel receipts database: Mang'ula, Ifakara, Mngeta, and Mlimba. This allowed for comparison of changes in vegetation cover made visible in the satellite images and the material we gathered from the parcel receipts, oral interviews, and field observations.

The satellite data showed that the most significant change in landscape cover was a conversion of grassland and bushed grassland to small-scale cultivation. Some woodlands and forests were also cleared for farming, but not as extensively. The satellite images also showed that cultivation intensity followed two main spatial patterns. The first spatial pattern showed the most intensive cultivation (and the highest level of grassland clearing) in the easternmost section of the railway corridor. Farming intensity decreased progressively to the southwest. The second spatial pattern was one of high farming density around town centers and large stations (for example, Ifakara) and lower density farther away from the railway line (a table showing landscape cover change is in appendix 3). The area around Mofu, for example, which is some distance from TAZARA, had lower levels of intensification than neighboring areas closer to the line of rail. There were some notable exceptions to this trend in areas with historically high agricultural potential—for example, the

Malinyi fan in Ulanga District, which was intensively cultivated and served by an active bicycle network out of Mlimba Station.[25]

Demographic data from national census reports and other sources show parallel patterns in the expansion of population and settlement in the TAZARA corridor. Using the results of the Tanzania National Census, we compared change during the first census decade following TAZARA's construction (1978–88) with that over the following twelve years (1988–2002). The data show that population increased over this period along the railway corridor, particularly in those areas adjacent to employment and trading opportunities and in areas of high agricultural productivity. Population levels grew at an accelerated pace in some areas after 1988, with Mbingu ward showing an annual growth rate of over 8.41 percent from 1988 to 2002. On the other side of the river in Ulanga District, growth was much slower. The average for Tanzania as a whole during that period was 2.8 percent, slightly higher than Ulanga District but significantly lower than Kilombero District.[26]

When these numbers are broken down by village and by ward, we can see that particular settlements in the railway corridor experienced more rapid growth than others. Remembering that these data were collected after the villagization efforts of 1974–75, we see for example that Kiberege Ward grew by 5.35 percent, Kibaoni by 4.37 percent, Idete by 5.9 percent, and Mlimba by 6.1 percent. The wards of Masagati and Mofu, in contrast, which lie some distance from the railway, saw growth of 1.53 percent and 2.37 percent respectively. Thus there were some settlements that experienced dramatic growth in the 1980s and 1990s compared with the national average. Some of these settlements, including Mlimba, were located in sparsely settled areas during the railway's construction. According to local accounts they were transformed from *pori* or "bush" to thriving towns in two decades, and therefore the rate of change taken alone (6.11%) may be somewhat misleading. Yet other settlements, for example Kiberege, that grew significantly during the same period (5.35%) had been important centers historically for trade and administration and were therefore well populated. If we calculate the rate of population change for the aggregated settlements located along the railway corridor we come up with a figure of 4.74 percent from 1978 to 2002. Density of population was also highest for Kilombero District: in 1988 density for Kilombero District was 9.8 per square kilometer, and for Ulanga District, 4.8.

In addition to the national census data, there are two independent evaluations of population change in Kilombero and Ulanga districts that show similar patterns. In a study carried out as part of a Selous conservation project in 2000, population change was calculated for six villages along the railway line, including Signali, Kiberege, Mkasu, and Ichonde.[27] These numbers confirm the general pattern of

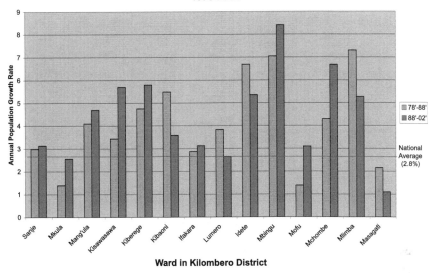

FIGURE 6.2. Population change for Kilombero District in the two decades after TAZARA's construction, compared with the national average. Tanzania National Census Reports. Analysis by Jennifer Monson-Miller.

population change that is expressed in the census data. The second independent study is the Demographic Surveillance System, or DSS, that was started in 1996 by researchers at the Ifakara Health Research and Development Center (IHRDC). While this project does not produce regular reports, data they collected showed population increases in the area surrounding Mngeta in the double digits from 1997 to 1999.[28]

When Mayombo did his demographic survey of the Kilombero valley in 1988, he concluded that the population remained sparsely dispersed in most rural parts of the valley, with the exception of the alluvial fans and river levees, where there were concentrated settlements. This description matched the observations of earlier visitors to the valley from the colonial period onward. By the time of the Selous management survey some thirteen years later, however, some areas in the valley were experiencing land shortages. In those villages without room for expansion residents described seeking second or third farm plots some distance from their original landholdings in order to maintain subsistence. This was especially true in areas where land shortage was aggravated by the proximity of nature reserve boundaries, where large numbers of people had decided to settle around employment opportunities, and where transportation options included both road and rail. The area that showed the most intensive cultivation in the satellite images—the Mang'ula complex—had all three of these attributes. Moreover, land in the Mang'ula complex was an extension of the broad floodplain of the Msolwa river and was described by farmers as having high levels of fertility due to annual flooding patterns. It was therefore a very attractive area for cultivators, and was also the closest to Dar es Salaam of our four study areas.

In these eastern areas of the valley that experienced high rates of settlement and limited room for expansion, farm plots had grown steadily smaller and more fragmented by the year 2001. While there were some farmers, mostly from outside the valley, who were able to purchase and operate larger farms, the majority of landholders cultivated between one and five acres per year. Many respondents to the Selous management survey stated that they had more than one plot in the village, while others had additional plots some distance away. While inheritance was one important source of land, 84 percent of respondents stated that they also obtained land by clearing unoccupied bush.[29] This information correlates with satellite data that show substantial bush clearing activity in the areas covered by the Selous survey, particularly in the Mang'ula complex. Newcomers to the valley were most likely to obtain their land by clearing open bush or grassland, or by purchasing land through village leaders.

It is difficult to document changes in farm size over time, because data from district agricultural files are inconsistent and independent studies vary greatly in their approaches and methodologies. A government report on rural development from July 2, 1984, showed varying plot sizes for selected villages in Kilombero district, from about 1.5 acres per person at Msolwa "A" and Sanje villages in the eastern Mang'ula complex, to 16 acres per person at Mlimba to the west.[30] A similar study conducted in 1999 for the purposes of famine relief listed both the area of land cultivated per village in the month of January, and the number of village households, showing that there were averages of half an acre of cultivated land per household at Msolwa "A" and 2.3 acres per household at Sanje. Toward Ifakara along the railway line, Kiberege had about half an acre per household and Signali about the same. To the far west at Mlimba, each household had cultivated more than 2 acres.[31] These two government reports cannot be easily compared because one measured total available land per capita while the other measured land by household under cultivation during a year of famine. Nevertheless, what they do confirm more broadly is the spatial distribution of landholding in the valley. Those villages located in the Mang'ula complex along the eastern section of the railway corridor showed the smallest and most fragmented farm plots, while those farthest to the west had larger plots, suggesting more land availability.

The sizes of farm plots throughout the eastern section of the study area were too small on average to sustain family subsistence. In some villages in the Mang'ula complex, there was severe land shortage—in Mhelule, for example, where a quarter of the population was found to be landless in 2000. The size of plots was one of the most important socioeconomic factors in household subsistence and sustainability in several studies. Kennedy Haule determined that the size of the plot for the primary crop, rice, was the most significant indicator of household income, followed by off-farm employment and beer brewing. The Selous study found that the majority of residents (71.8%) could not produce enough food for their own subsistence because of small farm sizes. Despite this, many farmers sold substantial proportions of their crops after harvest in order to raise cash needed for school fees, for medical expenses, and to pay off accumulated debts.[32]

Most respondents reported that they supplemented their farm income in various ways, most often by working as casual laborers on the farms of more wealthy neighbors or for other projects (75% of respondents), or by engaging in small-scale economic activities such as trade, beer brewing, brick-making, charcoal burning, and fishing. In Mikoleko village, 80 percent of farmers worked as casual laborers on the plots of wealthier landholders in order to sustain their households.[33] In villages of the most severe landlessness, residents migrated seasonally using the railway to the western parts of the valley to find available land or to work as casual farm labor. They traveled the length of the valley from Mang'ula to Mlimba, returning to their homes after the harvest.

Landscape Change and the Construction of Locality

From the time of the construction of the TAZARA railway to the end of the 1990s, the railway corridor experienced measurable demographic and environmental change. Areas that were once isolated and sparsely settled were becoming bustling trading centers surrounded by cultivated valley rice fields, upland maize farms, and banana gardens. Within the dense forests once filled with dangerous wildlife—such a formidable prospect for the railway construction workers and the *ujamaa* villagers of the 1970s—farms were being cleared and planted in the 1990s. As farmers and traders settled further and further westward in search of land and livelihood security, the density of settlement spread with them into formerly remote river valleys and grasslands.

In the context of these changes in demography and landscape, tensions developed over natural resource use, including access to farmland and to fisheries. These tensions were negotiated using a discourse of locality and belonging. Wage workers, retirees, and newcomers who acquired plots of land in the TAZARA corridor described feeling "at home" (rather than like "strangers") in a new place. Meanwhile, long-term residents of the region constructed their own identities as the "true locals" or indigenous people (*wenyeji*) of the Kilombero valley. These debates were frequently framed in ethnic terms. Those who laid claim to indigenous status (and had done so since the colonial period) identified themselves ethnically as Ndamba, best known for their fishing and rice-growing way of life along the waterways of the Kilombero River. Newcomers from the southern highlands identified as Nyakyusa (from Mbeya Region), or Bena or Hehe (from Iringa Region), and were associated with upland banana and maize cultivation. In some areas, such as Mbingu, so many newcomers from the southern highlands had resettled by 2001 that those who considered themselves to be the original inhabitants felt outnumbered. As Josefina Mwasulama put it, "the local people have become like strangers"[34]

In oral interviews about the history of natural resource use, those claiming indigenous status argued that outsiders were exploiting resources in indiscriminate ways that violated local custom and caused environmental degradation. Newcomers, on the other hand, claimed that Ndamba were backward and traditional farmers who stood to benefit from modernization in the form of new crops, marketing experience, and agrarian technology brought from the highlands. Framed as debates about ethnicity and resource use, these arguments engaged competing visions of the rural landscape of the railway corridor and its development.

Recent immigrants and long-term residents alike credited newcomers to the valley with introducing new crops and farming techniques. A resident of Mngeta said that it was good that people of different backgrounds had come into the valley, because when local people saw that traders were coming to purchase their crops, they began to grow maize and other crops that they had not grown in the past. They began to grow bananas, cassava, groundnuts, oranges, coconuts, and even onions. These crops were sold for sale rather than for consumption, and this increased the cash flow and therefore the development of the area. Outsiders even increased the production of the local staple food, rice, according to a district official interviewed in 2000: "People in Ifakara are now planting more rice, because now there is competition for rice production, and more and more people are growing surpluses of rice."[35] These discussions of agriculture and development portrayed the immigration of outsiders in a positive light, as having brought beneficial change to the Kilombero valley. The landscape vision they promoted was a modern one, in which crops were produced for market by industrious and experienced highland farmers. These discussions both implicitly and explicitly framed local Ndamba farmers as backward and traditional in their farming methods and outlook.

Many of those who identified themselves as Ndamba shared this positive view of the influence of outsiders on the landscape. Yet in discussions of resource exploitation, the influx of newcomers from other areas was viewed in more negative terms. Pastoralists who moved into the valley from the mid-1990s onward were described as having a destructive effect on the landscape, because they had large herds and were indifferent to the land use customs of the local farmers. Farmers accused them of overgrazing the landscape and destroying the rice fields. The commodities traders who brought development in the form of *"biashara"* (business/trade) were said to be contributing to the destruction of fisheries and other natural resources because they encouraged the overexploitation of the environment in order to make a profit. Timber cutters from the highlands had a reputation for felling forests indiscriminately, taking away the large hardwood trees that were most valued by locals for making into canoes. Fishermen from outside the valley were seen as the most destructive of all. In their rush to become wealthy, they ignored the customs and practices of the local fishing communities, using small-mesh drag nets that depleted fish stocks down to the smallest fingerlings.

Elders within the local community took these apprehensions still further. They were concerned that outsiders were disregarding important local fishing customs as well as ritual proscriptions against immoral behavior. The misbehavior of outsiders resulted in the inappropriate exploitation of natural resources, elders claimed, particularly in fishing camps. At the same time, they observed that outsiders violated the rules of the ancestral spirits, or *mahoka*, who controlled key aspects of the environment such as fertility and rainfall. The elders viewed themselves as important guardians both of the physical environment and of relationships with *mahoka*. Thus their complaints reflected concerns about the loss of authority and control among male elders in the context of rapid demographic and economic change. Because people no longer respected their authority or the authority of the *mahoka* for whom they mediated, they felt, the environment and the well-being of the local people were being destroyed.

At the center of their concerns about changing resource use were changes in fishing practices. Fishing and other customary uses of the Kilombero river and its tributaries were at the core of Ndamba identity and historical legitimacy. In the colonial period, an Ndamba historian wrote an ethno-history that recounted the ways his ancestors had used canoes, harpoons, traps, and weirs in the riverine environment to sustain their communities.[36] As new contests over natural resource use emerged in the 1990s, Ndamba activists once again incorporated the themes of identity, custom, and the appropriate exploitation of nature into the discourse of locality that they deployed. By looking more closely at debates over fishing practices, we can come closer to an understanding of both the way that resource use

FIGURE 6.3. A dugout canoe loaded with dried fish headed for market at Kivukoni river crossing, Ifakara, 2000. Photograph by Steven Davis.

changed after TAZARA's construction and also the larger meaning of these changes within communities.

Local fishermen believed that the increasing numbers of fishermen and the introduction of new fishing techniques from outside the valley reduced the fish harvest and threatened the very survival of the Kilombero fishery. They blamed the fishing practices of immigrants—particularly those from the shores of Lake Nyasa and from the Rufiji delta—for the declining numbers of fish. Atupele Mwakapala observed that

> People here have learned a lot about fishing from people from other areas— from the Ngoni from Songea, the people from Lake Nyasa at Kyela, and others. The people of the Ndengereko tribe from the Rufiji have brought a round net, called a *kimea*, that they throw out over the water and then tighten it. They use it when the water is lower, when the water is very shallow. Many fishermen have started using this type of net now. When people see new methods of fishing that other people are doing, they also start to do it.[37]

The nets were the main reason that fish stocks were declining and that fish were no longer as large as they used to be in the past, local fisherman claimed. Nets increased the size of the overall fish catch, and also increased the harvesting of breeding stock. This resulted in lower numbers of fish in the present and in a long-term decline in the sustainability of the fisheries into the future. The concerns of these fishermen appear to be confirmed by the preliminary results of a multi-year study of the Kilombero fishery carried out by volunteers from Frontier-Tanzania. They reported in 2002 that harvests from the Kilombero river fishery (9,500–12,000 tonnes per year) were exceeding its sustainable yield (believed to be 7,000 tonnes per year).[38]

Before the expansion of markets and fishing nets, Ndamba fishermen practiced what they call their "traditional" fishing techniques. These involved a system of traps, weirs, and lines in the faster-flowing waters, and scoop nets in the still waters and shallows. Atupele Mwakapala stated, "People here used to fish with *ndanga*, fish traps. Once the fish are trapped, they use another kind of net to scoop them out into the *mtumbwi* (dugout canoe) and they take them home. Now, people use fishing nets. Some people still use *ndanga*, because of tradition, but most younger people use *wavu* (nets)."[39]

The fishery was also affected by changes in the settlement practices of new immigrant communities living along the rivers. Prior to the demographic changes of the 1980s and 1990s, fishermen who went to the river stayed temporarily at fishing camps, leaving their wives and children at the rice farms or in the villages. Venance Lyapembile explained:

> The Wandamba are fishermen and farmers. After planting, they [the men] used to fish and then they came back to harvest, then they would go back to fishing again. . . . The problem people have here is cultural. Wandamba are fishermen who have special customs. The people who go there [e.g., to the fishing camps] were always men. Now, the Nyakyusa are doing the opposite. They go there and stay and make it into a village, when it is supposed to be a camp for people who are fishing. This will be the end of the village and of the customs of the Wandamba.[40]

According to Ndamba custom, the fishing camps were temporary accommodations where men would stay overnight for some days or weeks while fishing and fish trading. They were never intended to be permanent settlements. Newcomers from outside the valley, on the other hand, settled in some of the fishing camps along the river and made them into long-term residences. Some villages became registered with the state and had village government officers. With more people staying at some of the fishing camps year-round, in fact indefinitely, the threat to fishing stocks increased even further, according to Venance Lyapembile. The catches were diminished, he said, and the sizes of individual fish were growing smaller.[41]

The data collected by KVIEMP volunteers confirmed that those fishing settlements that were the most ethnically mixed were also those that had become
permanent villages. Of the eleven fishing camps in the study, the two that were
largest and most permanent were located downstream from Ifakara. These camps,
Mikeregembe and Ilua, had the largest numbers of Nyakyusa fishermen.[42] They
also had the largest fish catches in the study. Of the total fish catch that volunteers
weighed and measured in 1998–99 from the eleven sites, Mikeregembe accounted
for 29 percent, and Ilua for 17 percent.[43] Fishermen at Mikeregembe were most
likely to use nets to catch fish, and were also most likely to catch large numbers
of Bagrus (Kindamba, *kitoga*), Synodontis (Kindamba, *ngogo*), Mormyrus (Kindamba, *sura sura*), and *ndipi*. Differences in catch weight from the different fishing
camps in the study showed that fishing with nets sizably increased the catches.[44]
Thus the evidence from this study showed that Nyakyusa fishermen were indeed
making fishing camps into permanent, year-round villages. It confirmed that fishermen from these camps were most likely to use nets and were therefore making
the largest catches. The KVIEMP study also noted that the largest numbers of
fish traders were resident in Mikeregembe, rather than in the other camps along
the river.

Differences among the groups living in the fishing villages led to conflicts between local people and incoming migrants, conflicts that once again were negotiated in ethnic terms. In the late 1990s, there were conflicts between Ndamba and
Nyakyusa fishing groups living on the Kihansi River. Their disputes centered on
fishing methods, length of settlement at the camps, and moral behavior. In the
end, the fishermen divided into two separate camps, one for Nyakyusa fishermen
(Fibwe) and one for their Ndamba neighbors (Kihopa). Yet because they share the
same waterways, the conflicts continued.[45]

Demographic change in the TAZARA corridor also contributed to generational
tensions between youths and elders who utilized the fishery. Mr. Haule observed
that the customs that used to govern the behavior of fishermen were seen as old-
fashioned and out of date by younger people. The strictures of *masharti* and *mi-
iko* were being replaced by *elimu* (schooling, education), he said, intensifying the
differences between youth and elders. "Young people do not want to follow the
ways of long ago," he said. These generational tensions were exacerbated by the
immigration of young men from towns who had finished primary school (and in
some cases secondary school) and who sought a livelihood in the valley. Because
these young men had received *elimu*, they were less likely to value the customs of
the past. And because they were not local, they did not have the lineage or ethnic
ties that might incline them to show respect for the elders who traditionally held
positions of authority in the fishing camps.

There were also generational differences in the use of fishing technologies. Those who used the "traditional" Ndamba fishing techniques—traps and weirs, lines, spears—were mostly older local men. Those who preferred to use mesh nets were younger fishermen, the majority of whom were from outside the valley. Older men in the valley used to be respected for their wisdom and expertise in fishing technology, according to Leonard Likweti. Those with the most experience and skill in using traps and lines would obtain the largest fish and the biggest catch. Large fish were prized, not only because they would provide more protein for the family but also because it required skill and bravery to obtain them. With the advent of fishing nets, however, skill and expertise were no longer the primary determinants of a good catch. Harvesting a large number of fish became more important than bringing in one or two large specimens, once people began fishing for the market. And in turn, ownership of a net became the most important determinant of wealth. As Leonard Likweti observed, "A long time ago, people fished, and those with more experience and knowledge gained more. Now, those who gain are those who have access to nets."[46]

Those fishermen who owned nets, therefore, were those who made the largest profits. They were also able to employ other, less affluent fishermen to work for them. Large drag nets such as the *kokoro*, which swept up as many as three thousand fish at once, required six fishermen to handle them.[47] The fishing community thus became differentiated in new ways. In the KVIEMP study, researchers found that traders were in fact the most likely to be the owners of nets, while fishermen were more likely to be employed as workers. Some fishermen—rather than operating independently as in the past—therefore began to fish as employees of the fish traders, receiving a payment for their labor while the net owner made the profit. "Those who own the nets make larger profits," observed Leonard Likweti, "and those without nets remain poor."[48] In the past, male elders who had authority in the fishing camps could control the activities and therefore the labor of others. With the advent of fishing nets, those with access to these new forms of productive capital were able to mobilize labor. As demographic and economic change led to differentiation between those who owned fishing gear and those whom they employed, the role and authority of elders also diminished.

Over the course of their lives, Ndamba elders living in the Kilombero valley experienced significant changes in the utilization of natural resources. Following the construction of the TAZARA railway newcomers settled in the valley to take up farming and fishing, while traders shifted market relationships. Elders discussed these changes using the language of ethnicity and locality. They viewed themselves as important guardians of the well-being of the physical and sacred environments, or *mazingira*, and were critical of the immigrants and youths who disregarded their

customary functions. Newcomers, meanwhile, viewed themselves as bringing positive influences to the railway corridor in the form of market trading, new crops, and
farming practices. As they moved into landscapes that reminded them of home,
these settlers felt that they were themselves becoming local, and described feeling
like strangers when they visited their former homes in the highlands.

Conclusion

The mural painted on the wall of the KOTACO administration building revealed
one vision of landscape change and agricultural development in the TAZARA railway corridor; the satellite images taken between 1975 and 2001 revealed another.
What both of these landscape visions had in common was the presence of the
railway itself running through their centers. From KOTACO the railway pulled
wagonloads of rice, freshly harvested from the North Korean mechanized rice
scheme, toward the city of Dar es Salaam. From the smaller, irregularly shaped
farms represented in the satellite photographs, harvested rice was more likely to be
transported in gunnysacks, carried as parcels in the luggage wagon of the Ordinary
Train.

The Ordinary Train also carried farmers, fishermen, and traders, whether it
was transporting them to their dispersed outlying fields or connecting them with
their places of origin. The train moved people and their goods among the multiple spaces where they lived, farmed, fished, and traded. It allowed people from
the highlands to return home to join together with their families during times of
celebration and times of mourning. The TAZARA Railway was therefore not only
a source of physical mobility but also a vehicle through which one could create a
feeling of belonging. The train could facilitate becoming "local" or becoming a
"stranger," making it possible for individuals and for communities to redefine their
concepts of home and away.

At the same time, mobility and resettlement in the railway corridor led to dis-
cord over the meaning of locality, and over the rights to land and natural resources
that locality represented. Those who considered themselves to be the original, truly
local residents of the Kilombero valley critiqued the ways that changing patterns
of settlement and land use affected their control over nature. These tensions were
expressed in terms of ethnicity and generational difference, as Ndamba contested
the changing use of farmlands, forests, and fisheries. In this way, TAZARA played
a role in the construction as well as the negotiation of belonging.

7

Conclusion

Railway Visions

From the colonial period onward, successive regimes in East Africa imagined a southern railway that would link the Indian Ocean with the regions to the west beyond Lake Nyasa. Railway visions in colonial East Africa were connected to territorial rivalries and pan-territorial ambitions, whether these involved the German aspiration to span *Mittelafrika* or the British desire to create an Imperial Link between the settler colonies. At the time of independence, presidents Julius Nyerere and Kenneth Kaunda dreamed of a pan-territorial project that would end the "balkanization" of colonial spheres of influence while liberating the landlocked states of central Africa from their dependency upon routes through their still-colonized neighbors to the south. Each of these railway visions was constructed in a specific historical moment, reflecting the pressing political and economic issues of its time. The Imperial Link would have connected white settler interests in the southeastern African region; the post-colonial Freedom Railway sought to unravel them. Yet there was also continuity in these successive imaginings of a southern railway—not only in the mapping of the route itself, but also in the larger material and symbolic meanings that the southern railway held for states, subjects, and citizens.

Railway visions carried with them visions of development, visions that in the colonial period pitted white settler interests against the interests of those who sought to profit from an African peasant model of production. Thus the surveying and planning process in colonial railway development was contested by the individuals and interest groups who stood to benefit or to lose from the plan's ultimate implementation. While individual and collective stakeholders lobbied for their own interests, railways in the colonial and the post-colonial period remained projects of the state. As large-scale infrastructure investments, railways were material and symbolic expressions of state power: they held the potential to control the movements of people and goods, the locations of production and consumption, and the extraction of resources and labor.

The southern railway that was finally built in the 1960s and '70s could be viewed in this way as a classic model of a state-driven, large-scale infrastructure project. It came on the heels of other large-scale interventions in East African development, including the Groundnut Scheme and other projects of rural modernization that were instituted in Tanzania during the post–World War II period. As TAZARA's construction was completed, the railway stations on the Tanzanian side were incorporated into Julius Nyerere's vision of *ujamaa* villagization, a state-led rural resettlement project that had its predecessors in the colonial sleeping sickness campaigns of the 1940s and the agricultural resettlement schemes of the 1960s. TAZARA was built during the Cold War, when development visions were shaped by global rivalries; these rivalries played a pivotal role in the TAZARA project. They were part of the reason that TAZARA was dismissed by its critics as an ideological project (which it was in part), driven more by third world solidarities and pan-African aspirations than by economic common sense.

In this global context, the Chinese had articulated their own vision of development assistance in Africa through the Eight Principles of Development Assistance introduced during Zhou Enlai's tour of Africa in 1963–64. These principles reflected China's efforts to distinguish its approach to African development from those of the United States and the Soviet Union. Several of these principles had direct application to the TAZARA project, in particular the provision of an interest-free loan with a generous repayment schedule, the effort to promote self-reliance rather than dependency, the transfer of technical skills, and the expectation that Chinese technicians would have the same living standards as the African workers, without special amenities. These Chinese principles, together with Tanzanian and Zambian development ideals, became part of the state vision of railway development that shaped the TAZARA project.

This book goes beyond an analysis of state power and development "from above" in its approach to the history of the TAZARA railway project. While continuing to locate TAZARA in its historical context of post-colonialism and the Cold War, this book argues that a state-led development project in Africa could have outcomes that differed from the visions of its master planners. It does so by understanding the Freedom Railway from the perspective of the Ordinary Train—by recovering the railway's history from the memories of those who built it and from the life histories of its users. Further, this study uses new methodologies for reconstructing the history and outcome of a post-colonial development project, by collecting and analyzing the parcel receipts left behind at the individual stations along the railway corridor, and by comparing satellite images with field observations in order to document landscape change.

This approach helps us to understand the local experience of railway development in rural communities in East Africa, while showing at the same time that concepts of locality and belonging were negotiated and contested in the multispatial world of the railway corridor. It would be wrong, however, to think about this book merely as a local case study. The unexpected outcomes and the contradictions that accompanied railway development during this project were far broader in their scope. This history of the TAZARA railway raises larger questions about a wide range of historical issues, among them the history of development ideology as it was put into practice through technology transfer in Chinese aid to Africa, rhetorics of solidarity and practices of social cohesion during work on a transnational project, and the sustainability of relationships between people and the environment in the context of demographic transformation and landscape change.

Development, Ideology, and Technology Transfer

China was in the early stages of the Cultural Revolution when Tanzanian and Zambian delegations arrived in Beijing to sign the first railway construction agreement in September 1967.[1] During the 1960s and '70s China's model of rural development, in particular its experience with transforming rural agrarian production, was perceived positively by African visiting delegations. China intended to overcome its own "blank slate" of underdevelopment, and visitors to rural communes in China were impressed not only by the material technologies they witnessed there but also by the pace of change made possible, in their view, by the ideologies of hard work, solidarity, and self-reliance.

Thus, for newly independent African countries, one of the relevant aspects of China's experience with rural transformation was the Chinese emphasis on accelerated development. This could be seen in the effort made to complete the TAZARA project ahead of schedule: speed in construction would show the world what poor countries could do when they helped one another, as speechmakers announced; it was also a part of the discourse and practice of rural modernization. The combination of ideology and acceleration could be seen as having positive outcomes when ideology stressed hard work, solidarity, and the setting aside of negative attitudes. When it came to the development principles of training and skill development, on the other hand, and the creation of African self-reliance through the reduction of dependency upon outside experts, there were contradictions.

Despite these contradictions, the experience of railway construction and living along TAZARA was a transformative one for many African workers and for the rural communities of the railway corridor. And what of the Chinese railway workers from Tianjin, Chengdu, and Hebei who traveled to East Africa to work on the project for two to six years—in what ways might their work experience have also been transformative? Preliminary interviews with a small number of retired railway workers in China, while not representative, suggest that the experience of construction work was meaningful and did bring change to their lives and outlooks. Railway workers from Tianjin recalled that they had no other opportunity at the time to travel outside of China and little knowledge of what awaited them in East Africa. Yet they remember having had positive feelings about traveling abroad, with hopes of broadening their understanding of the world at a time when life in China was very difficult. Some described finding living conditions in East Africa that were more comfortable than those back at home, where food and other essential goods were rationed. Several Chinese railway workers decided to return to Africa after construction was completed, some of them several times, to work in the training workshop at Mpika, for example, or to join the Chinese Railway Experts Team that continued to maintain a presence in Dar es Salaam.

Solidarity

The TAZARA project's discursive foundations—including such slogans as "the poor helping the poor" and the ubiquitous usage of the terms "friend" and "friendship"— emphasized solidarity. This included solidarity among the workers on the project, between the pan-African partners of Tanzania and Zambia, and the larger networks of Afro-Asian and third world solidarity. Solidarity between the Chinese and African workers was emphasized at all levels of the project through speeches, worker meetings, news announcements, and even the Chinese comedic genre known as crosstalk, or *xiangsheng*. At the same time, observers of the project's social structures were struck by the high level of segregation in the work camps and in the off-duty behavior of the Chinese technicians. There was an apparent contradiction here: on the one hand, official statements and other forms of project rhetoric stressed friendship and solidarity. On the other hand, however, actual behavior indicated a Chinese reluctance to interact with African people.

In practice, TAZARA workers experienced both social cohesion and social distance while working on the project. Following their own initiative, workers built relationships that were neither envisioned nor initiated by the project's planners. They formed social groups on the basis of diverse ethnic and linguistic identities, groups that gave those far from home a feeling of belonging. At the same time, the formation of these social groups was a reminder of differences in worker identities, for both the African and the Chinese workers. Project planners had initially imagined that the African workers would eat their meals together in large dining halls, in what were called "family" or *ujamaa* groups, using the language of Julius Nyerere's African socialism. In practice, many workers organized smaller groups to carry out meal preparation and dining, based on connections with places of origin and particular staple foods. There were other ways that groups came together and acknowledged common identities or experiences during construction. Specific work sites and tasks could define identities. In particular, where work teams stayed together in one place for long periods of time—for example, in the tunnels section—stronger social bonds were created. The same was true for those who worked at the base camps in workshops and for those Africans who went abroad to China for further study.

Themes of social cohesion and social difference continued after the railway's construction as migrants came to the TAZARA corridor to settle and farm. While the initial settlement plans of the Tanzanian government had been based on the rural development vision of *ujamaa* villagization—a project through which a national concept of familyhood and belonging would be encouraged—over time the groups that settled along the railway moved to places where they lived among those who shared common languages, farming practices, food preferences, and social networks. Thus while the settlement plans that accompanied the railway's completion had a grand vision of government-led development through villagization, over time people grouped themselves in ways that associated place with identity. The migration and settlement patterns that followed TAZARA's construction led to conflicts between those who saw themselves as indigenous or local, and those who were newcomers, thereby reviving debates about belonging and difference that went back to the colonial and pre-colonial periods.

How the Railway Was Used

The planners of the TAZARA railway had a development vision of how the railway would be used. Those in the countryside who awaited the railway's completion also had visions of what the railway would bring to their communities and livelihoods. This was reflected in the anticipation that Carol Mpandamgongo remembers when local people first heard the news of TAZARA and cried out, "*Jamani!* Hey everyone! The railway is coming!" Paul Bolstad remembers that when he was a Peace Corps volunteer at Sonjo, he felt a similar sense of excitement along with the other leaders of the settlement and outgrower scheme where he worked. If the railway could be used to ferry sugar cane, they imagined, it could help to provide a vital link between the outgrowers and the sugar factory at Mkamba.

Twenty years later, the train was not carrying sugar through Sonjo and the other villages along the railway where the outgrowers lived. Rather, the Ordinary Train was carrying people and rice, ferrying passengers from the outgrower areas, where fields were taken up with sugar cane planting and where land was already in short supply, and taking them out to their outlying farms where there were also opportunities for casual labor and small-scale trading. The Ordinary Train could therefore be seen as serving the people and their economic needs. Yet the train, by serving this community of rural people, was also serving the sugar company and its labor casualization policies. For it was the availability of fertile farmland made accessible by the Ordinary Train that facilitated conversion to sugar cane on outgrower farms. The presence of the train cushioned the social and economic impact when the sugar company laid off workers who subsequently took up farming and trading or were hired back as casual labor for the company. Thus the Ordinary Train served the company not by carrying sugar but by supporting alternative livelihood options as Illovo reduced its commitment to long-term and short-term security for its workers.

The TAZARA railway facilitated the creation of multi-spatial rural livelihoods for its users in the context of economic uncertainty that accompanied Tanzania's liberalization and structural adjustment policies. It provided access to fertile farmland and to markets for agricultural products. Extractive products such as charcoal, timber, and dried fish were carried as parcels on the Ordinary Train. Yet as the spatial pattern of cultivation and settlement expands southeastward toward Mlimba and the steep escarpment below Makambako, the long-term sustainability of this livelihood strategy may be in question. Members of local communities have already expressed their concerns about the influx of immigrants who have brought with them different ways of farming, fishing, and trading. These concerns not only are about the numbers of people moving into the TAZARA corridor, but, just as importantly, are about methods of resource extraction—and the disregard for local practices—that outsiders bring with them. Newcomers bring development, local people say, but they also bring environmental degradation, revealing yet another contradiction of the railway's history. The same railway service that allows rural families to extend their settlement and productivity westward has resulted in new tensions and conflicts as the Kilombero valley fills in with new farms and farmers.

These tensions are related to measurable changes in landscape cover—including steep declines in grassland and wooded grassland vegetation—and in the availability of other natural resources that form the basis for rural livelihoods and environmental sustainability.

The Present and Future of TAZARA

By the time this book is published, it is possible that privatization of the TAZARA railway will be underway. Privatization has been agreed to in principle by China, Tanzania, and Zambia, and while a final decision has not yet been made, it appears likely that the railway will be taken over by a Chinese engineering company. Privatization will bring significant changes for a project that has been operated through a binational administrative body for over thirty years. TAZARA will join the Urafiki Textile Mill and other Chinese projects in Africa from the 1960s and '70s that have been handed over in recent years to private companies. As the "people's railway" becomes a commercial enterprise run by a private Chinese firm (if this is indeed what happens), it will be interesting to observe the ways that claims to ownership of the railway are framed by representatives of China, Tanzania, and Zambia, as well as by TAZARA workers and by the railway's users.

TAZARA now operates in the midst of an overall expansion of Chinese infrastructure projects in Africa, some of which will make direct connections to the TAZARA line as part of an extensive central African railway network. In this context, the history of TAZARA is important for understanding not only the past history of Chinese development assistance, but also its present and future. It reminds us that railway development takes place through the mobilization of technology and labor using historically specific social values and practices. By using life histories, parcel receipts, satellite images, and other methods, this book illustrates the importance of going beyond abstract generalizations about Chinese interventions in Africa to understand the way development assistance was experienced by the historical actors themselves.

At the same time, there are also historical continuities in the experience of Chinese development assistance. Many of China's present-day principles of nonintervention in the internal affairs of African states, for example, including a "no strings attached" approach to conditionality, were at the top of the list of the Eight Principles of Development Assistance distributed by Zhou Enlai during his African tour in 1963–64. The TAZARA project continues to retain symbolic significance in the framing of China's present and future relationship with Africa. This was made apparent in April 2008 when the Olympic torch relay was held in Dar es Salaam.

Tanzania was the only country in Africa selected to host the torch on its route to Beijing for the Olympics. The starting point for the torch relay in Dar es Salaam was the grand passenger terminal of TAZARA. The relay team ran with the torch from TAZARA through the old city to the newly built sports complex in Temeke, a project funded in 2005 with an 8.5-million-shilling gift from China.

The plans for the Olympic torch relay in Dar es Salaam were designed to chart a symbolic path of Chinese development assistance in Tanzania from TAZARA to the new sports stadium at Temeke. The relay route would thereby mark the passage of time as well as the continuity of Chinese commitment, as the torch would be carried from the flagship development project of the Cold War to the newest donation of China's wealth to the Tanzanian people. On one end of the spectrum, the TAZARA railway would symbolize an earlier period of assistance when resources were scarce and development aid involved "the poor helping the poor." The new sports complex, on the other end, could be seen as a marker of the possibilities of development for a new China and its relationship with Africa into the future. Whatever its other intended meanings, however, the relay evoked a collective memory in which the TAZARA railway holds primary place as an enduring symbol of Afro-Chinese friendship and development.

The torch relay celebrated one vision of TAZARA's development legacy, one that is referenced most often during state visits between Chinese and African officials. This book has shown that memories of TAZARA—and the visions of rural development that have accompanied them—are multiple. They include the remembered experience of the African and Chinese workers who built the project, as well as the stories of lives and livelihoods told by those who live alongside and use the railway. These life stories often share a development vision of progress and modernization that can mirror the vision of the state. At the same time, life stories contain reflections on the uncertainties and economic insecurity of everyday life in rural East Africa. In both kinds of stories—those of progress as well as those of uncertainty—the TAZARA railway plays a central role.

Postscript

When we completed the field research for this book project in 2002, our final interviews were carried out in the small railway stations along the TAZARA line between Msolwa and Makambako, in particular at those stations such as Mbingu that had experienced dramatic changes in demography, settlement, and economic activity by the end of the decade of the 1990s. During our last visit to Mbingu we had been impressed especially by the trade in green bananas and paddy rice that was attracting a large number of traders from outside the area and stimulating local agricultural production.

In the summer of 2010 we returned to Mbingu as part of a new TAZARA research project on technology and labor. We were amazed to find the station almost deserted, the once-bustling platform empty, and the offices of the railway authority locked up tight. No longer were there stacks of bananas being weighed and tabulated by the parcels clerk; there were no groups of young traders sitting in the shade of trees awaiting shipment of their gunny sacks filled with paddy.

We learned that since 2002, the services provided by TAZARA to local passengers and to small-scale traders had steadily declined. The *kipisi* shuttle train had already been eliminated due to the shortage of working locomotives that has plagued the railway for several years. By 2010 only two trains per week were serving passengers, both of them express trains. Only one of these trains stopped at the smaller stations on the Tanzanian side of the border, and this service was restricted to the return trip to Dar es Salaam (the express train on the Zambian side offered a similar service on its way from Tunduma to Kapiri Mposhi). Even these express trains were often held up by accidents and other delays that caused passengers and traders to wait for hours or even days for their goods to be shipped.

As passenger services to the smaller stations were reduced, the resident TAZ-ARA workforce was also reduced or even eliminated. A large number of stations were downgraded to "halt" stops where the train would only stop for a brief period of time. Meanwhile, the luggage vans available for shipping parcels were also in short supply, meaning that frequently there was only one luggage van (holding a maximum of 20 tons) per train or even no luggage van at all. Some traders responded by stuffing their products through the windows of the passenger carriages, where they filled the aisles and made boarding the train difficult, even dangerous. Others were forced to leave their parcels on the platforms to await the next train, in the process incurring the costs of several nights' subsistence in the local town as well as the risk of spoilage. One late night on the platform at Mlimba, we witnessed live chickens in cages, a shipment of papayas, and many other parcels left behind at the station by a passenger train already filled to capacity.

The closure of stations and the reduction of TAZARA services have affected passengers, traders, and agricultural producers alike. And just as they did in the past when station closures affected their livelihoods, communities of affected people have come together to protest the actions of the railway authority. Small-scale traders responded by writing letters to their local government officials. Farmers—in particular the retired civil servants (including a university professor) who have taken up commercial agriculture near the stations—also lodged a formal protest, first with TAZARA local staff and then with higher-level representatives. This effort resulted in the re-opening of two of the stations—Mbingu and Kiberege—so that they could retain enough staff to process tickets and parcels, and to inspect the railway line.

While the local picture at Mbingu looked grim in July 2010, there was an overall feeling of renewed optimism about the future of TAZARA following the adoption of "turnaround" policies under new Managing Director Akashambatwa Mbikusita-Lewanika, including the infusion of $40 million in interest-free loan support pledged by the Chinese government in December 2009. The railway is rehabilitating its existing rolling stock and hopes to take advantage of new markets for metals despite increasing competition from other infrastructure developments in the region. Even passenger services are due for a face-lift, in an ambitious effort to bring passenger traffic up to 1.5 million per year. Whether this rehabilitation will make a difference at the level of small stations like Mbingu, however, remains to be seen.

Appendix 1

*Eight Principles Governing China's Economic
and Technical Aid to Other Countries*

These principles were put forth by Zhou Enlai during his 1963–64 visit to Africa (English language version dated 1965, National Archives of Zambia, Ministry of Foreign Affairs, 1/64/1).

1. The Chinese Government always bases itself on the principle of equality and mutual benefit in providing aid to other countries. It never regards such aid as a kind of unilateral alms but as something mutual. Through such aid the friendly new emerging countries gradually develop their own national economy, free themselves from colonial control, and strengthen the anti-imperialist forces in the world. This is in itself a tremendous support to China.

2. In providing aid to other countries, the Chinese Government strictly respects the sovereignty of the recipient countries, and never asks for any privileges or attaches any conditions.

3. The Chinese Government provides economic aid in the form of interest-free or low-interest loans and extends the time limit for the repayment so as to lighten the burden of the recipient countries as far as possible.

4. In providing aid to other countries, the purpose of the Chinese Government is not to make the recipient countries dependent on China but to help them embark on the road of self-reliance step by step.

5. The Chinese Government tries its best to help the recipient countries build projects which require less investment while yielding quicker results, so the recipient government may increase its income and accumulate capital.

6. The Chinese Government provides the best-quality equipment and material of its own manufacture at international market prices. If the equipment and material provided by the Chinese Government are not up to the agreed specifications and quality, the Chinese Government undertakes to replace them.

7. In giving any particular technical assistance, the Chinese Government will see to it that the personnel of the recipient country fully master such techniques.

8. The experts dispatched by the Chinese Government to help in construction in the recipient countries will have the same standard of living as the experts of the recipient country. The Chinese experts are not allowed to make any special demands or enjoy any special amenities.

Appendix 2

Parcel Shipments to and from
Selected Rail Stations, 1998–2000

Appendix Table 2.1. Parcel Shipments from Mang'ula to Other Stations

	DSM[a]	Ifakara	Mngeta	Chita	Mlimba	Makambako
Maize	13	3	0	0	0	0
Rice	821	1	3	2	1	19
Paddy	118	12	0	0	6	· 5
Millet	0	0	1	0	0	0
Banana	20	0	0	0	0	2
Dried Fish	2	1	6	3	2	0
Tomatoes	0	0	0	0	0	0
Onions	0	0	0	0	0	0
Cabbages	0	0	0	0	0	0
Beans	0	0	0	0	1	0
Empty Crates	5	0	22	1	3	21
Consumer Goods	6	2	51	58	13	2
Bicycles	6	0	15	4	13	9

Notes: These tables represents the top thirteen items out of a total of forty-four different items shipped from the five primary stations included in the study. Because of its prominence as a destination, Dar es Salaam is also listed here. Each number represents one shipment of parcels of diverse weights and quantities; the total number of shipments in the database is 33,829.
a) Dar es Salaam

Appendix Table 2.2. Parcel Shipments from Ifakara to Other Stations
Goods Shipped as Parcels

	DSM	Mang'ula	Mngeta	Chita	Mlimba	Makambako
Maize	95	4	5	3	20	7
Rice	1348	0	7	2	15	83
Paddy	141	0	5	3	6	28
Millet	1	0	0	0	0	0
Banana	175	0	0	0	0	0
Dried Fish	201	6	0	3	14	45
Tomatoes	1	0	0	0	3	1
Onions	0	0	0	1	1	0
Cabbages	0	0	0	0	1	0
Beans	3	0	0	0	6	0
Empty Crates	7	1	7	8	20	214
Consumer Goods	24	0	6	14	50	38
Bicycles	26	1	24	35	94	24

Appendix Table 2.3. Parcel Shipments from Mngeta to Other Stations
Goods Shipped as Parcels

	DSM	Mang'ula	Ifakara	Chita	Mlimba	Makambako
Maize	42	39	36	0	19	6
Rice	291	1	0	0	0	16
Paddy	51	4	3	0	5	312
Millet	0	0	0	0	0	0
Banana	288	3	7	0	52	4
Dried Fish	109	7	1	0	10	4
Tomatoes	1	0	7	0	0	0
Onions	0	0	0	0	0	0
Cabbages	0	0	0	0	0	0
Beans	7	0	0	0	0	0
Empty Crates	1	1	1	0	0	0
Consumer Goods	0	0	0	0	0	0
Bicycles	4	1	1	0	6	5

Appendix Table 2.4. Parcel Shipments from Chita to Other Stations
Goods Shipped as Parcels

	DSM	Mang'ula	Ifakara	Mngeta	Mlimba	Makambako
Maize	16	0	24	0	0	1
Rice	675	1	2	0	3	161
Paddy	37	0	32	0	2	180
Millet	0	0	0	0	0	0
Banana	32	0	4	0	1	2
Dried Fish	24	2	0	0	5	0
Tomatoes	0	0	0	0	1	0
Onions	0	0	0	0	0	0
Cabbages	0	0	0	0	0	0
Beans	2	0	0	0	0	0
Empty Crates	0	0	0	0	0	3
Consumer Goods	2	0	2	0	3	1
Bicycles	2	0	2	0	3	8

Appendix Table 2.5. Parcel Shipments from Mlimba to Other Stations
Goods Shipped as Parcels

	DSM	Mang'ula	Ifakara	Mngeta	Chita	Makambako
Maize	16	2	1	0	1	15
Rice	99	0	1	0	0	44
Paddy	2	0	0	0	0	8
Millet	0	0	0	0	0	0
Banana	2	0	0	0	0	0
Dried Fish	7	0	0	0	0	16
Tomatoes	0	0	1	0	0	0
Onions	0	0	0	0	0	0
Cabbages	0	0	0	0	0	0
Beans	1	0	0	0	0	0
Empty Crates	14	0	3	1	1	10
Consumer Goods	0	0	1	0	0	2
Bicycles	0	0	1	0	0	3

Appendix Table 2.6. Parcel Shipments from Makambako to Other Stations
Goods Shipped as Parcels

	DSM	Mang'ula	Ifakara	Mngeta	Chita	Mlimba
Maize	43	61	206	135	180	887
Rice	6	0	0	0	0	2
Paddy	0	0	0	0	0	1
Millet	20	15	47	149	196	279
Banana	1	0	2	0	0	1
Dried Fish	2	0	0	4	4	23
Tomatoes	516	51	460	77	276	608
Onions	11	2	30	112	136	233
Cabbages	1	13	131	90	55	101
Beans	63	10	110	99	176	322
Empty Crates	0	1	4	6	16	33
Consumer Goods	3	1	68	274	296	220
Bicycles	2	3	12	20	19	135

Appendix 3

Land Cover Change, Kilombero Valley Study Area

Note: Differences in total Land Cover Type reflect small variations in computing individual land covers. Data collected by Jesse Grossman.

Appendix Figure 3.1. Kilombero Valley landscape change, 1975–2001.
Analysis by Jesse Grossman.

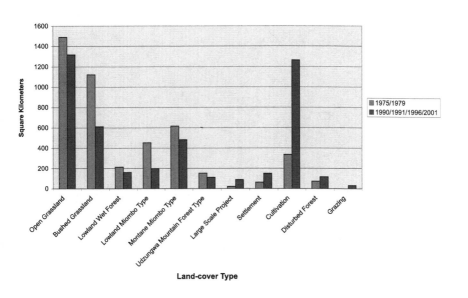

Appendix Figure 3.2. Mlimba-Mngeta area landscape change, 1975–1991.
Analysis by Jesse Grossman.

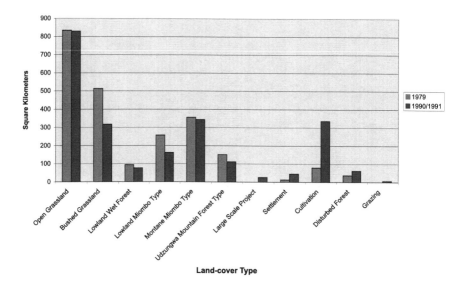

Tazara Rural History Survey, Jamie Monson and Jesse Grossman, 2002

Appendix Figure 3.3. Ifakara-Mang'ula area landscape change, 1975–1996.
Analysis by Jesse Grossman.

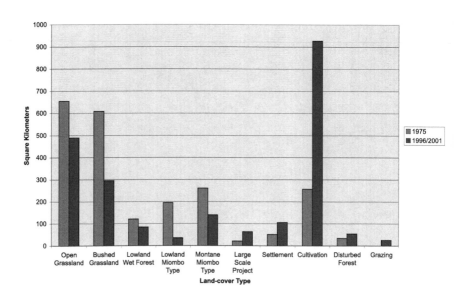

Tazara Rural History Survey, Jamie Monson and Jesse Grossman, 2002

Appendix Table 3.1. Land Cover Change in Mlimba, 1979–1990

Land Cover Type	1979	1990
	Area, Square Kilometers	Area, Square Kilometers
Open Grassland (Seasonally Inundated)	349	325
Bushed Grassland	88	25
Lowland Wet Forest	52	46
Lowland Miombo	204	123
Montane Miombo	281	271
Udzungwa Mountain Forest	29	28
Settlement	1	3
Cultivation	49	212
TOTAL	1053	1033

Appendix Table 3.2. Land Cover Change in Mngeta, 1979–1990/91

Land Cover Type	1979	1990–91
	Area, Square Kilometers	Area, Square Kilometers
Open Grassland (Seasonally Inundated)	485	504
Bushed Grassland	425	291
Lowland Wet Forest	41	29
Lowland Miombo	53	38
Montane Miombo	74	72
Udzungwa Mountain Forest	122	82
Large Scale Project	0	25
Settlement	11	42
Cultivation	30	124
Disturbed Forest	37	61
Grazing	0	6
TOTAL	1278	1274

Appendix Table 3.3. Land Cover Change in Ifakara, 1975–1996

Land Cover Type	1975	1996
	Area, Square Kilometers	Area, Square Kilometers
Open Grassland (Seasonally Inundated)	597	469
Bushed Grassland	447	295
Lowland Wet Forest	88	73
Lowland Miombo	146	35
Montane Miombo	207	139
Large Scale Project	4	25
Settlement	43	85
Cultivation	148	542
Disturbed Forest	34	39
Grazing	0	25
TOTAL	1714	1727

Appendix Table 3.4. Land Cover Change in Mang'ula, 1975–2001

Land Cover Type	1975	2001
	Area, Square Kilometers	Area, Square Kilometers
Open Grassland (Seasonally Inundated)	57	19
Bushed Grassland	161	0
Lowland Wet Forest	32	11
Lowland Miombo	49	0
Montane Miombo	53	0
Large Scale Project	17	38
Settlement	8	20
Cultivation	109	385
Disturbed Forest	0	15
TOTAL	486	488

Notes

1. Introduction

1. Tanzania Zambia Railway Authority, *Archives Booklet (draft)* (2007), 29, courtesy of James Mwitangeti; James Mwitangeti, personal communication, 16 August 2007.

2. "The Tortoise and the Hare," *Newsweek,* 25 October 1971, 56. See also Philip Snow, *The Star Raft: China's Encounter with Africa* (New York: Weidenfeld and Nicolson, 1988), 165.

3. Servacius B. Likwelile, interview by author, Dar es Salaam, April 2000. See also Servacius B. Likwelile, "An Analysis of Efficiency in the Trucking Industry in Tanzania" (Ph.D. thesis, University of Dar es Salaam, 1996).

4. U.S. Congress, *Congressional Record—House* (Washington: U.S. Government Printing Office, 18 January 1973), H 286.

5. George T. Yu, *China's African Policy: A Study of Tanzania* (London: Praeger, 1975), 132.

6. Kim Jaycox, telephone interview by author, 26 October 1999; "Highway, Railroad Compete in Tanzania," *Christian Science Monitor,* 27 December 1972, 4; Alan Hutchinson, *China's African Revolution* (London: Hutchinson, 1975), 270.

7. Servacius B. Likwelile, interview by author, Dar es Salaam, April 2000.

8. Wang Qinmei, interview by author, Beijing, 29 June 2007.

9. *The Nationalist,* 2 October 1969; emphasis in original.

10. Thomas Land, "Chinese Working on the Railroad," *The Nation,* 19 October 1970, 371.

11. J. M. Mukama, "Mwenyekiti wa Kamati ya Suala la Kufungwa kwa Stesheni ya Mbingu, to Mbunge wa Kilombero, Wilaya ya Kilombero, Re: Kufungwa kwa Stesheni ya TAZARA—Mbingu," 1 August 1994. Kilombero District File R.40/6.

12. CIA Special Report, "Tanzania Taking the Left Turn," 21 May, 1965.

13. "Red Guard Line Chugging into Africa," *Wall Street Journal,* 29 September 1967.

14. "Comrades-in-Arms: Tanzania in Front Line of the People's Fight," *The Nationalist*, 7 June 1965, 2.

15. Yu, *China's African Policy*, 108.

16. Du Jian, interview by author, Dar es Salaam, July 2000.

17. Raymond Ndimbo, interview by author, Mbeya, 29 July 2006.

18. Tanzania National Archives (TNA) C/2112/71, IS/I.317, 23 September 1971.

19. D. D. S. M. Mumello, "Final Report on Tunnels Construction, Mkela Base Camp," 1972.

20. This has been documented by Lisa Lindsay, in her work on masculinity and colonial railway labor in West Africa. Lisa Lindsay and Stephan Miescher, eds., *Men and Masculinities in Modern Africa* (Portsmouth, N.H.: Heinemann, 2003). For Tanzania, see Thaddeus Sunseri, *Vilimani: Labor Migration and Rural Change in Early Colonial Tanzania* (Portsmouth, N.H.: Heinemann, 2002).

21. A description of the application of this Chinese development model of labor in Africa can be found in Deborah Bräutigam, *Chinese Aid and African Development: Exporting Green Revolution* (New York: St. Martin's, 1998), 148–151.

22. Dick Foeken and Samuel Owuor, "Multi-spatial Livelihoods in Sub-Saharan Africa: Rural Farming by Urban Households—The Case of Nakuru Town, Kenya," in *Mobile Africa: Changing Patterns of Movement in Africa and Beyond*, ed. Mirjam de Bruijn, Rijk van Dijk, and Dick Foeken (Boston: Brill, 2001); Deborah Bryceson, "Multiplex Livelihoods in Rural Africa: Recasting the Terms and Conditions of Gainful Employment," *Journal of Modern African Studies* 40, no. 1 (2002): 1–28.

23. A large section of the railway between Msolwa and Dar es Salaam runs mostly through the Selous Reserve and is therefore uninhabited.

24. Susan Geiger, *TANU Women: Gender and Culture in the Making of Tanganyikan Nationalism, 1955–1965* (Portsmouth, N.H.: Heinemann, 1997); Stephan Miescher, Louise White, and David Cohen, eds., *African Lives, African Voices: Critical Practices in Oral History* (Bloomington: Indiana University Press, 2001).

25. Elizabeth Tonkin, *Narrating Our Pasts: The Social Construction of Oral History* (Cambridge: Cambridge University Press, 1992). See also Kathleen Canning, "Feminist History after the Linguistic Turn: Historicizing Discourse and Experience," *Signs* 19, no. 2 (1994): 368–404.

26. The thesis of Ali Mohamed Sendaro is an unusually helpful source for this reason. A. M. Sendaro, "Workers' Efficiency, Motivation and Management: The Case of the Tanzania-Zambia Railway Construction" (Ph.D. diss., University of Dar es Salaam, 1987).

27. George Yu, "Dragon in the Bush: Peking's Presence in Africa," *Asian Survey* 8 (1968): 1025–1026.

28. Scholars and journalists wishing to write about Chinese-Tanzanian relations were treated with suspicion in the late 1960s and early 1970s. The Nigerian scholar Alaba Ogunsanwo, whose work is cited in this book, was arrested and detained in 1969 while carrying out his doctoral thesis on China in Africa. Alan Hutchison describes being arrested at Dar es Salaam harbor while photographing the off-loading of Zambian copper. Hutchinson, *China's African Revolution*, 267.

2. Railway Visions

1. The southern African network used the wide gauge (3'6"), while the eastern network used the meter or 3'3" gauge.

2. "Kaunda on Completion of Uhuru Railway: Great Victory for the People," *Daily News*, 24 October 1975.

3. *CIA Intelligence Report*, "Prospects for the Tan-Zam Railway," 8 November 1965.

4. Tonderai Makoni, "The Economic Appraisal of the Tanzania-Zambia Railway," *The African Review* 2, no. 4 (1972): 606.

5. The Tanga line was initiated with private capital early in the 1890s, then taken over by the German imperial government in 1899. According to Clements Gillman, the Tanga line was an important stimulus for German plantation development in the Tanga hinterland. Clements Gillman, "A Short History of the Tanganyika Railways," *Tanganyika Notes and Records* 13 (1942): 14.

6. For example, the surveys of Paul Fuchs, "Die wirtschaftliche Erkundung einer ostafrikanischen Südbahn," *Beiheft zum Tropenplanzer* 6, no. 4/5 (1905), and "Wirtschaftliche Eisenbahn-Erkundigen in mittleren und nördlichen Deutsch-Ostafrika," *Beiheft zum Tropenpflanzer* 11, no. 8 (1907). See also Juhani Koponen, *Development for Exploitation: German Colonial Policies in Mainland Tanzania, 1884–1914* (Helsinki: Lit Verlag, 1994), 303–307.

7. Fuchs, "Die wirtschaftliche Erkundung," 3.

8. For a summary of German policy on *Mittelafrika* see Helmuth Stoecker, *German Imperialism in Africa* (London: 1986), 250–263. Koponen argues that the *Mittelafrika* concept was more important to politicians than to investors; Koponen, *Development for Exploitation*, 314. Clements Gillman meanwhile denied that the concept of *Mittelafrika* had any role in German colonial railway policy; Gillman, "A Short History,"15.

9. See for example G. Lieder, "Zur Kenntnis des Karawanenwege im südlichen Teile des ostafrikanischen Schutzgebietes," *Mitteilungen aus den Deutschen Schutzgebieten* 7 (1894): 271–282; G. Lieder, "Beobachtungen auf der Ubena-Nyasa Expedition, November 1893 bis 30 Marz 1894," *Mitteilungen aus den Deutschen Schutzgebieten* 7 (1894): 271–277.

10. Fuchs, "Wirtschaftliche Eisenbahn-Erkundungen"; Fuchs, "Die wirtschaftliche Erkundung."

11. Clements Gillman later scoffed at these "misconceptions," especially the "pitifully exaggerated notion of the fertility of tropical soils, of teeming millions of population, or unbounded dormant wealth, both agricultural and mineral." Gillman, "A Short History," 15.

12. Koponen, *Development for Exploitation*, 302.

13. M. F. Hill, *Permanent Way II: The Story of the Tanganyika Railways* (Nairobi: 1967), 101.

14. F. D. Hammond, "Report on the Railway Systems of Kenya, Uganda and Tanganyika" (London: 1921); Edward Grigg, "Railways" (Nairobi, 1926), 4.

15. Werner Biermann, *Tanganyika Railways—Carrier of Colonialism: An Account of Economic Indicators and Social Fragments* (Munster: Afrikanische Studien, 1995), 38. Gillman argued that the hinterland of Tanganyika would never be able to support a railway in the way that the interior of Kenya and Uganda could. Gillman, "A Short History," 36–37.

16. East African Railways and Harbors Administration, *Report on an Engineering Survey of a Rail Link between the East African and Rhodesian Railway Systems* (Nairobi: Government Printing Office, June 1952).

17. "Uhuru Railway Opens Today," *Tanzania Daily News*, 23 October 1975.

18. R. M. Bostock, "The Transport Sector," in *Constraints on the Economic Development of Zambia*, ed. Charles Elliot (Oxford: Oxford University Press: 1971), 323–376.

19. Bostock, "The Transport Sector," 323–376. See also Tonderai Makoni, "The Economic Appraisal of the Tanzania-Zambia Railway," *African Review* (1972). For an overview of Rhodesian railway construction see Jon Lunn, "The Political Economy of Primary Railway Construction in the Rhodesias, 1890–1911," *Journal of African History* 33, no. 2 (1992): 239–254.

20. Bostock, "The Transport Sector," 370.

21. J. S. Lemkin, "Memorandum on Certain Constitutional Aspects Concerning Rhodesian Railways and Proposed New Railway," London, 19 March 1965, NAZ MFA 1/41/1.

22. "North-East Rail Link," Permanent Secretary, Ministry of Foreign Affairs to All Heads of Zambian Missions, National Archives of Zambia, Ministry of Foreign Affairs (NAZ MFA) 1/103/107A, n.d.

23. Minutes of Meeting of Zambian Ministers with the Rt. Hon. Mrs. Barbara Castle, British Minister of Overseas Development, 25 April 1965, NAZ MFA 1/41/16. Ngila Mwase, "The Tanzania-Zambia Railway: The Chinese Loan and the Pre-Investment Analysis Revisited," *Journal of Modern African Studies* 21, no. 3 (1983): 537.

24. M. B. Gleave, "The Dar es Salaam Transport Corridor: An Appraisal," *African Affairs* 91 (1992): 249–267.

25. Ngila Mwase, "The Future of TAZARA in a Post-Apartheid Southern Africa," *Southern African Perspectives* (Cape Town: Center for Southern African Studies, University of the Western Cape, March 1993), 2–3. Bostock, "The Transport Sector," 356–357.

26. Meeting of Zambian ministers with the Rt. Hon. Mrs. Barbara Castle, British Minister of Overseas Development, 25 April 1965. NAZ MFA 1/41/16.

27. Under-Secretary of Foreign Affairs to Permanent Secretary, 7 August 1965, NAZ MFA 1/41/40.

28. "Tanzania Rail Link," 28 September 1965, NAZ MFA 1/41/88–92.

29. "North-East Rail Link," Foreign Affairs Zambia to All Heads of Zambian Missions, NAZ MFA 1/103/107A, n.d.

30. "Tanzania Rail Link," 28 September 1965, NAZ MFA 1/41/88–92; Zambian High Commission, Dar es Salaam, to Foreign Ministry, Lusaka, telegram received 24 August 1965, NAZ MFA/1/41/66; George Yu, *China's African Policy*, 128–129.

31. Zambian Embassy Washington to Foreign Ministry Lusaka, telegram received 17 November 1967, NAZ MFA 1/103/144.

32. Kaiser Engineers International, Inc., to Kenneth Kaunda, 28 April 1967, NAZ MFA 1/103/86/1.

33. Government of the Republic of Zambia, Cabinet Minutes, *Railways: Zambia Tanzania Rail Link Project*, NAZ MFA 1/103/157 and *Railways: Zambia Tanzania Rail Link Project: The Maxwell Stamp Report*, NAZ MFA 1/103/162.

34. Tanza [sic] representative Peking to Foreign Affairs Lusaka, telegram received 5 September 1967, NAZ MFA 1/103/109.

35. Zambian Embassy Washington to Foreign Affairs Lusaka, telegram received 1 November 1967; "Peking Woos Africa Coyly: Tanzam Railway Backed," *Christian Science Monitor*, 10 October 1967.

36. "Supplementary Report," A. M. Chambeshi, Acting High Commissioner Dar es Salaam, to Foreign Affairs Lusaka, 19 September 1967, NAZ MFA 1/103/126.

37. Permanent Secretary Foreign Affairs to Minister Foreign Affairs, 19 September 1967, NAZ MFA 1/103/115.

38. "Africa's Progress in Transportation, Communications Reported," *North China News Agency* (NCNA), 1 August 1975.

39. "All Africa Is Standing Up," NCNA, 31 July 1975.

40. NCNA, 31 July 1975.

41. Philip Snow, *The Star Raft: China's Encounter with Africa* (New York: Weidenfeld and Nicolson, 1988), 166.

42. *Youyi de Caihong Bianji Xiaozu* [Editors of *Rainbow of Friendship*], *Youyi de Caihong* [*Rainbow of Friendship*]. Beijing: Renmin Wenxue Chubanshe, 1975.

43. Ian Taylor, *China and Africa: Engagement and Compromise* (London: Routledge, 2006), 25, citing NCNA, 4 February 1964.

44. Ian Taylor, *China and Africa: Engagement and Compromise*, 29; Warren Weinstein, ed., *Chinese and Soviet Aid to Africa* (New York: Praeger, 1975).

45. Speech made by Fang Yi, Minister of Economic Relations with Foreign Countries, during a state visit to Beijing by seven Tanzanian delegates. NCNA, 17 September 1975.

46. Oginga Odinga, *Not Yet Uhuru* (London: Hill and Wang, 1967), 190.

47. "Political and Economic Organisation in China and North Korea," report prepared after visit to China by Kenneth Kaunda and delegation, 9 May 1974, UNIP 6/7/50/25/1.

48. "To Serve the World's People with Sincerity," *Renmin Ribao*, 15 March 1968.

49. Kim Jaycox remembers that at the Chinese restaurant on the rooftop of the New Africa Hotel in Dar es Salaam, Mao's teachings and Mao buttons were distributed freely, and "the back streets were filled with revolutionaries" (telephone interview, 26 October 1999). Lorne Larson also remembers ubiquitous Mao buttons in Tanzania at the same time (personal communication).

50. "Rendering Full-Hearted Service to the World's People," *Renmin Ribao*, 26 September 1969.

51. Tariq Ismael, "The People's Republic of China and Africa," *The Journal of Modern African Studies* 9, no. 4 (1971): 526; Yu, *China and Tanzania*, 74.

52. "Crosstalk" recording by Ma Ji and Tang Jiezhong, http://www.haoting.com/hao123/126. htm.

53. George Yu, *China's African Policy*, 75.

54. Sunil Kamar Sahu, "Sino-Tanzanian Relations," *United Asia* 3, no. 2 (1971): 79.

55. Alaba Ogunsanwo, *China's Policy in Africa, 1958–71* (Cambridge: Cambridge University Press, 1974), citing NCNA, 18 June 1966; George Yu, *China's African Policy*, 85.

56. Cited in George Yu, *China and Tanzania*, 46.

57. Mwase, "The Tanzania-Zambia Railway," 539.

58. Personal communication with Saxton Kendrick, USAID railway maintenance specialist, 3 January 2002; Philemon Kaduma, interview with the author, Mbeya, 1998; Mwase, "The Tanzania-Zambia Railway," 539–540.

59. "Tanzania-Zambia Railway Project—Credit Commodity Arrangements," Ministry of Development and Finance to Permanent Secretary, Ministry of Foreign Affairs, 3 October 1969, NAZ MFA 1/286/23.

60. "Commodity Purchases from China," Ministry of Development and Finance to Permanent Secretary, Ministry of Foreign Affairs, 1 December 1969, NAZ MFA 1/286/116.

61. Mwase, "The Tanzania-Zambia Railway," 540.

62. "Bill for an Act to Provide for . . . the Establishment of the Tanzania-Zambia Railway Authority," effective as of 12 March 1968. NAZ MFA 103/209.

63. "Supplementary Agreement between the Government of the People's Republic of China and the Governments of the United Republic of Tanzania and the Republic of Zambia on the Construction of the Tanzania Zambia Railway," 14 November 1969, NAZ MFA 1/286/115.

64. "Proceedings of the First Meeting [of the RLC]," 12 April 1965, NAZ MFA 1/41/3.

65. "Meeting of Zambian Officials and the EAC on Harbours of 6th May, 1969 held in Dar es Salaam," NAZ MFA 1/286/69.

66. *CIA Intelligence Report*, "Communist Aid to Less Developed Countries of the Free World, 1974," 1 June 1975, 13.

67. "Jin Hui . . . the person who dreams about the Tanzania-Zambia Railroad," *People's Daily*, overseas edition, 25 January 2007; the same figure is also cited in Hu Zhichao, "The

Past, Present and Future of the Tanzania-Zambia Railroad," *Economic Research of Railroads* (2000): 46–47. At the peak of construction in 1972 there were 16,000 Chinese workers, according to Jin Hui, while the TAZARA annual report for 1972–73 lists a high of 13,500 in July 1972 declining to 11,500 in 1974. See also Zhang Tieshan, *Youyi Zhi Lu: Yuanjian Tanzan Tielu Jishi [Road of Friendship: The Memoirs of the Development Assistance of the Tanzania-Zambia Railroad]* (Beijing: Zhongguo Duiwai Jingji Maoyi Chubanshe, 1975) for more specific details and statistics.

68. "Red Guard Line Chugging into Africa," *Wall Street Journal*, 29 September 1967.

69. Wenping He, "Fifty Years through Wind and Rain," unpublished paper presented to International Conference on Blacks and Asians: Encounters through Time and Space, Boston University, April 2002.

3. Building the People's Railway

1. Zambian High Commission Dar es Salaam to Foreign Lusaka, 24 August 1965, NAZ MFA 1/41/66; R. Hall and H. Peyman, *The Great Uhuru Railway* (London: Gollancz, 1976), 107–108; Ali Mohamed Sendaro, "Workers' Efficiency, Motivation and Management: The Case of the Tanzania-Zambia Railway Construction" (Ph.D thesis, Department of Management, University of Dar es Salaam, 1987), 250; George Yu, *China's African Policy: A Study of Tanzania* (New York: 1975), 128.

2. "Communist Aid," *Kenya Weekly News*, 29 April 1966, 29.

3. "China's Gold-Tipped Wand Hovers over Eastern Africa," *The Economist*, 12 August 1967, 565.

4. This first survey preceded the lengthy negotiations that later took place between China, Tanzania, and Zambia. It did not cross the border into Zambia.

5. Clements Gillman, "A Short History of the Tanganyika Railways," *Tanganyika Notes and Records* 13 (1942): 51.

6. East African Railways and Harbors Administration, "Report on an Engineering Survey of a Rail Link between the East African and Rhodesian Railway Systems," Nairobi, June 1952, 11–12.

7. "Tanzania, Zambia Celebrate Railway Completion," NCNA, 24 October 1975.

8. Alaba Ogunsanwo, *China's Policy in Africa, 1958–71* (Cambridge: Cambridge University Press, 1974), 207–208. According to George Yu the completion of survey and design work had been announced publicly in April 1970; the Chinese account *Road of Friendship* lists the completion date as June of that year. George Yu, *China's African Policy*, 131; *Road of Friendship*, 388. The TAZARA *Annual Report for 1973–4* lists the survey and design phase as starting in May 1968 and finishing in May 1970.

9. "TAZARA—Lusaka Branch, Base Camp Number 2—Mpika, Progress Report for the Quarter Ending September 30, 1969," NAZ MFA 1/286/85.

10. Carol Mpandamgongo, interview by author, Ikule, 14 July 2000; Martin Mtwanga, interview by author, Mchombe, 9 July 2000.

11. Philemon Kigola, interview by author, Mang'ula, 5 August 2000.

12. "Jin Hui . . . The Person Who Dreams about the Tanzania-Zambia Railroad," *People's Daily*, overseas edition, 25 January 2007; Zhang Tieshan, *Youyi Zhi Lu: Yuanjian Tanzan Tielu Jishi [Road of Friendship: The Memoirs of the Development Assistance of the Tanzania-Zambia Railroad]* (Beijing: Zhongguo Duiwai Jingji Maoyi Chubanshe, 1975); Group interview in Beijing, 5 July 2007: Jin Hui, Lu Datong, Du Jian, Zhang Zhiying; Wang Hui Min, interview by author, Tianjin, 6 July 2007; Li Jin Wen, interview by author, Tianjin, 6 July 2007.

13. This plant, known botanically as *Mucuna*, is still ubiquitous throughout this section of the railway corridor. If the windows of the train compartment are left open, small irritating fibers can blow in and settle on blankets and clothing where it is impossible to see or remove them.

14. An encounter between a Chinese driver, Mr. Li, and *upupu* is described in Zhang, *Youyi Zhi Lu [Road of Friendship]*, 233. See also Hall and Peyman, *The Great Uhuru Railway*, 108–109.

15. Zhang, *Youyi Zhi Lu [Road of Friendship]*, 178–179; trans. Lingque Hu.

16. "They Are True Friends: Stories of Chinese and Tanzanian Workers in Rescuing Each Other," *Renmin Ribao*, 18 July 1972, 6; trans. Gu Yi.

17. Rogatus Nyumayo, interview by author, Mlimba, 26 July 2000.

18. Group interview in Beijing, 5 July 2007: Jin Hui, Lu Datong, Du Jian, Zhang Zhiying; Wang Hui Min, interview by author, Tianjin, 6 July 2007; Li Jin Wen, interview by author, Tianjin, 6 July 2007; Zhang, *Youyi Zhi Lu [The Road of Friendship]*, 209.

19. "Local Workers Participation in the Railway Construction," TAZARA Brief Progress Report, 3 March 1970, NAZ MFA 1/286/144, 4.

20. Benedict Mkanyago, interview by author, Mchombe, 7 July 2000.

21. Andrew John Mangile, interview by author, aboard *kipisi* train, 26 July 2000.

22. Rogatus Nyumayo, interview by author, Mlimba, 26 July 2000.

23. Salum Mwasenga, interview by author, Mang'ula, 30 July 2000.

24. Sendaro, "Workers' Efficiency," 199–205; D. D. S. M. Mumello, "Final Report on Tunnels Construction, Mkela Base Camp," 1972, 13; *The Standard*, 19 February 1970.

25. Mumello, "Final Report on Tunnels Construction."

26. "Administrative Assistant's Report from Kiberege Camp," November 1971, cited in Sendaro, "Workers' Efficiency," 201.

27. John Gilbert, interview by author, 20 April 2000.

28. Christian Bulaya, interview by author, Mchombe, 16 July 2000.

29. John Gilbert, interview by author, Ifakara, 20 April 2000.

30. Chinese project leader Jin Hui recalls that there was high turnover among the African workforce, and therefore the project was continuously recruiting new applicants. Jin Hui, interview by author, Beijing, 5 July 2007. See also "Jin Hui . . . The Person Who Dreams about the Tanzania-Zambia Railroad," *People's Daily*, overseas edition, 25 January 2007.

31. Mumello, "Final Report on Tunnels Construction," 3.

32. In the German period, "The greatest limitation to widespread availability of local day labor was plantation dependence on food supplies to feed their workers." Thaddeus Sunseri, *Vilimani: Labor Migration and Rural Change in Early Colonial Tanzania* (Portsmouth, N.H.: Heinemann, 2002), 55; similar patterns are described in Thomas Spear, *Mountain Farmers* (Berkeley: University of California Press, 1997), 87.

33. Base Camp No. 1, Report No. 14 of 1969, cited in Sendaro, "Worker's Efficiency," 210.

34. Philip Snow, *The Star Raft*, 162.

35. *TAZARA Annual Report*, 1973/4, 6.

36. Lao Wan, interview by author, Ifakara, July 2000; Du Jian, interview by author, Dar es Salaam, April 2000; Hall and Peyman, *The Great Uhuru Railway*, 122; *Drum Magazine*, November 1973, quoted in *The Story of Julius Nyerere: Africa's Elder Statesman* (Dar es Salaam, 1993), 186–187; Bruce Larkin, *China and Africa* (Berkeley: University of California Press, 1971), 99; personal communication with Thomas Spear, who witnessed the unloading of Chinese ships at Kurasini harbor in the early 1970s.

37. Julius Nyerere, *Freedom and Development* (Oxford: Oxford University Press, 1973), 239; Mumello, "Final Report on Tunnels Construction," iii.

38. Dexter Tiranti, "The Chinese in Africa," *New Internationalist*, May 1973, 12.

39. Salum Mwasenga, interview by author, Mang'ula, 30 July 2000; D. S. M. Mumello, interview by author, Njombe, July 2002; Mumello, "Final Report on Tunnels Construction," iii.

40. Benedict Mkanyago, interview by author, Mngeta, 7 July 2000.

41. Sendaro, "Workers' Efficiency," 169; D. S. M. Mumello, interview by author, Njombe, July 2002.

42. "Speed Along, Train of Friendship," *Renmin Ribao*, 4 February 1973, 4. I am grateful to Li Baoping for his assistance with this citation.

43. Moses Hassan and Benedict Mkanyago, group interview by author, Mngeta, 7 July 2000; Beatus Lihawa, interview by author, Mlimba, 20 July 2000; group interview in Beijing, 5 July 2007: Jin Hui, Lu Datong, Du Jian, Zhang Zhiying.

44. Mumello, "Final Report on Tunnels Construction," 14. Rogatus Nyumayo, interview by author, Mlimba, 26 July 2000.

45. Mumello, "Final Report on Tunnels Construction."

46. TAZARA Annual Report and Accounts for 1973–74, 11; Simon Katzenellenbogen, "Zambia and Rhodesia: Prisoners of the Past: A Note on the History of Railway Politics in Central Africa," *African Affairs* 73, no. 290 (January 1974), 63–66.

47. Sendaro, "Workers' Efficiency," 239.

48. Salum Mwasenga, interview by author, Mang'ula, 30 July 2000.

49. Letter from Administrative Assistant, 17 May 1971, cited in Sendaro, "Workers' Efficiency."

50. Raphael Chawala, interview by author, Ifakara, 20 April 2000.

51. Rogatus Nyumayo, interview by author, Mlimba, 26 July 2000; Salum Mwasenga, interview by author, Mang'ula, 30 July 2000; Hashim Mdemu, interview by author, Ifakara, June 2000. Hall and Peyman, *The Great Uhuru Railway*, 128.

52. Hashim Mdemu, interview by author, Ifakara, June 2000.

53. John Gilbert and Hosea Mngata, interview by author, Ifakara, 20 April 2000.

54. Rogatus Nyumayo, interview by author, Mlimba, 26 July 2000.

55. Beatus Lihawa, interview by author, Mlimba, 20 July 2000; Mumello, "Final Report on Tunnels Construction," 9.

56. Salum Mwasenga, interview by author, Mang'ula, 30 July 2000.

57. Andrew J. Mangile, interview by author, Mlimba, 26 July 2000.

58. Yu, *China's African Policy*, 142–143.

59. Sendaro, "Workers' Efficiency," 187; Philip Snow, *The Star Raft: China's Encounter with Africa* (New York: Weidenfeld and Nicolson, 1988), 173; Keletso Atkins, *The Moon Is Dead, Give Us Our Money! The Cultural Origins of a Zulu Work Ethic* (Portsmouth, N.H.: Heinemann, 1993); Frederick Cooper, "Colonizing Time: Work Rhythms and Labor Conflict in Colonial Mombasa," in *Colonialism and Culture*, ed. Nicholas Dirks (Ann Arbor: University of Michigan Press, 1992), 209–246.

60. Sendaro, "Workers' Efficiency," 233; Mumello, "Final Report on Tunnels Construction," 2. There are suggestions from worker interviews that a range of conflicts arose as a result of the disparities between the Tanzanian and Chinese approaches to labor and workers' rights; this topic will merit further investigation when archival resources are made available to scholars.

61. Snow, *The Star Raft*, 164.

62. Raphael Chawala, interview by author, Ifakara, 20 April 2000.

63. Salum Mwasenga, interview by author, Mang'ula, 30 July 2000.

64. Chart from Makambako Field Report of 31 August 1973, reproduced in Sendaro, "Workers' Efficiency," 166. In the CRWT staff chart, "trainees" were African workers learning skills.

65. Zhang, *Youyi Zhi Lu [Road of Friendship]*, 258.

66. Minutes from Makambako base camp file, TBC/15, from Sendaro, "Workers' Efficiency," 183.

67. Mumello, "Final Report on Tunnels Construction," 2, 40.

68. Mumello, "Final Report on Tunnels Construction," 2.

69. "Quarterly Monthly Report: Camp Base No. 3, Kasama, July to September, 1969," 23 September 1969, NAZ MFA 1/286/85.

70. Sendaro, "Workers' Efficiency," 224–227.

71. Sendaro, "Workers' Efficiency," 230.

72. Sendaro, "Workers' Efficiency," 231.

73. John Gilbert and Hosea Mngata, interview by author, Ifakara, 20 April 2000; Rogatus Nyumayo, interview by author, Mlimba, 26 July 2000.

74. Group interview in Beijing, 5 July 2007: Jin Hui, Lu Datong, Du Jian, Zhang Zhiying.

75. Tiranti, "The Chinese in Africa," 15.

76. *TAZARA Annual Report and Accounts for 1973–74*, 6.

77. Zhang, *Youyi Zhi Lu [Road of Friendship]*, 259.

78. Sendaro, "Workers' Efficiency," 243.

79. Beatus Lihawa, interview by author, Mlimba, 20 July 2000; Mumello, "Final Report on Tunnels Construction."

80. John Gilbert, Hosea Mngata, and Raphael Chawala, interview by author, 20 April 2000. Sunil Sahu wrote that Chinese workers engaged on the railroad construction were instructed to stay clear of politics and propaganda. Supposedly Chairman Mao assured Nyerere that "any hint of subversion reported to him would be immediately dealt with." Sunil Kumar Sahu, "Sino-Tanzanian Relations," *United Asia* 23, no. 2 (1971): 78–80.

81. Yu, *China's African Policy*, 142.

82. Moses Hassan and Benedict Mkanyago, group interview by author, Mngeta, 7 July 2000.

83. John Gilbert, interview by author, Ifakara, 30 July 2000.

84. John Gilbert and Hosea Mngata, group interview by author, Ifakara, 20 April 2000; Moses Hassan and Benedict Mkanyago, interviews by author, Mngeta, 7 July 2000; Sendaro, "Workers' Efficiency," 185; group interview in Beijing, 5 July 2007: Jin Hui, Lu Datong, Du Jian, Zhang Zhiying.

85. Lao Wan, interview by author, Ifakara, 2000; Raphael Chawala, interview by author, Ifakara, 20 April 2000.

86. Benedict Mkanyago, interview by author, Mngeta, 7 July 2000.

87. John Gilbert, interview by author, Ifakara, 30 July 2000; Salum Mwasenga, interview by author, Mang'ula, 30 July 2000.

88. Samuel Undole, interview by author, Chita, 11 July 2000.

89. Group of women, interviews by author, Mchombe, 16 July 2000.

90. Mumello, "Final Report on Tunnels Construction," 4.

91. Salum Mwasenga, interview by author, Mang'ula, 30 July 2000.

92. Meat was the most difficult food item to obtain at the outlying camps. A butchery project started in June 1972 at Ludilo Power Station Base Camp was closed after two months due to shortages of livestock. Mumello, "Final Report on Tunnels Construction," 5.

93. Mumello, "Final Report on Tunnels Construction," 4; Moses Hassan and Benedict Mkanyago, group interview by author, Mngeta, 7 July 2000.

94. Benedict Mkanyago, interview by author, Mngeta, 7 July 2000.

95. Kasuka S. Mutukwa, "Imperial Dream Becomes Pan-African Reality," *Africa Report*, January 1972, 12.

96. Group interview in Beijing and Tianjin, July 2007: Jin Hui, Lu Datong, Du Jian, Zhang Zhiying.

97. Hall and Peyman, *The Great Uhuru Railway*; Blasius Undole, interview by author, Chita, 22 July 2000.

98. Zhang, *Youyi Zhi Lu [Road of Friendship]*, 171; Li Baoping, personal communication.

99. Zhang, *Youyi Zhi Lu [Road of Friendship]*, 230–232.

100. Group interview in Beijing and Tianjin, July 2007: Jin Hui, Lu Datong, Du Jian, Zhang Zhiying. Hall and Peyman, *The Great Uhuru Railway*, 129.

101. Samuel Undole, interview by author, Chita, 11 July 2000.

102. Yohina Protas Msaka, interview by author, Mchombe, 16 July 2000.

103. Benedict Mkanyago and Moses Hassan, group interview by author, Mngeta, 7 July 2000.

104. Samuel Undole, interview by author, Chita, 11 July 2000.

105. Mumello, "Final Report on Tunnels Construction," 3.

106. TAZARA Report, "Transportation of food stuffs for resale to local workers assigned on Mlimba/Makambako stretch, as from 1st January 1972 to 31st December, 1974"; Moses Hassan and Benedict Mkanyago, group interview by author, Mngeta, 7 July 2000; Beatus Lihawa, interview by author, Mlimba, 20 July 2000.

107. Blasius Undole, interview by author, Chita, 22 July 2000. Jin Hui described these hand-rolled cigarettes as "trumpets" in our interview in Beijing, July 2007.

108. Hall and Peyman, *The Great Uhuru Railway*, 129.

109. Benedict Mkanyago, interview by author, Mngeta, 7 July 2000.

110. Lisa Lindsay, "Money, Marriage and Masculinity on the Colonial Nigerian Railway," in *Men and Masculinities in Modern Africa*, ed. Lisa Lindsay and Stephan Miescher (Portsmouth, N.H.: Heniemann, 2003), 150.

111. D. E. Stambuli, "Staff Commentary," appendix 9 in Mumello, "Final Report on Tunnels Construction."

112. Carol Mpandamgongo, interview by author, Ikule, 14 July 2000. The practice of *ngoma* was defined as "an indigenous ritual of healing, dance, rhythm and rhyme" in a recently published collection: R. van Dijk, R. Reis, and M. Spierenburg, *The Quest for Fruition through Ngoma* (Oxford: Oxford University Press, 2000), iii.

113. John Gilbert and Hosea Mngata, group interview by author, Ifakara, 20 April 2000.

114. These will be dealt with more fully in a subsequent chapter.

115. Johanes Mhiliwa, interview by author, Segelea, 1998.

116. "Tunnels along the Uhuru Railway," appendix A in Mumello, "Final Report on Tunnels Construction," 31.

4. Living along the Railway

1. As construction passed into Zambia, the Tanzanian workforce was reduced from a high of 35,900 in the second half of 1972 to 13,600 at the end of June 1974. Meanwhile Zambian workers increased from 2,100 to 13,000 over the same period. Tanzania Zambia Railway Authority [hereafter TAZARA] Annual Report and Accounts for 1973/74, 12.

2. "Vijiji vya Ujamaa Kando Kando ya Reli ya Uhuru," CCM Archives Accession No. 5 File 1008, 15. Many thanks to James Giblin for access to this document.

3. Tanzania African National Union, "Muhtasiri wa Mkutano Mkuu wa 15 uliofanyika Dar es Salaam 1971" 18–26 September 1971, 8, TNA Accession No. 550, C/2112/71, IS/I.317. Juma's reference to "capitalists" here was apparently a reference to commodity traders and shopkeepers; in a subsequent report Juma referred to this form of capitalism as *unyonyaji*, a term that was used at the time to describe Asian traders. "Akumbusha Siasa ya Tanzania Katika Ujenzi wa Reli," TNA Accession 550, A/1027/72, IS/I.331, 1 May 1972.

4. "Wito wa Kuanza Vijiji vya Ujamaa Kando ya Reli ya Uhuru," 19 June 1971, TNA, Accession 550, A/1382/71, IS/I.329.

5. "Idete ni Kijiji Bora Zaidi Mkoani Morogoro," 30 June 1971, TNA, Accession 550, A/1457/71, IS/I.329. The village of Idete was supported by Swiss development assistance.

6. "Vijiji vya Ujamaa Kando Kando ya Reli ya Uhuru," CCM Archives, Dodoma, Accession 5, File 1008, 14; "Operation Vijiji-Kando ya Reli," Kilombero District File D.40/2/vol. 2.

7. James Scott, *Seeing like a State: How Certain Schemes to Improve the Human Condition Have Failed* (New Haven, Conn.: Yale University Press, 1998), 227–229.

8. "Vijiji vya Ujamaa Kando Kando ya Reli ya Uhuru," CCM Archives, Dodoma, Accession 5, File 1008, 15.

9. Paul Fuchs, "Die wirtschaftliche Erkundung einer ostafrikanischen Sudbahn," *Beiheft zum Tropenpflanzer* 6, no. 4/5 (1905): 13. Fuchs believed that Nyamwezi laborers were best suited for this purpose, and proposed that they be recruited first to build the railway and then encouraged to stay on as settlers through a temporary hut tax reprieve and other measures.

10. "Vijiji vya Ujamaa Kando Kando ya Reli ya Uhuru," CCM Archives, Dodoma, Accession 5, File 100p, 14.

11. Yusufu Lawi, "Tanzania's Operation *Vijiji* and Local Ecological Consciousness: The Case of Eastern Iraqwland, 1974–1976," *Journal of African History* 48 (2007): 69–93. Lawi describes similar processes and local experiences in northern Tanzania.

12. An example is *Karte: Nyasa-Expedition des Gouverneurs Obersten Freiherrn von Schele*, H. Ramsay and Richard Kiepert, *Mitteilungen aus den deutschen Schutzgebieten*, Band 7, 1894.

13. Gideon von Grawert, "Bericht über die Bezirksbereisung," 17 November to 18 December 1903, G1/91, Ulanga-Perondo, *Mahenge-Verwaltungsangelegenheiten*, 1894–1906, Band 1.

14. Mahenge District Annual Report, 1919/1920, TNA SMP 1733/1/8; cited in Lorne Larson, "A History of the Mahenge (Ulanga) District, c. 1860–1957" (Ph.D. diss., University of Dar es Salaam, 1996), 221.

15. Towegale Kiwanga to Eastern Province PC, 9 November 1935; Letter from Mtwa Sapi Mkwawa to D. O. Iringa, Mgololo, 1 August 1934; Memorandum on the Bena-Hehe Dispute, Culwick, Kiberege, 8 December 1936; Ulanga District Books, Inter-Tribal Boundaries.

16. Dean E. McHenry, *Tanzania's Ujamaa Villages: The Implementation of a Rural Development Strategy* (Berkeley: University of California, 1979), 25.

17. A. T. Culwick, Annual Report, Mahenge Division of Ulanga District, 1941. TNA 61/141/H/I.

18. Andrew Burton, "The Haven of Peace Purged: Tackling the Undesirable and Unproductive Poor in Dar es Salaam, c. 1950s–1980s," *International Journal of African Historical Studies* 40, no. 1 (2007): 119–150.

19. Paul Bolstad, "Recollections and Observations: October 1966–1968, Kilombero Settlement Scheme, Ulanga District, Tanzania," unpublished manuscript of former Peace Corps volunteer, 2001; Paul Bolstad, interview by author, Northfield, Minn., 2001; Juma Juma Kiswanya, interview by author, Mgudeni, 2001; Robert Chambers, *Settlement Schemes in Tropical Africa: A Study of Organizations and Development* (London: Routledge, 1969), 151.

20. There is a large literature on the villagization period in Tanzania. In addition to archival materials and oral interviews, I have relied here on Dean McHenry, *Tanzania's Ujamaa Villages: The Implementation of a Rural Development Strategy* (Berkeley: Institute of International Studies, 1979); Dean McHenry, *Limited Choices: The Political Struggle for Socialism in Tanzania* (Boulder: L. Rienner, 1994); Jannik Boesen, Birgit S. Madsen, and Tony Moody, *Ujamaa—Socialism from Above* (Uppsala: Nordiska Afrikainstitutet, 1977); and Idris Kikula, *Policy Implications on Environment: The Case of Villagisation in Tanzania* (University of Dar es Salaam, 1997), among others.

21. "Kijiji cha Chita," 28 September 1973, Kilombero District File, D40/40/vol. 2.

22. Samuel Mihanji Undole, interview by author, Chita, 7 November 2000.

23. "Kijiji cha Chita," 28 September 1973, Kilombero District Books, D40/40/vol. 2.

24. Maulidi Mustafa Majiji, interview by author, Mngeta, 7 July 2000; Mtwanga family group, interview by author, Mngeta, 9 July 2000.

25. Maulidi Mustafa Majiji, interview by author, Mngeta, 7 July 2000.

26. Godfrey Mwakyoma, interview by author, Mngeta, June 2000.

27. Venance Michael Lyapembile, interview by author, Mchombe, 16 July 2000.

28. Yohina Msaka, interview by author, Mchombe, 16 July 2000.

29. Godfrey Mwakyoma, interview by author, Mchombe, June 2000.

30. Joseph Haule, interview by author, Ifakara, 21 May 2001.

31. Mzee Moyo, interview by author, Ifakara, 25 May 2001.

32. Brother Edwin von Moos, interview by author, Ifakara, May 2000.

33. "Draft of Final Report, Selous Game Reserve Management Project, Socio-Economic Survey of the Buffer Zone of Selous Game Reserve, Volume 3: Village Socio-Economic Profiles, Kilombero and Ulanga Districts," Department of Sociology, University of Dar es Salaam. Many thanks to Dr. Simeon Mesaki for sharing this report.

34. R. P. Mayombo, "Economic Structural Changes and Population Migration in Kilombero Valley" (M.A. thesis, University of Dar es Salaam), 58; Philemon Kigola, interview by author, Mang'ula, 5 August 2000.

35. Paul Bolstad, interview by author, Northfield, Minn., 2001.

36. Juma Juma Kiswanya, interview by author, Mgudeni, 8 August 2000.

37. Zhang Tieshan, *Youyi Zhi Lu [Road of Friendship]*, 381.

38. Julius Nyerere, *Freedom and Development: A Selection from Writings and Speeches 1968–1973* (Oxford: Oxford University Press, 1973), 237.

39. "Lindeni Reli," 14 October 1971, TNA Accession No. 550, A/2272/71, IS/I.322.

40. Mumello, "Final Report on Tunnels Construction," 20.

41. "Tulinde Reli ya Uhuru," *Ngurumo*, 1973, no. 4476, 1.

42. Regional Commissioner, Morogoro (Anna Abdallah) to District Commissioner, Ifakara, "Ajali za Treni katika Reli ya TAZARA, 1-4-81," Kilombero District File 40/6.

43. Carol Mpandamgongo, interview by author, Ikule, 14 July 2000.

44. Many people sleep at the TAZARA stations while waiting for a train or for arriving passengers, or because it is a peak trading season and there is no available shelter, or because, like Rehema, they have no other secure place to rest.

45. "Uchotaji wa Maji," 13 August 1992, Kilombero District File 40/6.

46. Waziri Juma had endeavored in June 1971 to squelch rumors that the railway belonged to the Chinese, urging citizens of Morogoro region "not to accept the rumors that are circulated by some people who say that this railway belongs to the Chinese; rather they should understand that it is the wealth of Tanzanians and Zambians." "Habari Kutoka Mikoani: Morogoro: Reli ya Tanzania/Zambia Mali Yetu," 2 June 1971, TNA Accession no. 550, A/1239/71, IS/I.379.

47. Mkuu wa Polisi TAZARA, Mlimba to Mkuu wa Wilaya, Kilombero Re: Hujuma Dhidi ya Reli ya Uhuru TAZARA Kipindi cha 1988/89, 6 September 1989, Kilombero District File 40/6.

48. Ibid.; Samuel Undole, interview by author, Chita, 11 July 2000; Telephone operators at Makambako, interview by author, Makambako, 2000.

49. Benedict Mkanyago, interview by author, Mngeta, 7 July 2000.

50. Mkuu wa Polisi TAZARA, Mlimba to Mkuu wa Wilaya, Kilombero, Re: Hujuma Dhidi ya Reli ya Uhuru TAZARA Kipindi cha 1988/89, 6 September 1989, Kilombero District File 40/6.

51. Samuel Undole, interview by author, Chita, 11 July 2000.

52. Mkuu wa Wilaya Kilombero, E. F. Tumbo to District Traffic Superintendent, Makambako, "Re: Ziara kwenye Vijiji Kando Kando ya Reli Uhuru Kudhibiti Hujuma," Kilombero District File 40/6.

53. J. M. Mukama, Mwenyekiti wa Kamati ya Suala la Kufungwa kwa Stesheni ya Mbingu, to Mheshimiwa, Mbunge wa Kilombero, Wilaya ya Kilombero, Re: Kufungwa kwa Stesheni ya TAZARA—Mbingu, 1 August 1994, Kilombero District File 40/6.

54. "TAZARA Closes Nine Stations," *Business Times*, 5 August 1994, 3.

55. District Traffic Inspector Mlimba to District Traffic Supervisor Mlimba/Makambako, "Report on Request for Passenger Halts in Mlimba District for Kilombero District," 3 April 1990, Kilombero District File 40/6.

56. Ibid, 5.

57. H. B. Jumaa, District Traffic Superintendent Mlimba, to Regional Manager TAZARA, Dar es Salaam, "Re: District Commissioner Ifakara Request of Opening Halts along the Railway Line," 17 April 1990, Kilombero District File 40/6.

58. A. Saidi, TAZARA Passenger Services, to District Commissioner Kilombero, "Re: Kufunguliwa Kwa Vituo Vidogo kwa Ajili ya Treni Ndogo," 28 July 1998, Kilombero District File 40/6.

5. The Ordinary Train

1. "Chinese-built Tanzam Railway Trains Run Ontime at £ 5.50 Fare for 1.162-mile Journey," *The Times*, 26 July 1976, 5.

2. Jamie Monson, "Maisha: Life History and the History of Livelihood along the TAZARA Railway," in *Sources and Methods in African History: Spoken, Written, Unearthed*, ed. Toyin Falola and Christian Jennings (Rochester, N.Y.: University of Rochester Press, 2003), 312–330.

3. Samuel Mihanji Undole, interview by author, Chita, 11 July 2000.

4. Michael Gleave, "The Dar es Salaam Transport Corridor: An Appraisal," *African Affairs* 91 (1992): 249–267; *Railway Gazette International* 134, no. 8 (1978): 548.

5. "Who Speaks for TAZARA?" *Daily News*, 22 April 1981, 1.

6. "Zambia's Fertilizer 'Out of Danger,'" *Daily News*, 8 April 1978, 3.

7. "Record of the Minutes of the Call by his Excellency Mr. Ke Pu-Hai, Ambassador of the People's Republic of China on the Ambassador Mr. G. R. Zimba, Under-Secretary (Political)," Wednesday, 18 October 1978; UNIP 7/23/65/32.

8. "Chinese Help for Broken Down Tanzam Trains," *The Times*, 3 September 1980, 7; "China yaombwa kusaidia TAZARA: Lusaka, Zambia," *Uhuru*, 26 August 1980; "Kikao cha TAZARA leo: Wajumbe 14 Toka China Kuchunguza Taarifa ya Reli Hiyo," *Uhuru*, 25 August 1980.

9. "Donors Breathe Life into TAZARA," *Railway Gazette International*, 144, 12 December 1988, 823–825.

10. "TAZARA to Get 1250m/= grants," *Daily News*, 17 September 1987, 1; "US Provides 3 bn/= to TAZARA," *Daily News*, 1 October 1987, 1.

11. Tanzania Zambia Railway Authority, *Ten Years of TAZARA Operations: Review and Perspective* (Lusaka and Dar es Salaam, 1986), 16.

12. John Briggs, "The Tanzania-Zambia Railway," *Geography* 77 (1992): 267.

13. "TAZARA Hauls Part of Stranded Maize," *Daily News*, 30 December 2000, 1; "TAZARA Draws New Market Plan," *Daily News*, 5 February 1992, 1; "TAZARA Nets Record Profit," *Daily News*, 6 January 1990, 1.

14. Zhang Dacheng, "China Promises Aid for Reviving Tanzania-Zambia Railway," *Xinhua News Agency* (Dar es Salaam), 19 July 2001.

15. C. G. Mung'ong'o, "Coming Full Circle: Agriculture, Non-Farm Activities and the Resurgence of Out-Migration in Njombe District, Tanzania," Working Paper 26 (Leiden: Afrika-Studiecentrum), 1998.

16. David Booth, "Why Tanzanian Society Is Not Experiencing Structural Adjustment: The Case of Iringa," in *The Tanzanian Peasantry: Economy in Crisis*, ed. P. Forster and S. Maghimbi (Aldershot, Hants.: Avebury, 1992), 256; Stefano Ponte, *Farmers and Markets in Tanzania* (Oxford: James Currey, 2002), 74–75. Migrants from the highlands who were interviewed in the Kilombero valley cited agricultural price constraints as well as the shortage of fertile land as reasons for their resettlement in the TAZARA corridor: e.g., Brown Mwasonge, interview by author, Ifakara, 30 April 2000.

17. Mboya S. D. Bagachwa, "The Rural Informal Sector in Tanzania," in *Farewell to Farms: De-Agrarianisation and Employment in Africa*, ed. Deborah Fahy Bryceson and Vali Jamal (Leiden: African Studies Center, 1997), 137–154.

18. Ngila Mwase, "The Future of TAZARA in a Post-Apartheid Southern Africa," Southern African Perspectives Working Paper 21, Center for Southern African Studies, University of the Western Cape, South Africa, 1993.

19. "TAZARA Donors Meet Tuesday to Review Progress," *Daily News*, 1 February 1992, 3.

20. "TAZARA Layoffs No Surprise," *Daily News*, 9 March 1995, 1; see also "TAZARA to Lay Off 2,600," *Daily News*, 8 March 1995, 1; "Hatua za kuboresha TAZARA zachukuliwa," *Mzalendo*, 6 August 1995, 3; "Dar, Lusaka Reaffirm Commitment to Maintain TAZARA," *Daily News*, 15 January 1994, 3.

21. Philemon Kaduma, interview by author, Mbeya, 24 August 1998.

22. Rashid Shabani Rajabu, interview by George Mwombeta, Mbingu, 25 July 2002.

23. It would have been very helpful if we had been able to make connections between the individual traders in the receipt books and the traders we interviewed; unfortunately most records contain common names (frequently first names), and these are not specific or consistent enough for accurate comparisons.

24. Selemani Issa Mwelela, interview by George Mwombeta, Mlimba, 16 July 2002.

25. *Ukindu* collectors, interview by author, Mgudeni, on bicycle trip to the river from KOTACO in July 2000; Kennedy Haule, "Wildlife Prospects in Kilombero Game Controlled Area, Tanzania: Traditional vs. State Management" (M.S. thesis, Centre for International Environment and Development Studies, Agricultural University of Norway, 1977), 34; Thierry Freyvogel, "A Collection of Plaited Mats from the Ulanga District of Tanganyika," *Tanganyika Notes and Records* 57 (1961): 139–148.

26. Balista Idifonce Kidehela, interview by George Mwombeta, Mbingu, 28 July 2002.

27. Rehema P. Mwabutwa, interview by George Mwombeta, Mlimba, 16 July 2002.

28. Mwamini Salehe, interview by George Mwombeta, Mlimba, 16 July 2002.

29. John Emmanueli Mbwilo, interview by George Mwombeta, Mlimba, 16 July 2002. We have seen the way that Balista and Mwamini used similar strategies within marriage.

30. Eddy Nyaruke, interview by George Mwombeta, Mlimba, 17 July 2002.

31. Mwajuma Malangu, interview by George Mwombeta, Mbingu, 27 July 2002. Mwajuma harvests only six bags of grain from her one-acre rice plot per year, but is able to earn about 1,000 shillings per day from her cooking business.

32. Pekka Seppälä, *Diversification and Accumulation in Rural Tanzania: Anthropological Perspectives on Village Economics* (Uppsala: Nordiska Afrikainstitutet, 1998), 27.

33. Brown Mwasongwe, interview by author, Ifakara, 30 April 2000.

34. Form Four is the final year of secondary school and Form Six the last year of high school in Tanzania. Both are considered to be important educational milestones, particularly Form Six.

35. Anua Mtengela, interview by author aboard *kipisi* shuttle train, 26 July 2000.

36. Michael Mweji, interview by George Mwombeta, Mbingu, 26 July 2002.

37. Lazaro Mbilinyi, interview by author, Ifakara, June 2000.

38. This argument goes back to Sara Berry's formative work: Sara Berry, *No Condition Is Permanent: The Social Dynamics of Agrarian Change in Sub-Saharan Africa* (Madison: University of Wisconsin Press, 1993).

39. Michael Mweji, interview by George Mwombeta, Mbingu, 26 July 2002.

40. See, especially, Julius Nyerere, *Ujamaa, Essays on Socialism* (Oxford: Oxford University Press, 1967).

41. Yohana Paul Nyakunga, interview by George Mwombeta, Mlimba, 18 July 2002.

42. Ibid.

43. Rehema Mwabutwa, interview by George Mwombeta, Mlimba, 16 July 2002. Rehema's life story is also one of enormous fluctuations in socioeconomic status and geographical mobility. She began her working life as a telephone operator, while her husband earned a good income as a driver for the FAO. Following his death she was able to earn enough money trading rice in Tunduma that she bought a small home and lived there with her children. Unfortunately, a harsh case of malaria forced her to return to live with her parents and incapacitated her for several years. It was after this episode (which was according to her own account also a period of emotional suffering due to the circumstances of her husband's death) that she moved to Mlimba.

44. Michael Mweji, interview by George Mwombeta, Mbingu, 26 July 2002.

45. Selous Game Reserve Management Project (SGMP), *Socioeconomic Survey of the Buffer Zone of the Selous Game Reserve, Final Report 2* (Department of Sociology, University of Dar es Salaam, November 2001). Courtesy of Dr. Simeon Mesaki.

46. Michael Mweji, interview by George Mwombeta, Mbingu, 26 July 2002.

47. Selemani Mwelela, interview by George Mwombeta, Mlimba, 16 July 2002.

6. Landscape Visions

1. Government of Tanzania, "Second Five-Year Plan for Economic and Social Development," vol. 1 (Dar es Salaam: Government Printing Office, 1 July 1969–30 June 1974), 40.

2. Moses Kisugite, interview by author, Mngeta, 10 July 2000.

3. C. Bekker, W. Rance, O. Monteuuis, "Teak in Tanzania: II. The Kilombero Valley Teak Company," *Bois et Forêts des Tropiques* 249 (2004): 11–21.

4. The term is from Dennis Cordell, Joel Gregory, and Victor Piché, eds., *Hoe and Wage: A Social History of a Circular Migration System in West Africa* (Boulder, Colo.: Westview, 1996).

5. Rudolf Peter Mayombo, "Economic Structural Changes and Population Migration in Kilombero Valley" (M.A. thesis, Department of Demography, University of Dar es Salaam, 1990), 75.

6. Augustine Magwaja, interview by George Mwombeta, Mlimba, 17 July 2002; Bernard Katabi, interview by author, Msolwa 12 August 2002; Shabani Sulemani Mseja, interview by George Mwombeta, Mlimba, 17 July 2002.

7. Kennedy Haule, "Wildlife Prospects in Kilombero Game Controlled Area, Tanzania: Traditional vs. State Management" (M.S. thesis, Centre for International Environment and Development Studies, Agricultural University of Norway, 1997), 104.

8. Faustine Rwambali, "State Lays Off All 3000 Kilombero Sugar Workers," *The East African*, 3 July 2000. In interviews people also complained that the sugar company was enforcing harsh regulations in worker housing compounds—for example, restricting the presence of extended family members and forbidding the keeping of chickens for home consumption.

9. Interviews at Msolwa by George Mwombeta, 12 August 2002, and at Mwaya by George Mwombeta, 14 August 2002.

10. Mung'ong'o, C. G., "Coming Full Circle: Agriculture, Non-Farm Activities and the Resurgence of Out-Migration in Njombe District," Tanzania, ASC Working Paper 26, Leiden, 1997.

11. Elisha Kidumba, interview by George Mwombeta, Mwaya, 14 August 2002.

12. Richard Mwailunda, interview by author, Mwaya, 14 August 2002.

13. Martin Kabida, interview by George Mwombeta, Sonjo, 13 August 2002.

14. Sugar cane outgrowers were listed as company labor in Illovo's official reports (www.illovosugar.com).

15. Interviews with members of sugar cane outgrowers association, interview by author, Mkamba, April 2000.

16. Shaha Salum Mnauye, interview by George Mwombeta, Mlimba, 26 July 2002; Gerod: Pius Mikupi, interview by George Mwombeta, Mlimba, 18 July 2002.

17. Michael Noah Mwaniko, interview with George Mwombeta, Mbingu, 28 July 2002.

18. Josefina Jackson Mwasulama, interview with author, Dar es Salaam, May 2001.

19. Shabani Sulemani Mseja, interview with George Mwombeta, Mlimba, 17 July 2002.

20. Hamisi Mkoka, interview with George Mwombeta, Mbingu, 27 July 2002.

21. Yohana Paul Nyakunga, interview with George Mwombeta, Mlimba, 18 July 2002.

22. Mohamed Juma Manjenga, interview with George Mwombeta, Mlimba, 18 July 2002.

23. Hussein Ally Mgeni, interview with George Mwombeta, Mbingu, 25 July 2002.

24. The determination of vegetation categories and the analysis of the satellite images were conducted by Jesse Grossman.

25. The fertility of the Malinyi fan made it a site of bitter contestation over land and labor resources in the colonial period: see Lorne Larson, "A History of the Mahenge (Ulanga) District, c. 1860–1957" (Ph.D. diss., University of Dar es Salaam, 1976); Jamie Monson, "The Tribal Past and the Politics of Nationalism in Mahenge District, 1940–1960," in *In Search of a Nation: Historians and Nationalism in Tanzania*, ed. Gregory Maddox and James Giblin (Oxford: James Currey, 2005).

26. Government of Tanzania, National Census Reports, 1978, 1988, 2000 (www.tanzania.go.tz/census).

27. Selous Game Reserve Management Project (SGMP), *Socio-Economic Survey of the Buffer Zone of the Selous Game Reserve, Final Report* 2 (Department of Sociology, University of Dar es Salaam, November 2001). Courtesy of Dr. Simeon Mesaki.

28. Demographic Surveillance Survey, IHRDC, 1997–2000. Courtesy of Dr. Rose Nathan.

29. Selous Game Reserve Management Project, *Socio-Economic Survey*; Kilombero District Agricultural Office, "Mahitaji ya Chakula cha Njaa na Mbegu za Kupanda 1998/99," mimeo.

30. "Uchaguzi wa Vijiji Vya Mfano kwa Ajili ya Maendeleo Wilayani," 2 June 1984. Kilombero District Files D.40/3.

31. Kilombero District Agricultural Office, "Mahitaji ya Chakula cha Njaa na Mbegu za Kupanda 1998/99," mimeo.

32. Selous Game Reserve Management Project, *Socio-Economic Survey*.

33. Selous Game Reserve Management Project, *Socio-Economic Survey*.

34. Josefina Mwasulama, interview by author, Dar es Salaam, May 2001.

35. Mr. Manusa and Mrs. Abdalla, interview by author, District Development Office, Ifakara, 20 April 2000.

36. Anton Ngwawe Mwilenga, *Historia Fupi ya Wandamba*, n.d.

37. Atupele Mwakapala, interview by author, Ifakara, 3 May 2000.

38. The KVIEMP study is doing a valuable service by examining the relationships between different types of fishing gear and the size of fish catches. Volunteers measure and record the fish catches in four permanent fishing settlements. See R. Jenkins, K. Roettcher, G. Corti, and E. Fanning, *The Kilombero River Fishery*, Annual Report, KVIEMP, October 2000. Conversation with Richard Jenkins, Dar es Salaam, August 2000.

39. Atupele Mwakapala, interview by author, Ifakara, 3 May 2000.

40. Venance M. Lyapembile, interview by author, Mchombe, 16 July 2000.

41. Ibid.

42. Jenkins et al., *The Kilombero Fishery: Annual Report*, 22–23.

43. Ibid., 11.

44. Ibid., 20.

45. Interview with *ukindu* weavers at Mgudeni, interview by author, on bicycle trip to the river from KOTACO in July 2000. Despite the rhetoric about Ndamba custom in arguments over these two fishing camps, many people were observed drinking alcohol at Kihopa and women were sleeping overnight during a visit in July 2000.

46. Leonard Likweti, interview by author, Ifakara, 5 May 2000.

47. Ibid.

48. Ibid.; Jenkins et al., *The Kilombero Fishery: Annual Report*, 21.

Bibliography

Armstrong, Allen. "Urban Control Campaigns in the Third World: The Case of Tanganyika." *Glasgow University Occasional Papers* 19 (1987): 15.

Atkins, Keletso. *The Moon Is Dead, Give Us Our Money! The Cultural Origins of a Zulu Work Ethic.* Portsmouth, N.H.: Heinemann, 1993.

Bagachwa, Mboya S. D. "The Rural Informal Sector in Tanzania." In *Farewell to Farms: De-Agrarianisation and Employment in Africa,* ed. Deborah Fahy Bryceson and Vali Jamal. Leiden: African Studies Center, 1997.

Bailey, Martin. *Freedom Railway: China and the Tanzania-Zambia Link.* London: Rex Collings, 1976.

Barkan, Joel, ed. *Beyond Capitalism vs. Socialism in Kenya and Tanzania.* Boulder, Colo.: Lynne Rienner, 1994.

Barnes, John, and Louise Lief. "Africa Makes a Hard Choice: Can a Bitter Dose of Capitalism Fix What's Broken after Decades of Socialism and Failure?" *U.S. News and World Report,* 27 June 1988, 28.

Bassett, Thomas. *The Peasant Cotton Revolution in West Africa: Cote D'Ivoire, 1880–1995.* Cambridge: Cambridge University Press, 2001.

Berry, Sara. *No Condition Is Permanent; The Social Dynamics of Agrarian Change in Sub-Saharan Africa.* Madison: University of Wisconsin Press, 1993.

Biermann, Werner. *Tanganyika Railways—Carrier of Colonialism: An Account of Economic Indicators and Social Fragments.* Münster: Afrikanische Studien 9, 1995.

Boesen, Jannik, Birgit S. Madsen, and Tony Moody. *Ujamaa: Socialism from Above.* Uppsala: Nordiska Afrikainstitut, 1977.

Bolstad, Paul. "Recollections and Observations: October 1966–1968, Kilombero Settlement Scheme, Ulanga District, Tanzania." Unpublished manuscript, 2001.

Booth, David. "Why Tanzanian Society Is Not Experiencing Structural Adjustment: The Case of Iringa." In *The Tanzanian Peasantry: Economy in Crisis*, ed. P. Forster and S. Maghimbi. Aldershot, Hants.: Avebury, 1992.

Bostock, R. M. "The Transport Sector." In *Constraints on the Economic Development of Zambia*, ed. Charles Elliott. Oxford: Oxford University Press, 1971.

Bräutigam, Deborah. *Chinese Aid and African Development: Exploring Green Revolution.* New York: St. Martin's, 1999.

Brennan, James. "Blood Enemies: Exploitation and Urban Citizenship in the Nationalist Political Thought of Tanzania, 1958–1975." *Journal of African History* 47, no. 3 (2006): 387–411.

Bruijn, Mirjam de, Rijk van Dijk, and Dick Foeken. *Mobile Africa: Changing Patterns of Movement in Africa and Beyond.* Boston: Brill, 2001.

Bryceson, Deborah Fahy. "De-agrarianisation in Sub-Saharan Africa: Acknowledging the Inevitable." In *Farewell to Farms: De-Agrarianisation and Employment in Africa*, eds. Bryceson and Vali Jamal. Leiden: African Studies Center, 1997.

———. "Multiplex Livelihoods in Rural Africa: Recasting the Terms and Conditions of Gainful Employment." *Journal of Modern African Studies* 40, no. 1 (2002): 1–28.

Burton, Andrew. "The Haven of Peace Purged: Tackling the Undesirable and Unproductive Poor in Dar es Salaam, c. 1950s–1980s." *International Journal of African Historical Studies* 40, no. 1 (2007): 119–150.

Canning, Kathleen. "Feminist History after the Linguistic Turn: Historicizing Discourse and Experience." *Signs* 19, no. 2 (1994): 368–404.

Chambers, Robert. *Settlement Schemes in Tropical Africa: A Study of Organizations and Development.* London: Praeger, 1969.

Charnley, Susan. "Cattle, Commons and Culture: The Political Ecology of Environmental Change on a Tanzanian Rangeland." Ph.D. thesis, Stanford University, 1994.

———. "The Opening of an African Commons: Pastoralism, Property Rights, and Rangeland Degradation in Tanzania." Unpublished manuscript, 1998.

Cheng-chih, Liao. *The Chinese People Resolutely Support the Just Struggle of the African People.* Chinese-African Friendship Association. Peking: Foreign Languages Press, 1961.

Chitukiro, Jacob Kilandio. "The Impact of the Uhuru Railway on Agricultural Development in the Kilombero District." M.A. thesis, Dar es Salaam, 1976.

Cooper, Frederick. "Colonizing Time: Work Rhythms and Labor Conflict in Colonial Mombasa." In *Colonialism and Culture*, ed. Nicholas Dirks. Ann Arbor: University of Michigan Press, 1992.

———, and Randall Packard. *International Development and the Social Sciences.* Berkeley: University of California Press, 1997.

Cordell, Dennis, Joel Gregory, and Victor Piché, eds. *Hoe and Wage: A Social History of a Circular Migration System in West Africa.* Boulder, Colo.: Westview, 1996.

Coulson, Andrew. *Tanzania: A Political Economy.* Oxford: Oxford University Press, 1982.

Cowen, Michael, and Robert Shenton. "The Invention of Development." In *Power of Development*, ed. Jonathan Crush. London: Routledge, 1995.

Crush, Jonathan, ed. *Power of Development.* London: Routledge, 1995.

Dacheng, Zhang. "China Promises Aid for Reviving Tanzania-Zambia Railway." *Xinhua News Agency*, Dar es Salaam, 19 July 2001.

Donham, Donald. *Marxist Modern.* Berkeley: University of California Press, 1999.

East African Railways and Harbors Administration. "Report on an Engineering Survey of a Rail Link between the East African and Rhodesian Railway Systems." Nairobi, June 1952.

Escobar, Arturo. *Encountering Development: The Making and Unmaking of the Third World.* Princeton, N.J: Princeton University Press, 1995.

Ferguson, James. *The Anti-Politics Machine: "Development," Depoliticization, and Bureaucratic Power in Lesotho.* Minneapolis: University of Minnesota Press, 1994.

Freyvogel, Thierry. "A Collection of Plaited Mats from the Ulanga District of Tanganyika." *Tanganyika Notes and Records,* University of Dar es Salaam 57 (1961): 139–148.

Fuchs, Paul. "Wirtschaftliche Eisenbahn-Erkundigen in mittleren und nördlichen Deutsch-Ostafrika." *Beiheft zum Tropenpflanzer* 11, no. 8 (1907).

——. "Die wirtschaftliche Erkundung einer ostafrikanischen Sudbahn." *Beiheft zum Tropenpflanzer* 6, no. 4/5 (1905).

Geiger, Susan. *TANU Women: Gender and the Making of Tanganyikan Nationalism, 1955–1965.* Portsmouth, N.H.: Heinemann, 1997.

Giblin, James. *A History of the Excluded: Making Family a Refuge from State in Twentieth Century Tanzania.* Athens: Ohio University Press, 2004.

Gillman, Clements. "A Short History of the Tanganyika Railways." *Tanganyika Notes and Records* 13 (1942): 14.

Gleave, M. B. "The Dar es Salaam Transport Corridor: An Appraisal." *African Affairs* 91 (1992): 249–267.

Government of Tanzania. "Second Five-Year Plan for Economic and Social Development." Vol. 1. Dar es Salaam: Government Printing Office, 1 July 1969–30 June 1974.

Green, Maia. "Witchcraft Suppression Practices and Movements: Public Politics and the Logic of Purification." *Comparative Studies in Society and History* 39, no. 3 (1997): 319–345.

Griggs, John. "The Tanzania-Zambia Railway: Review and Prospects." *Geography* 77 (July 1992): 264–268.

Hall, R., and H. Peyman. *The Great Uhuru Railway.* London: Gollancz, 1976.

Hammond, F. D. "Report on the Railway Systems of Kenya, Uganda and Tanganyika." London: Government Printer, 1921.

——. "Report on the Railway System of Tanganyika Territory." London: Government Printer, 1930.

Hance, William, and Irene van Dongen. "Dar es Salaam, the Port and Its Tributary Area." *Annals of the Association of American Geographers* 48, no. 4 (1958): 419–435.

Haule, Kennedy. "Wildlife Prospects in Kilombero Game Controlled Area, Tanzania: Traditional vs. State Management." M.S. thesis, Centre for International Environment and Development Studies, Agricultural University of Norway, 1997.

He, Wenping. "China-Africa Relations Facing the 21st Century." In *Africa beyond 2000,* Institute of West Asian and African Studies, Chinese Academy of Social Sciences, October 1998. 393–412.

Henn, S. H. H. "Appendices to the Report of the Tanganyika Railway Commission, Contains Oral Evidence and Memoranda." London: Crown Agents for the Colonies, 1930.

——. "Report of the Tanganyika Railway Commission." London: Crown Agents for the Colonies, 1930.

Hill, M. F. *Permanent Way II: The Story of the Tanganyika Railways.* Nairobi, 1967.

Hodgson, Dorothy. *Once Intrepid Warriors: Gender, Ethnicity, and the Cultural Politics of Maasai Development.* Bloomington: Indiana University Press, 2001.

——, and Monica von Beusekom. "Lessons Learned? Development Experiences in the Late Colonial Period." *Journal of African History* 41 (2000): 29–33.

Hu, Zhichao. "The Past, Present and Future of the Tanzania-Zambia Railroad." *Economic Research of the Railroads* (2000): 46–47.

Hutchinson, Alan. *China's African Revolution.* London, 1975.

Ismael, Tareq Y. "The People's Republic of China and Africa." *The Journal of Modern African Studies* 9, no. 4 (1971): 507–529.

Jenkins, R., R. Roettcher, G. Corti, and E. Fanning. *The Kilombero Fishery: Annual Report.* Kilombero Valley Integrated Environmental Management Programme (KVIEMP), October 2000.

Katzenellenbogen, Simon. "Zambia and Rhodesia: Prisoners of the Past: A Note on the History of Railway Politics in Central Africa." *African Affairs* 73, no. 290 (January 1974): 63–66.

Kikula, Idris. *Policy Implications on Environment: The Case of Villagisation in Tanzania.* University of Dar es Salaam, 1997.

Koponen, Juhani. *Development for Exploitation: German Colonial Policies in Mainland Tanzania, 1884–1914.* Helsinki: Finnish Historical Society, 1994.

Land, Thomas. "Chinese Working on the Railroad." *The Nation,* 19 October 1970, 371.

Larkin, Bruce. *China and Africa, 1949–1970.* Berkeley: University of California Press, 1971.

Larson, Lorne. "A History of the Mahenge (Ulanga) District, c. 1860–1957." Ph.D. thesis, University of Dar es Salaam, 1976.

Lawi, Yusufu. "Tanzania's Operation *Vijiji* and Local Ecological Consciousness: The Case of Eastern Iraqwland, 1974–1976." *Journal of African History* 48 (2007): 69–93.

Lieder, G. "Beobachtungen auf der Ubena-Nyasa Expedition, November 1893 bis 30 Marz 1894." *Mitteilungen aus den Deutschen Schutzgebieten* 7 (1894): 271–277.

———. "Zur Kenntnis des Karawanenwege im sudlichen Theile des ostafrikanischen Schutzgebietes." *Mitteilungen aus den Deutschen Schutzgebieten* 7 (1894): 271–282.

Likwelile, S. B. "An Analysis of Efficiency in the Trucking Industry in Tanzania." Ph.D. thesis, University of Dar es Salaam, 1996.

Lindsay, Lisa, and Stephan Miescher, eds. *Men and Masculinities in Modern Africa.* Portsmouth, N.H.: Heinemann, 2003.

Lofchie, Michael. "Tanzania's Agricultural Decline." In *Coping with Africa's Food Crisis,* ed. N. Chazan and T. M. Shaw. Boulder: University of Colorado Press, 1988.

Lunn, Jon. "The Political Economy of Primary Railway Construction in the Rhodesias, 1890–1911." *Journal of African History* 33, no. 2 (1992): 239–254.

Makoni, Tonderai. "The Economic Appraisal of the Tanzania-Zambia Railway." *The African Review* 2, no. 4 (1972): 606.

Matzke, Gordon. "The Development of the Selous Game Reserve." *Tanzania Notes and Records* 79/80 (1976): 37–41.

———. *Wildlife in Tanzanian Settlement Policy: The Case of the Selous.* Foreign and Comparative Studies/Africa Series 28. Syracuse University, 1977.

Mayombo, Rudolf Peter. "Economic Structural Changes and Population Migration in Kilombero Valley." M.A. thesis, University of Dar es Salaam, 1990.

McHenry, Dean E. *Limited Choices: The Political Struggle for Socialism in Tanzania.* Boulder, Colo.: Lynne Rienner, 1994.

———. *Tanzania's Ujamaa Villages: The Implementation of a Rural Development Strategy.* Berkeley: University of California Press, 1979.

Miescher, Steven, Louise White, and David Cohen, eds. *African Lives, African Voices: Critical Practices in Oral History.* Bloomington: Indiana University Press, 2001.

Monson, Jamie. "Defending the People's Railway in the Era of Liberalization." *Africa* 76, no. 1 (January 2006): 113–130.

———. "Maisha: Life History and the History of Livelihood along the TAZARA Railway." In *Sources and Methods in African History: Spoken, Written, Unearthed,* ed. Toyin

Falola and Christian Jennings. Rochester, N.Y.: University of Rochester Press, 2003. 312–330.

———. "Memory, Migration and the Authority of History in Southern Tanzania, 1860–1960." *Journal of African History* 41 (2000): 347–372.

———. "Relocating Maji Maji: The Politics of Alliance and Authority in the Southern Highlands of Tanzania, 1860–1918." *Journal of African History* 39 (1998): 95–120.

———. "The Tribal Past and the Politics of Nationalism in Mahenge District, 1940–1960." In *In Search of a Nation: Histories of Authority and Dissidence in Tanzania*, ed. Gregory Maddox and James Giblin. Oxford: James Currey, 2005.

Msabaha, Ibrahim. "Contribution to International Relations." In *Mwalimu: The Influence of Nyerere*, ed. Colin Legum and Geoffrey Mmari. London: Oxford Journals, 1995.

Mumello, D. D. S. M. "Final Report on Tunnels Construction, Mkela Base Camp." 1972.

Mung'ong'o, C. G. "Coming Full Circle: Agriculture, Non-Farm Activities and the Resurgence of Out-Migration in Njombe District, Tanzania." ASC Working Paper 26. Leiden, 1997.

Mutukwa, Kasuka S. "Imperial Dream Becomes Pan-African Reality." *Africa Report* (January 1972), 12.

Mwase, Ngila. "The Future of TAZARA in a Post-Apartheid Southern Africa." Southern African Perspectives Working Paper 21. Center for Southern African Studies, University of the Western Cape, South Africa, 1993.

———. "The Tanzania-Zambia Railway: The Chinese Loan and the Pre-Investment Analysis Revisited." *Journal of Modern African Studies* 21, no. 3 (1983): 535–543.

Ndulu, Benno. "Economic Stagnation and the Management of Change: Reducing Macro-Micro Conflicts of Interest." In *What Went Right in Tanzania: People's Response to Directed Development*, eds. M. L. Swantz and A. M. Tripp. Dar es Salaam: University of Dar es Salaam Press, 1996.

Nettleton, John G. "The Tanzam Railroad: The PRC in Africa versus United States Interests." Research Study, Air Command and Staff College, Maxwell Air Force Base, Alabama, 1974.

Neumann, Roderick P. "Africa's 'Last Wilderness': Reordering Space for Political and Economic Control in Colonial Tanzania." *Africa* 71, no. 4 (2001): 641–665.

Nyerere, Julius. *Freedom and Development: A Selection from Writings and Speeches 1968–1973*. Oxford: Oxford University Press, 1973.

Odinga, Oginga. *Not Yet Uhuru*. London: Hill and Wang, 1967.

Ogusanwo, Alaba. *China's Policy in Africa 1958–71*. Cambridge: Cambridge University Press, 1974.

Ponte, Stefano. *Farmers and Markets in Tanzania*. Oxford: James Currey, 2002.

Raikes, Phil. "Eating the Carrot and Wielding the Stick: The Agricultural Sector in Tanzania." In *Tanzania: Crisis and Struggle for Survival*, ed. J. Boesen, K. J. Havnevik, J. Koponen, and R. Odgaard. Uppsala: Nordiska Afrikainstituetet, 1986.

Ramsar Convention Bureau. "Information Sheet on Ramsar Wetlands (RIS), May 2002, 11.

Rwambali, Faustine. "State Lays Off All 3000 Kilombero Sugar Workers." *The East African*, 3 July 2000.

Sahu, Sunil Kumar. "Sino-Tanzanian Relations." *United Asia* 23, no. 2 (1971): 78–80.

Scott, James. *Seeing like a State: How Certain Schemes to Improve the Human Condition Have Failed*. New Haven, Conn.: Yale University Press, 1998.

Selous Game Reserve Management Project. *Socio-economic Survey of the Buffer Zone of Selous Game Reserve*. Unpublished report. University of Dar es Salaam, November 2001.

Sendaro, Ali Mohamed. "The Great Uhuru Railway (Tanzam): A Project for Achievement in the Ten Years of the Arusha Declaration." Unpublished paper. Dar es Salaam, 1977.
———. "Workers' Efficiency, Motivation and Management: The Case of the Tanzania-Zambia Railway Construction." Ph.D thesis, University of Dar es Salaam, 1987.
Seppälä, Pekka. *Diversification and Accumulation in Rural Tanzania: Anthropological Perspectives on Village Economics*. Uppsala: Nordiska Afrikainstitutet, 1998.
Sheridan, Michael. "The Environmental Consequences of Independence and Socialism in North Pare, Tanzania, 1961–1988." Boston University Working Paper 233, 2000.
Snow, Philip. *The Star Raft: China's Encounter with Africa*. New York: Weidenfeld and Nicolson, 1988.
Spear, Thomas. *Mountain Farmers*. Berkeley: University of California Press, 1997.
Stanford Research Institute (SRI). "Middle Africa Transport Survey." Stanford, Calif., 1968.
Stoecker, Helmuth. *German Imperialism in Africa*. London: C. Hurst, 1986.
Sunseri, Thaddeus. *Vilimani: Labor Migration and Rural Change in Early Colonial Tanzania*. Portsmouth, N.H.: Heinemann, 2002.
Tanzania Ministry of Lands, Housing and Urban Development and Finland Ministry for Foreign Affairs. *Uhuru Corridor Regional Physical Plan*. Sectoral Studies II: Settlement Patterns and Physical Infrastructures. August 1978.
Tanzania Zambia Railway Authority. *Annual Reports and Accounts for 1973/4*.
———. *Ten Years of TAZARA Operations: Review and Perspective*. Lusaka and Dar es Salaam, 1986.
Taylor, Ian. *China and Africa: Engagement and Compromise*. London: Routledge, 2006.
Tiranti, Dexter. "The Chinese in Africa." *New Internationalist* (May 1973): 12.
Tonkin, Elizabeth. *Narrating Our Pasts: The Social Construction of Oral History*. Cambridge: Cambridge University Press, 1992.
Tripp, Aili. *Changing the Rules: The Politics of Liberalization and the Urban Informal Economy in Tanzania*. Berkeley: University of California Press, 1998.
U.S. Congress. *Congressional Record—House*. Washington, D.C.: Government Printing Office, 1973.
Vail, Leroy. "The Making of an Imperial Slum: Nyasaland and Its Railways, 1895–1935." *Journal of African History* 16, no. 1 (1975): 89–112.
Van Dijk, R., R. Reis, and M. Spierenburg. *The Quest for Fruition through Ngoma*. Oxford: Oxford University Press, 2000.
Von Beusekom, Monica. *Negotiated Development: African Farmers and Colonial Experts at the Office du Niger, 1920–1960*. Portsmouth, N.H.: Heinemann, 2002.
Watts, Michael. "A New Deal in Emotions: Theory and Practice and the Crisis of Development." In *Power of Development*, ed. Jonathan Crush. New York: Routledge, 1995.
Weinstein, Warren, ed. *Chinese and Soviet Aid to Africa*. New York: Praeger, 1975.
———. "Contemporary Relations between China and Africa: Fifty Years in Wind and Rain." Unpublished paper presented to International Conference on Blacks and Asians: Encounters through Time and Space. Boston University, April 2002.
World Bank, *World Bank Mission's Report on the North East Rail Link*, 1963, cited in Bostock, "The Transport Sector," 367.
World Bank Group, "Kilombero Business Linkages: Outgrower Schemes, Tanzania, Proposed Project." http://www.ifc.org/sme/Linkages/html/agribusiness.html.
Youyi de Caihong Bianji Xiaozu [Editors of *Rainbow of Friendship*]. *Youyi de Caihong [Rainbow of Friendship]*. Beijing: Renmin Wenxue Chubanshe, 1975.

Yu, George T. *China and Tanzania: A Study in Cooperative Interaction*. Chinese Research Monograph Number 5. Center for Chinese Studies, University of California, Berkeley, 1970.
——. *China's African Policy: A Study of Tanzania*. London: Praeger, 1975.
——. "Dragon in the Bush: Peking's Presence in Africa." *Asian Survey* 8 (1968): 1025–1026.
——. "Working on the Railroad: China and the Tanzania-Zambia Railway." *Asian Survey* 11, no. 11 (1971): 1101–1117.
Zhang Tieshan. *Youyi Zhi Lu: Yuanjian Tanzan Tielu Jishi [Road of Friendship: The Memoirs of the Development Assistance of the Tanzania-Zambia Railroad]*. Beijing: Zhongguo Duiwai Jingji Maoyi Chubanshe, 1975.

Interviews

Ameir, Ally Nassor. Ifakara. 24 June 2000.
Banda, Ahmadi. Msolwa. 12 August 2002.
Bolstad, Paul. Northfield, Minnesota. 2001.
Bulaya, C. V. Mchombe. 16 July 2000.
Chawala, Raphael. Ifakara. 20 April 2000.
Du Jian. Dar es Salaam. April 2000.
Gilbert, John, and Hosea Mngata. Ifakara. 20 April 2000.
Group interview at Msolwa village. 12 August 2002.
Group interview at Mwaya village. 14 August 2002.
Group interview with *ukindu* weavers at Mgudeni. July 2000.
Group interview with women at Mchombe. 16 July 2000.
Hassan, Moses, and Benedict Mkanyago. Mngeta. 7 July 2000.
Haule, Joseph. Ifakara. 21 May 2001.
Jaycox, Kim. Telephone interview. 26 October 1999.
Kabida, Martin. Sonjo. 13 August 2002.
Kaduma, Philemon. Mbeya. 24 August 1998.
Kalonga, Joseph. Sonjo. 13 August 2002.
Kaparape, Mohammed Chandi. 13 August 2002.
Katabi, Bernard. Msolwa. 12 August 2002.
Kidehela, Balista Idifonce. Mbingu. 28 July 2002.
Kidumba, Elisha. Mwaya. 14 August 2002.
Kigola, Philemon. Mang'ula. 5 August 2000.
Kikoko, Abdallah. Mwaya. 14 August 2002.
Kisugite, Moses. Mngeta. 10 July 2000.
Kiswanya, Juma Juma. Mang'ula. 8 August 2000.
Kiswanya, Juma Juma. Mgudeni. 2001.
Kupaya, Salumu. Msolwa. 12 August 2002.
Li, Jin Wen. Tianjin, China. 6 July 2007.
Lihawa, Beatus. Mlimba. 20 July 2000.
Likwelile, S. B. Dar es Salaam. April 2000.
Likweti, Leonard. 5 May 2000.
Liuka, Abdallah. Sonjo. 13 August 2002.
Luwangu, Meshack. Sonjo. 13 August 2002.
Lyapembile, Venance Michael. Mchombe. 16 July 2000.
Magwaja, Augustini. Mlimba. 17 July 2002.

Majiji, Maulidi Mustafa. Mngeta. 7 July 2000.

Malangu, Mwajuma. Mbingu. 27 July 2002.

Malowe, Abdallah Hassani. Msolwa. 12 August 2002.

Mangile, Andrew J. Mlimba. 26 July 2000.

Manjenga, Mohamed Juma. Mlimba. 18 July 2002.

Matthei, Hosana. Sonjo. 13 August 2002.

Mazengo, Abdul Abdallah. Msolwa. 12 August 2002.

Mbilinyi, Lazaro. Ifakara. June 2000.

Mbwilo, John Emmanueli. Mlimba. 16 July 2002.

Mdae, C. Mlimba. June 2002.

Mdemu, Hashim. Ifakara. June 2000.

Melela, Selemani. Mlimba. 16 July 2002.

Members of Sugar Cane Outgrowers Association. Mkamba. 2000.

Mgei, Hussein Ally. Mbingu. 25 July 2002.

Mgomba, Abdul Yusufu. Mbingu. 27 July 2002.

Mhiliwa, Johanes. Segelela. August 1998.

Mikupi, Gerald Pius. Mlimba. 18 July 2002.

Mkanyago, Benedict. Mngeta. 7 July 2000.

Mkoka, Hamisi. Mbingu. 27 July 2002.

Mkwaya, Omar. Mofu. 19 August 2002.

Mnauye, Shaha Salum. Mbingu. 26 July 2002.

Momello, Daniel S. M. Njombe. July 2002.

Moos, Brother Edwin von. Ifakara. May 2000.

Moyo, Mzee. Ifakara. 25 May 2001.

Mpandamgongo, Marian Kassian, and Carol Mpandamgongo. Ikule. 14 July 2000.

Msaka, Aurelia Protas. Mchombe. 16 July 2000.

Msaka, Yohina. Mchombe. 16 July 2000.

Mseja, Shaban Suleiman. Mlimba. 17 July 2002.

Msemakweli, Khalifa Kibarana. Mwaya. 14 August 2002.

Mtahune, Saidi. Mwaya. 14 August 2002.

Mtuluku, Felician. Mofu. 17 August 2002.

Mtwanga extended family. Mngeta. 9 July 2000.

Mushi, Amadeus. Ifakara. July 2000.

Mwabutwa, Rehema P. Mlimba. 16 July 2002.

Mwailunda, Richard. Mwaya. 14 August 2002.

Mwakapala, Atupele. Ifakara. 3 May 2000.

Mwakyoma, Godfrey. Mngeta. June 2000.

Mwamiiko, Michael Noah. Mbingu. 28 July 2002.

Mwasenga, Salum. Mang'ula. 30 July 2000.

Mwasonge, Brown. Ifakara. 30 April 2000.

Mwasulama, Josefina. Dar es Salaam. May 2001.

Mweji, Michael. Mbingu. 26 July 2002.

Mwelela, Selemani Issa. Mlimba. 16 July 2002.

Ndimbo, Raymond. Mbeya. July 2006.

Ngakorwa, Kombo Nasolwa. Msolwa. 12 August 2002.

Ngenza, Julius. Ifakara. 9 May 2000.

Ngula, Cletus Robert, Mbingu. 26 July 2002.

Nyakunga, Yohana Paul. Mlimba. 18 July 2002.

Nyaruke, Eddy. Mlimba. 17 July 2002.
Nyota, Mariamu. Sonjo. 13 August 2002.
Nyumayo, Rogatus. Mlimba. 26 July 2000.
Nyumile, Suleiman. Mngeta. July 2000.
Rajabu, Rashid Shabani. Mbingu. 25 July 2002.
Salehe, Mwamini. Mlimba. 16 July 2002.
Sanka, Grace. Mngeta. June 2000.
Songo, Charles. Mlimba. 20 July 2000.
Undole, Blasius. Chita. 22 July 2000.
Undole, Samuel Mihanji. Chita. 11 July 2000.
Wan, Lao. Ifakara. July 2000.
Wang, Hui Min. Tianjin, China. July 2007.
Wang, Qinmei. Beijing, China. June 2007.
Yongding, Yu. Beijing, China. August 2003.

Index

Note: Page numbers in *italics* refer to illustrations.

JAMIE MONSON is Professor of History at Macalester College. She is editor of *Women as Food Producers in Developing Countries* and *Maji Maji: Lifting the Fog of War.* She is past president of the Tanzania Studies Association.